AESTHETIC AUTOBIOGRAPHY

Also by Suzanne Nalbantian and from St. Martin's

SEEDS OF DECADENCE IN THE LATE
NINETEENTH-CENTURY NOVEL

Aesthetic Autobiography

From Life to Art
in
Marcel Proust, James Joyce,
Virginia Woolf and Anaïs Nin

SUZANNE NALBANTIAN

St. Martin's Press   New York

First published in the United States of America in 1994

Printed in Great Britain

ISBN 0–312–12170–9

Library of Congress Cataloging-in-Publication Data
Nalbantian, Suzanne, 1950–
Aesthetic autobiography : from life to art in Marcel Proust, James
Joyce, Virginia Woolf, and Anaïs Nin / Suzanne Nalbantian.
p. cm.
Includes bibliographical references and index.
ISBN 0–312–12170–9
1. English prose literature—20th century—History and criticism.
2. Novelists, English—20th century—Biography—History and
criticism. 3. Autobiographical fiction—History and criticism.
4. Novelists—Biography—History and criticism. 5. Woolf, Virginia,
1882–1941—Biography. 6. Proust, Marcel, 1871–1922—Biography.
7. Joyce, James, 1882–1941—Biography. 8. Nin, Anaïs, 1903–1977–
–Biography. 9. Self in literature. 10. Autobiography. I. Title.
PR756.A9N35   1994
823' .9129353—dc20   94–9925
                                                            CIP

To my dear husband
David S. Reynolds

Contents

Preface

Autobiography, in the popular form, is the rage of our era. Public figures inevitably resort to this form to reveal aspects of their lives after they have been at centre stage. It has become one of the most consumer-oriented media, ranking high on the best-seller lists and lying on coffee tables ready to be devoured. A random list would be quite lengthy, including names from politicians to actresses, from rock stars to military heroes. The sensational nature of the beast prompts distortions of truth, even as perspectives are altered, so that this traditionally 'non-fiction' form often opens up into the domain of fiction. In fact, this medium has become so popular that even literary critics have mingled their literary criticism with life stories.

But such autobiographies are not the subject of this book. Instead, I delve into the literary manifestation of autobiographical writing as developed by a cluster of modernist novelists of the first half of the twentieth century. A question which immediately arises is how can one isolate such a group and derive paradigms from it? Many will say that *all* novels are autobiographical to some degree, and valid and interesting examples will immediately follow from the history of literature. One cannot deny such an assertion. I would argue that the four particular writers scrutinised in the pages that follow – two of whom are men and two women – infused their lives artistically into their fiction in a manner without precedent. The Comparatist act of bringing these four well-known writers together from this point of view, never previously contemplated, sheds new light on a common aesthetics of transmutation in fiction.

Since three of the four writers are so well known, and perhaps so nationally identified, they have been appropriated by their respective organisational societies and readership and to some extent kept isolated from each other. Those very active and interesting literary societies of critics of Joyce, Woolf and Proust meet separately, conduct annual tours of significant locales, and remain unaware of a certain aesthetic affinity which existed unconsciously among the writers. The case of Nin is yet to be seen, since she, unlike the other three, was bicultural and may actually 'belong' to the literary criticism coterie of two countries.

Furthermore, with the temporary exception of Nin, for there are several biographies in progress, these are writers who have been extensively studied from the biographical point of view. In the case of Nin, I feel I have compensated somewhat for the absence of a biography by having had the good fortune to know her; she wrote that she would have wanted me to be her daughter. As for the other three writers, the biographical critics have carefully studied their lives and have provided ample evidence of parallels between their lives and fiction. But again, no parallels between such parallels have been discussed, because the writers have been isolated from each other.

My book, however, goes on to another step in seeking to extract from these writers the aesthetic element of transmutation. For from such parallels actual distortions can be detected which lead to the 'higher truths' of fiction. That is to say, the artistic manipulation of life facts through a set of techniques which I uncover intertextually divulges a common aesthetics among these writers that created a self-referentiality of another degree. I am speaking here of the creative process – of the transformation of life into art. A primary link between these writers is the fact that they include in their fictional works a self-reflexive commentary on their very method so that the aesthetics within are clues to the interpretation of their work.

A principal motive for such dissemblance on the part of the authors may well have been subterfuge. In the process of 'using' their lives as raw material for their fiction, they may have been trying to hide certain facts, often out of reticence or for the sense of privacy. Fortuitously perhaps it was this very constraint which led, in each case, to artistic ingenuity, for the 'cover-up' was inevitably achieved through an artistic artifact or process. This tension between the revealing and the concealing in these four artists creates the rich ambiguity and the symbolic artistry of their writing.

My chapter 'A Theory of Aesthetic Autobiography' uncovers the common techniques derived from these four authors, which contribute to what I call a 'transformation theory'. As will be seen, it is a theory of transmutation and transposition which constitutes the aesthetic element in this fiction. Selection, substitution, distancing, abstraction, the creation of composites, multiplication, diffusion, misrepresentation, mythification – these are some of the techniques which are amply analysed and illustrated throughout the book. The reader may well compare the implementation of such approaches with the different life materials of each writer.

I have divided the book into seven sections. Beginning with a selective history of autobiography proper, I have distinguished that formal genre from the 'aesthetic autobiographies' which follow. The purpose, however, in surveying this genre 'with a history', is to present the paradigms established as a gauge for the artistic ones which I locate in the fictional mode. In the formal genre, writers coped with a certain selection process as well, deciding what part of their lives to feature, but the selectivity was very different from that of the novelistic orientation seen in the fictional genre. Following this chapter, I give a perspective on the scholarly research on autobiography which has abounded in the last two decades. I then present my own theory of aesthetic autobiography: to orient the reader in what is to follow in the examination of the four individual writers – Proust, Joyce, Woolf, Nin – and their techniques. These chapters are journeys into the intimate lives and fictive processes of these writers. My method is ultimately summed up in the Envoi.

I would add that each of the four writers provides an enormous and stimulating body of material to study and analyse, that it is almost traumatic to leave one for another, and that the only consolation is that they are equally fascinating and provocative. In the years of preparation for this book I was able to travel to each of the four writers' locales and habitats, from Illiers to Cabourg, to St Ives, to Louveciennes, to Dublin, to Clongowes, reliving the texts in those sites and pondering the transformations that occurred in the fiction. Having taken the standard tour of Illiers and its environs, in 1987 I had the unexpected experience of staying in the room opposite Proust's room – number 414 – in the Grand Hotel of Cabourg and being hosted by Michel Moles, the then mayor of that seaside resort. There was also the visit to the still-existing boarding school of Clongowes Wood College, hidden away in County Kildare, and talks with the Jesuit priests about their former 'notorious' student. It was compelling to trace Joyce's footsteps through the streets of Dublin on Bloomsday in 1985, to take a bus ride out to the Martello tower at Sandycove, and to take train rides to Blackrock and on to Bray where I visited the attached house at 1 Martello Terrace facing Bray Head. I also had the peaceful sensation of staying at a hotel at St Ives bay in Cornwall, staring both day and night at the Godrevy lighthouse, attempting to recapture Virginia Woolf's childhood vision. And then, too, there was the more enigmatic trip to Louveciennes, the sleepy suburban town outside of Paris, where the mysterious house of Nin still stands, covered by ivy and hidden behind a forbidding stone wall.

Such trips, however pleasurable, did not detract from the fundamental motive of detecting alteration and creativity in the re-presentation of such sites by the authors in question. It is that process of transmutation, of which only the true artist is capable, applied to various aspects of life, that I now offer to the reader.

1

Historical Paradigms

Formal autobiography has always been assumed to be a genre of its own, even though it is said that it was not until 1809 that the English writer Robert Southey coined the word in the *Quarterly Review*. The twentieth-century critics have called it autobiography 'proper', 'standard', 'strictly speaking', or in French *proprement dite* – to distinguish it from either the autobiographical novel or that more facile mode of popular autobiography which is proliferating worldwide. The evolution of the genre well before the word, in the general terms of Philippe Lejeune's definition – retrospective prose narrative concentrating on the history of an individual personality – can be traced from Saint Augustine onward to another writer from Africa, Wole Soyinka. And indeed, many critics have carved out certain portions of the genesis of the form. Many have also concurred with William Spengemann's clear-cut notion that a certain evolution occurred from the religious to the secular and even the poetic. At the same time, however, there can be uncovered certain common elements or paradigms germane to Western autobiography as a whole. For in the juxtaposition of some of the most obvious titles, common internal laws, conventions and structures can be discerned and afterwards measured as a backdrop against the sister genre of fictional autobiography.

I shall be necessarily selective in considering classic examples from prose in the Western heritage such as those of Saint Augustine, Cellini, Rousseau, Franklin, Gosse, Gide, Stein, Leiris, Sartre and Soyinka. They have been chosen for the light they shed on the continuity in structural elements in the developing genre. There is no question that autobiography is a larger experience than prose narrative, as evidenced in the grand poetic examples of Wordsworth's *The Prelude* and T. S. Eliot's *The Four Quartets*. However, since the purpose here is to identify narrative patterns which pertain, by comparison, to the autobiographical novel, narratives are the focus.

A first observation in such scrutiny of prose autobiographies of the Western heritage is that for the most part they have been written

1

well after the experiences which actually turned the writers into public figures. Benvenuto Cellini made a point of spelling out an age and 'vita' requirement for the genre:

> All men of whatsoever quality they be, who have done anything of excellence, or which may properly resemble excellence, ought, if they are persons of truth and honesty, to describe their life with their own hand; but they ought not to attempt so fine an enterprise till they have passed the age of forty.[1]

With such a perspective, there arises a distinction between the past self and the present self, and the past self is often coloured by the writing self – as can be seen in the disparate instances of Saint Augustine and Sartre. The span of time treated in these autobiographies varies from those which bring the narrative up to the time of writing and the more modern ones which treat a formative 'slice of life'. But unlike the autobiographical novelist, whose motive, as shall be seen, is to hide, embellish and transform, the strict autobiographer writes on the assumption of a truth claim, as if his writings were to be received in the same manner as historical fact. There is the accepted illusion of mimesis, with the 'I' in a referential position. The autobiographer also relishes the opportunity of speaking directly to the reader of certain recognised accomplishments.

Many of the classic autobiographies dwell on the period of childhood, so much so that the French, with their gift of classification, have often labelled them as *récits d'enfance*. Richard Coe's book *When the Grass was Taller* has gone so far as to view this concentration in autobiography as creating an autonomous literary genre which he labels for the English-speaking context 'The Childhood'. Coe naturally places Rousseau's *Confessions* at the source of this specific literary form and then traces it on to Michel Leiris's *La Règle du jeu*. It is true that, in general, the Romantic writers themselves, represented most vocally by Wordsworth's ringing phrase 'The Child is father of the Man', developed the genre as a process of the organic growth of a personality from the seeds of early childhood. It does seem more than a coincidence that many of the crucial incidents in the standard autobiographies occur around the age of six – as do those in the aesthetic autobiographies that follow. In fact, this is a point of convergence between the two.

The next memorable age, recounted in classic autobiographies, seems to be sixteen – what becomes an age of crisis experience. Such

experiences are turned into paradigms of turning points in the lives and in the narrative. Here the examples are many, as will be seen in the following: St Augustine's theft from the pear tree and his period of sensual indulgence as he 'walked the streets of Babylon' (really Carthage), Cellini's departure from his father and his native Florence for Rome, Franklin's flight from his brother's tyranny and entry into Philadelphia with his three pennyworth of bread, Rousseau locked out of the gates of his beloved Geneva and his decision never to return to his master, Gosse's denial of his father's religion while at boarding school. Many of these incidents are acts of rebellion involving the severance of certain relationships and therefore a significant turning point in the development of the personality in question.

The vividness of such incidents varies according to the authors, yet they are *potentials* for what Wordsworth calls 'spots of time', what Joyce terms 'epiphanies', or what Woolf describes as 'scene making'. Whereas, for the most part, the literal transcription of them is the concern of the standard autobiographer, the embellishment and transformation of such scenes is the material for the aesthetic autobiographer. In an example which will be discussed, Joyce takes his crisis of religion, which occurred at the age of sixteen, and elaborates it in several chapters of *A Portrait of the Artist as a Young Man*.

CONVERSION PARADIGM

The *Confessions* of Saint Augustine, often regarded as the first formal autobiography in the Western tradition, introduces the conversion paradigm, which will be turned into the crisis experience of the later secular models. To have a work so heavily devoted to an author's life was a novel idea for Augustine's time. On the other hand, the work became a historical document for the spread of Christianity through the Roman world. But Saint Augustine's personal struggle with sin and knowledge individualises him and manifests itself in terms of a quest rather than a chronicle. Unlike the spiritual autobiographies that were to follow, this early religious one necessarily addresses itself to God although the narrative strategy is to induce the reader to follow the pathway of confession, humility and thanks.

The autobiography proceeds in the first nine books through retrospective narration and then moves on in the last four books,

dismissing chronology altogether, to a philosophical meditation. What separates these two parts is the crucial conversion scene, as the narrative self, aged 44, converted and religious, overrides the protagonist self, aged from one to 33, pagan and sinful. After the conversion, the chronology and narration stop, as there is no longer need for time since Augustine's relationship with his God is cast in terms of eternity.

The philosopher Paul Ricoeur, in his studies of time and narrative, has assigned the notion of *aporia* or irreconcilable paradoxes to the tensions between time and eternity in Augustine's *Confessions*. The nagging question of Book Eleven, 'What, then, is time?', is mediated by Augustine's notion of memory:

> My own childhood, which no longer exists, is in past time, which also no longer exists. But when I remember those days and describe them, it is in the present that I picture them to myself, because their picture is still present in my memory.[2]

The 'converted' self is justifying the narration and chronology of the first nine chapters of the book or the autobiography itself.

But it is this narrative first section which is most pertinent to the discussion of the genre since certain pristine patterns emerge. 'Spots of time' could describe the incidents of theft from Augustine's parents' larder and from the pear tree. The 'Babylonian wanderings' in Carthage and the conflict between the opposing poles of the pagan father and the Christian mother provide material for crisis experience. Augustine's eventual conversion to Christianity is equivalent to identity formation.

In the early chronological sequence, it is youth rather than childhood *per se* which is dwelt upon, perhaps in this first case since the innocence of childhood is dismissed on the doctrinal grounds of the notion of original sin. The rhetorical question 'Can this be the innocence of childhood? Far from it, O Lord!'[3] accounts for the sparse treatment of that period of life. Much later, Rousseau will do the reverse in intentionally secularising his confessions. Dwelling on childhood, the later autobiographer will, more characteristically for the genre as a whole, make the passage from childhood a turning point, marked by the theme of 'injured innocence'.

In fact, since Augustine's intention is to dramatise the great conflicts he had prior to his conversion, he extends the period of adolescence forward and does not allow manhood to emerge before the

age of 29. The ten-year period prior to that age covers his bout with Manicheanism, his interest in the theatre, his indulgence in carnal pleasures, and his liaison with his concubine mistress. The lustful activity stemming from his stay in Carthage and elsewhere as a teenager wallowing in sensuality is described in terms of the metaphor of Babylon:

> I walked the streets of Babylon. I wallowed in its mire as if it were made of spices and special ointments, and to fix me all the faster in the depths of sin the unseen enemy trod me underfoot and enticed me to himself.

It is especially worth noting that Joyce's *A Portrait of the Artist as a Young Man* presents Stephen Dedalus in a similar way at the same age but on the streets of Dublin instead of Carthage. Although the same situation is presented, of a youth wallowing in sinful activity, in the modern autobiographical novel the persona is thereafter converted out of religion into art, art taking the place of religion. Joyce may well have subversively undermined the earlier model, in taking part of the pattern and reversing the outcome. As will be seen, the secular rendition is much more interiorised, as it dramatises the psychological dilemmas and the epiphanies which ensue.

Aside from introducing the structure of conversion, Augustine's autobiography gives early expression to a substantive element indigenous to the genre, that of parental relationships. He reveals himself as vacillating at first between the forces of a pagan father and a Christian mother. If his father Patricius encourages him in his lustfulness, his mother Monica dreams of his future conversion. Eventually, in this case, the relationship with the mother is the lasting one. In the autobiographies which follow, it will be noted that at least one parental relationship is the focus. Also, in the particular aesthetic autobiographies that are examined, the conflict between parents are often dramatised, but also universalised in terms of social stereotype or mythic figure.

In his narrative Augustine also seems to be establishing a paradigm for what later will be called 'scene making', even though he does not fully structure and elaborate such scenes. The two memorable incidents of Augustine's autobiography are the theft from the pear tree (at the age of sixteen) and the actual conversion in the Garden of Milan (at the age of 32). Given the repercussions of such

incidents, Augustine is noticeably sparse in the treatment of these scenes – unlike later autobiographical novelists who would seize the opportunity to elaborate on such rich material. The focal point in the case of the theft from the pear tree is the generalisation of a category of sin rather than the exploration of a feeling experienced. Augustine, along with his mischievous companions, stole for the sole sake of stealing: 'we took away an enormous quantity of pears, not to eat ourselves, but simply to throw them to the pigs'.[4] The scene is at the service of such a statement.

As for the conversion scene in the Garden of Milan in Book Eight, Augustine uses a *locus classicus*. But he does not dwell long enough on it to interiorise it as an epiphany precisely because it is not a question of the psychological self but of the soul's maturation to faith. In order to remain true to the Christian guidelines of humility, Augustine minimizes the ego's role, much in distinction to the autobiographies to follow. The scene remains an external one, as a succinct spot of time which is charted in the narrative. Following the chance reading of Saint Paul's *Epistles*, Augustine is instantly converted and the 'darkness of doubt was dispelled'. Augustine purposely minimises this moment of narrated time in contrast to the scheme of eternity which follows the conversion.

These innovative elements in this pristine autobiography become conventions in those that follow. Of course, there are many later variations on the conversion narrative in America by such writers as Jonathan Edwards and John Woolman, and journals abound. But the conversion factor as a structural rather than religious ingredient has a distinct role in the sequence of autobiographical narrative, as will be seen in the manipulation of it by such moderns as Edmund Gosse and James Joyce. As Susanna Egan has confirmed in her study of nineteenth-century autobiographies, conversion prevails as an archetypal pattern because it represents an aspect of the maturing process and a move toward self discovery.[5] Moreover, specific facets of Augustine's autobiography seem to have elicited very conscious responses in the classic autobiographies that followed his, so that he becomes an implicit frame of reference for the genre. The scene of theft illustrated by the pear tree incident, for example, has far-reaching repercussions in secular descendants – the stealing of the ribbon in Rousseau, the ruin of the rockery in Gosse, and the neglect of the rose bush by Soyinka. So, too, do the secular versions of autobiography become more focused on events in the lives.

LARGER THAN LIFE

In contrast to the intensely religious, primordial form of the genre, there is the secular form which develops in the Renaissance with Benvenuto Cellini's *Life*, even though the work itself did not become widely known until the nineteenth century. Cellini's outright motive is to chronicle the great achievements of his life, artistic and otherwise, and to assure his place in history as he defends his status against a society which failed fully to appreciate him. Accordingly, this autobiography dwells exclusively on the chronological narration of events, as it presents a typical, extroverted Renaissance personality in 'larger than life' proportions. This epic dimension becomes the prime feature of his autobiography. Dictating his life events up to the age of 62, he embellishes them with novella-like detail of protracted plot description and exaggerated drama. He adorns the story of his life with extraneous detail, as he moves from one digression to the next, in a a manner similar to the fiction of his countrymen, Boccaccio and Castiglione. But at the same time, he continuously claims his veracity in recounting facts as they really occurred. It can be argued, of course, that his narrative had only followed the perspective of his sculpture – the larger-than-life dimensions of his statues.

But in the course of such entertaining descriptions of events and actions, only superficially does the reader get to know this public personality. In fact, a major criticism of this autobiography by John Addington Symonds, Cellini's nineteenth-century British translator, was how little introspective he was:

> No one was less introspective than this child of the Italian Renaissance. No one was less occupied with thoughts about thinking or with the presentation of psychological experience. Vain, ostentatious, self-laudatory, and self-engrossed as Cellini was, he never stopped to analyze himself.[6]

On the other hand, another commentator, the nineteenth-century French sociologist Hippolyte Taine, had praised the work precisely for its informative externality and cultural relevance. In his view, Cellini's account is an example of a document reflecting the entire spirit of an age: 'I would give fifty volumes of charters and a hundred volumes of diplomatic papers for the memoirs of Cellini' ('*Je donnerai cinquante volumes de chartes et cent volumes de pièces diplomatiques pour*

les mémoires de Cellini'[7]). Although historians have contested the heroic role that Cellini claims in the Sack of Rome, the cultural significance of the autobiography remains authentic and secure.

It is true that the distinct Renaissance signature is there from the start of the work – that of an individual within a society of individuals. Cellini begins by boasting of his distinguished genealogy in a manner comparable to Rabelais's fictional family history in *Gargantua* and *Pantagruel*. But since he is concerned with revealing his professional accomplishments rather than the growth of his character, his childhood is not featured. The autobiography is full of comical, anecdotal tales in which Cellini comes out the abused – so that ultimately the narrative reads as a defence or apology. In dictating the events of his life to a scribe, he creates a demotic, conversational style, contrived with *sprezzatura* to appear as natural as possible. At several points in the narrative, he emphasises that he does not wish to depart from a steady account of the progress of his profession as artist, sculptor and goldsmith, even though at those very points he digresses to adorn the story of his life with extraneous detail.

Because of his external motives, it can be well understood why Cellini falls short of revealing the formation of his personality. In the course of his *Life* there is no transformation of character but sheer repetition of it in parallel situations and predicaments. Nor is there a single crisis or turning point. Instead, he shows how time and time again he is mistreated and undervalued by rivals or superiors in instances of jealousy or malice, whether it be in the company of Pope Clement VII, King Francis I or the Grand Duke Cosimo. Struggling against all odds, he creates a heroics of life in an epic-like battle against mankind. With this exaggeration of proportion, the life transcends itself, although the character remains identifiable and typical of its age. Cellini lends vivacity to the genre, highlighting the exterior events and the chronology of the narrative.

THE EXEMPLARY LIFE

If Cellini allows his ego to saturate his narrative, Ben Franklin distances his own through a persona which embodies selective elements of his life and exemplary patterns of behaviour. This distancing process removes the personal ingredients from the narrative, creating a model persona which imbibes the superego. Many

have criticised this autobiography on the very grounds that it lacks sincerity and depth. D. H. Lawrence led such attacks in noting from the Freudian perspective that Franklin suppressed his 'id' in his autobiography, and that it is therefore a cover-up of a hidden self. Lawrence detested Franklin's ultrarational approach in the analysis of exemplary behaviour.

The tripartite narrative, written at separate times and places, from England to France to the US, from 1771 to 1789, is sparse, simple and factual, reminiscent of Puritan prose style. Unlike his predecessor Cellini, Franklin avoids any digression or ornamentation of event. Also in contrast to Cellini, Franklin stops his chronological narrative just at the period of perhaps his greatest professional achievement: the beginning of his career as a diplomat. Although the autobiography covers the first 51 years of Franklin's life, from the point of view of a man of 65 to 72 years of age, it omits his accomplishments of his later years and especially the fact of Franklin's eventual rebellion against the British.

A crisis experience, worthy of scene making, is an incident in the autobiography which has since been turned into American folklore. Franklin's entry into Philadelphia at the crucial age of seventeen with three pennyworth of rolls in his hand is recounted as a factual event. Behind this event lie problematic relationships: his feud with his overbearing brother James and his rift with his unsupportive father. But these relationships are never deeply probed; instead they are dealt with as obstacles which Franklin surmounts in advancing in his printing career. It is after fleeing his brother's printing house in Boston that Franklin arrives in Philadelphia. Franklin does not convey this pivotal episode of his life, however memorable it may be, into a 'spot of time' or 'epiphany', as later writers would have done. Regarding it in thematic terms rather than psychological ones, Franklin creates a Horatio Alger motif (*avant la lettre*) and fits it neatly into the retrospective, chronological narration of selected events.

Since the outright purpose of this autobiography is to instruct and to offer a program of moral reform to the readers, the first one being his own son William, Franklin uses a segment of his own life to explore moral values. But he makes an interesting analogy between his life and the written text. The durability of his life is insured by the simple narrative recording the facts and not by any artistic process, as later writers would have it. He speaks metaphorically, using his printer's vocabulary, of his desire to live a 'second edition' of his

life, in which he would correct the 'errata' of the first and be even more selective in his transcription of events. But since such a repetition is impossible, he accepts the printed recollection as the next best alternative:

> the next Thing most like living one's Life over again seems to be a Recollection of that Life; and to make that Recollection as durable as possible, the putting it down in Writing.[8]

His identification of only three 'errata', however, has called into question the sincerity of his work. Franklin's biographers know that he was responsible for more grievous errors than he reported, especially with respect to fathering an illegitimate son and abandoning his wife during the period of his diplomatic appointments. With such omissions, he is viewed as showing only partial truths. He has produced a persona to follow the path of a curriculum vitae, and only partially at that, since the narrative does not cover a span long enough to include all his accomplishments. The complexity of such a multi-talented man is not touched upon; instead a preconceived public identity is imposed upon the selection of life facts to make of himself a model for history.

THE TRUTH CLAIM

Jean-Jacques Rousseau, Franklin's contemporary, does not sidestep the question of truth in autobiography, as does Franklin. Quite the contrary, Rousseau's overriding position is that of truth-telling, wishing to make his soul transparent to the reader, an approach to autobiography which is consistent with the typical attitude of Romanticism. Unlike Franklin, Rousseau refuses to allow any gap in his imposing autobiographical narrative, *Les Confessions*. In Rousseau's view, the reader must be presented with *all* the life facts in order to arrive at a judgement of the life:

> It is not for me to judge of the relative importance of events; I must relate them all, and leave the selection to him . . . I have only one thing to fear in this enterprise; not that I may say too much or tell untruths, but that I may not tell everything and may conceal the truth.[9]

This statement reads like a response to Franklin, who would impose his own selectivity on an already incomplete account. In contrast, Rousseau desires to be fully accountable to his reader.

Les Confessions have been considered the first modern autobiography and the most acknowledged prototype of the genre. Rousseau himself was self-conscious of his role in the development of the genre, aiming to revolutionise it. He was radical in shunning any intended falsification, ornamentation or artifice in a virtual Romantic manifesto of sincerity and authenticity. He was effusive in displaying his emotions at every turn and in every reaction, even admitting to contradictions in his behaviour. And he paraded in this autobiography nothing but his egotistical self – exactly what the later autobiographical novelists, as we shall see, were out to avoid.

Rousseau's claims at the beginning of the widely read two-part work are typically sweeping and questionable. First, he sees no historical precedents, whereas there are obvious allusions to Saint Augustine's model in the very undermining of the notion of a confession to God; the work is the confession of 'truths' to the reader. Secondly, Rousseau foresees no imitators, yet he creates some of the most lasting paradigms which are adopted by autobiographers to follow. His opening statement reveals his commitment to the genre and to himself:

> I have resolved on an enterprise which has no precedent, and which, once complete, will have no imitator. My purpose is to display to my kind a portrait in every way true to nature, and the man I shall portray shall be myself.[10]

In critical commentary on autobiography, this celebration of the individual self has been labelled as 'Rousseauean', and considered prototypical for the genre. Some critics have gone on to charge Rousseau's autobiography with being egotistical in its obsessive self-reference. If historical critics have hailed Rousseau as representing the height of Western individualism, others have attacked him for being limited to the expression of a unitary selfhood, based on the notion of an essentialist self. The fact is that, throughout the narrative, Rousseau remains the child-self, even after the point at which he alleges that childhood is over.

Rousseau's is the first autobiography to contain an historical self-consciousness of the genre itself. Throughout the narrative there is a self-conscious commentary on his own process of recollection.

Rousseau also appears to critique and surpass his predecessors in statements he makes. For example, the comment 'I never promised to present the public with a great personage. I promised to depict myself as I am' seems to counter Cellini's act of self-aggrandizement and Franklin's display of exemplary behaviour. Similarly, Rousseau's closing of Part One with the statement 'such were the errors and faults of my youth' overrides the selection of a few errata by his contemporary Ben Franklin. On the other hand, Part Two becomes a virtual defence, reminiscent of Cellini, against a society of political enemies who Rousseau believes form a conspiracy to mar his reputation.

But it is the original model of Augustine's autobiography that is most alluded to by Rousseau, as he attempts to take the genre into a secular mode. For example, Rousseau elaborates on the initial paradigm of the stolen fruit, devised by Saint Augustine, and turns it into a convention for the genre as a whole. Both authors admit stealing in their youth, respectively in the incidents of the pear and asparagus thefts. At the beginning of his narrative, Rousseau describes his impulsive nature in terms which call Augustine to mind: 'I would have stolen fruit or sweets or any kind of eatable', but then he qualifies the Augustine allusion: 'but I never took delight in being naughty or destructive'.[11] Dismissing the theological grounds of Augustine's acts, that of the doctrine of original sin, Rousseau suggests his social theory that transgressions such as stealing are acquired acts prompted by society's inequalities and corruptions. In fact, his being an accomplice in the theft of asparagus from a neighbouring garden derived from a certain need and outside instigation.

Rousseau does introduce elements of scene making, even though in his case such scenes are substantive – for example, at the service of social theory rather than structural composition. Rousseau features two analogous scenes from his youth as illustrations of acts of injustice. In the incident of Mademoiselle Lambercier's comb, the eight-year-old Rousseau is the victim of such an act; in the case of Mademoiselle Pontal's ribbon, the nineteen-year-old Rousseau is the perpetrator. First, Rousseau describes an incident in the household of a pastor Lambercier at Bossey, Rousseau's guardian at that time. Fifty years later, Rousseau is protesting that as a young boy he was unjustifiably accused of breaking the teeth of the pastor's sister's comb and severely punished: 'I had not broken, nor so much as touched the comb.'

Despite his alleged innocence, Rousseau uses this incident to chart the end of an idyllic childhood: 'There ended the serenity of my childish life.' The subsequent incident occurs when Rousseau is nineteen while serving as a secretary in a household in Turin. In a vivid account, Rousseau admits 40 years later that he actually stole a worthless little pink ribbon from a Mademoiselle Pontal and then impulsively accused the young cook Marion of the theft. Rousseau magnifies this incident as a supreme example of injured innocence and as the impetus behind his confessions:

> The burden, therefore, has rested till this day on my conscience without any relief; and I can affirm that the desire to some extent to rid myself of it has greatly contributed to my resolution of writing these *Confessions*.

In retrospect, this scene becomes something like a 'spot of time' with the suggestion of an awakening. Such emotional moments occur throughout the *Confessions*, framed by highly visual scenes and reflecting the movement of the author's sensibility.

Other scenes mark crucial stages in his life. Rousseau recounts how at the age of sixteen he gets locked out of the gates of his native city Geneva and begins his live as a fugitive in the countryside of France. Another such scene, in Book Eight, dramatises his choice of vocation. Sitting under an oak tree, aged 37, during a journey to visit Diderot, Rousseau reads the *Mercure de France*, chances on the question of the Dijon Academy, and develops his ideas for the first *Discourse*: 'The moment I read this I beheld another universe and became another man.'[12] In retrospect, Rousseau attributes to his prize-winning essay both the recognition and misfortunes of his subsequent life. It is noteworthy to identify such an instance of 'calling', sparse though it may be in this case, since later autobiographical writers and even novelists, as will be seen, elaborate such scenes of flight and calling in the literary terms of an epiphany.

Rousseau's main contribution to the genre is to use chronology in a new way, to trace the succession of feelings, not of events. In contrast to the autobiographies before his, Rousseau's envisages the genre as charting the organic development of a personality from the early beginnings of childhood. It is in this Romantic context that the genre acquires its most common definition. And in this respect Rousseau makes a significant statement regarding the purpose of autobiography:

I may omit or transpose facts, or make mistakes in dates; but I cannot go wrong about what I have felt, or about what my feelings have led me to do; and these are the chief subjects of my story. The true object of my confessions is to reveal my inner thoughts exactly in all the situations of my life. It is the history of my soul that I have promised to recount.

It can be readily seen how Rousseau opened up the form to successors such as Thomas de Quincey and Oscar Wilde, to name but two, who though less comprehensive in their account of their lives, would use the form as a vehicle for unleashing their feelings and divulging their souls, with the freedom and bravura of unchecked sincerity.

PSYCHIC FACTS

Despite the fact that Rousseau has been dubbed the father of modern autobiography, historically oriented critics have been quick to single out generic revisionism in the second half of the nineteenth century. On the one hand, William Spengemann has traced the evolution of 'poetic' autobiography; on the other hand, Linda Peterson has identified the development of positivistic, scientific autobiography. In this latter connection, along with names such as Darwin, Butler, Spencer, is most notably Edmund Gosse. For if the scientifically oriented writers were recounting their discovery of scientific facts, Gosse was assembling a series of psychic facts as if they were scientific. But it can be argued that the process of focusing on psychic facts in Gosse's *Father and Son* (1907) brings this autobiography closer to the fictional ones that were developing simultaneously. On the one hand, Gosse was charting the evolution of an identity, in Darwinian fashion, but on the other hand, he was chronicling a narrative of dramatic events, adding an intensity in the presentation of them that seemed to anticipate the treatment of events fictionalised by Proust and Joyce specifically.

The tone of Gosse's autobiography is distinctive and takes the genre to another stage in the early twentieth century. For although Gosse treats telling psychic moments, he deals with them in an objective, detached fashion which is unsentimental and factual. It would appear that he was attacking specifically the influence of Rousseau on the genre in the statement he makes in the Preface to

Father and Son: 'Perhaps an even more common fault in such autobiographies is that they are sentimental, and are falsified by self-admiration and self-pity.'[13] As for himself, he insists that he has not tampered with precise facts; what he has to say about his relationship with his father reflects the problematics of his society at large. Comparing his work to the contemporary fiction of his time, he pledges that his account is 'scrupulously true' because it is presented as a sociological document, 'as the diagnosis of a dying Puritanism'. Gosse writes his autobiography from a Positivistic viewpoint which bears the marks of Taine's 'race–moment–milieu' theory.

On the other hand, the very material of Gosse's autobiography – the nocturnal dreams, the negative epiphany regarding religion, the experiments with paganism in the idolatry of the chair, and the contemplation of the pagan idols – are all material for fiction. It is as if Gosse's unique mixture of the scientific (as he charts the stages of evolution of his identity) and the literary (the scene making) is a result of his intellectual movement away from the religious and scientific elements of his father's background to the literary orientation which he himself adopts. Therefore, although this autobiography is constructed on grounds of scientific documentation, it contains literary potential beyond the mere automatic, retrospective narration of events. For, while charting in Darwinian fashion the evolution of his own identity into manhood, he was creating a narrative of dramatic events which, intense as they are, are actually similar to those fictionalised by such contemporaries as Proust and Joyce.

This representatively modern autobiography is selective in treating a slice of life from the ages of three to seventeen. Psychic facts are featured as emerging from traumatic experiences of early childhood and are dealt with analytically by the author:

> In the course of this, my sixth year, there happened a series of minute and soundless incidents which, elementary as they may seem when told, were second in real importance to none in my mental history.[14]

Gosse seems to multiply and intensify events pertaining to the age of six – the heresy of the chair, the ruin of the rockery, and the discovery of the father's lack of omniscience. These scenes are presented as focal points of rebellion and scepticism emerging in early childhood and protracting the narrative of that segment of life. For

example, in hoisting a chair on to a table and then praying to it, the young Gosse does not incur the wrath of God as his father had warned. In recounting such an act of idolatry, Gosse notes that it only served to increase his scepticism about his father's omniscience. Such experiences culminate in the crisis scene at the age of seventeen when Gosse, in the last year of what he calls his 'boyish life', alone in his boarding school classroom, totally dismisses the God of his father and turns agnostic. Such dramatic identity-forming shifts seem to be charted in all the autobiographies, formal and even fictional, but they become more climactic when images are produced to describe these pivotal experiences.

It has been pointed out that Gosse undercuts the conversion convention of spiritual autobiographies by offering an earlier conversion scene to be followed by a radical reversal of de-conversion. As such, it can be considered a parody of spiritual autobiography. An analogous approach could be seen in the case of Sartre who, half a century later, denies his allegiance to the literary work nurtured in childhood as he reverts to dehumanisation in existentialist fashion.

Yet in heightening the notion of identity formation, this autobiography reflects the developing psychological theory of its time, which was to be most notably exposed by Freud. Gosse formally offers 'a study of the development of moral and intellectual ideas during the progress of infancy'.[15] He recalls early childhood experiences which had lasting impacts on his life. He recounts how at the age of seven, he endured the illness and death of his mother. Then when he was nine, there were the nightmare visions and nocturnal episodes – hints of a repressed imagination and symptomatic perhaps of an artistic sensibility. Repeated disappointments in his father's Calvinist religion create a crisis of faith and prepare the way for the eventual rejection of his father's dogma and the ultimate adoption of an agnostic vision.

Accompanying such psychological material is the appearance of the technique of epiphany, what Joyce was virtually defining at this same time. After all, *Father and Son* appeared at the time Joyce was writing *Stephen Hero*, his draft for *A Portrait of the Artist as a Young Man*. Gosse's rejection at the age of seventeen of his father's religion is described in a three-paragraph passage and cast in terms of a negative epiphany. Because of similar themes and practices, there is here an intersection between what is still in the category of the conventional genre and what was simultaneously developing as an aesthetic one. But whereas Joyce, as we shall see, proceeds with the

elaboration of the epiphany in fictionalisation, Gosse clings to the factual basis for his moment of awakening, as he documents it with time, place and elaboration of sentiment.

The comparison of these two contemporary autobiographical writers, whose autobiographies both range from the early years of childhood to the age of 20 or 21, suggests that the notion of epiphany, which was to become a distinct structural element in fictional autobiographies, grew out of real life experience. As in Gosse's case, it was seen as emerging in a scientific, factual 'slice of life' autobiography with a strong truth claim. As fictional autobiography begins to develop, it becomes contaminated with elements of the factual and acquires a hybrid make-up.

Gosse's succinct autobiography suggests where autobiography proper was arriving in the early twentieth century. Its slice-of-life span ending in crisis had replaced the extended narrative of a continuous life that was typical of previous autobiographical narrative. Psychic intensity – the concentration on significant moments – was replacing extrinsic reportage of events. Autobiography was on the verge of annulling the notion of single selfhood as its basis, and a dialectical movement was about to replace the standard linear chronology of the narrative. Eventually, the mode would turn upon itself in autocriticism.

AUTOCRITICISM

A number of reputable twentieth century self-conscious autobiographies introduce an element of autocriticism in connection with the genre. In the years after Gosse's autobiography and certain literary memoirs such as those of Moore and Yeats, the first edition of Gide's sensational autobiography *Si le grain ne meurt* appeared in 1920. As a contemporary and editor of Proust, Gide opposed Proust's secretive attitude toward his personal life and manifested this contrast through the outright frankness and candour of his own life writing. With respect to his novel *L'Immoraliste*, for example, Gide declared that the germ of his character Michel existed in himself so as to expose his homosexuality at that time. If, as we shall see, in the process of aesthetic autobiography Proust was veiling his life through the subterfuge of art, Gide was using autobiography in all forms to feature the truth-telling process. The two French writers were going in opposite directions in their different practices of the

autobiographical mode. Also, while the aesthetic autobiographers were creating a hybrid genre, as shall be seen, the practitioners of autobiography proper were working to secure the boundaries between their genre and fiction.

Gide's work provides a significant stage in the evolution of autobiography in the twentieth century because he was obsessed throughout his life with autobiographical expression and experimented with the various forms it could take. He created transparent fictional characters and used the confessional form in *Les Cahiers d'André Walter* and *L'Immoraliste*, produced 60 years of running autobiographical commentary in his journal, and authored a strict autobiography, *Si le grain ne meurt*. It is interesting that he arrives at writing autobiography proper during his period of maturity at the age of 57. In writing the account of his youth which he labels as a narrative or *récit*, he qualifies it as *véridique* rather than *vrai*. *Véridique* is a word used by twentieth-century French writers to indicate the feeling of truth, rather than simply truthful. Gide obviously regards the question of truth to be a complicated matter, insisting on the truthfulness of his autobiography but speculating that his novel comes closer to the truth than the memoir. He was perhaps suggesting that his novel *L'Immoraliste*, for example, had used no literary techniques to hide an identity as had been the case with Proust and others. For Gide's work did not aim at aesthetic priorities.

Gide also insists that his autobiography proper is *not* a literary composition. Saying that he wrote those recollections as they came to him, he admits that the chronological tradition that he adheres to actually hinders him:

> *Le plus gênant c'est de devoir présenter comme successifs des états de simultanéité confuse. Je suis un être de dialogue; tout en moi combat et se contredit. Les Mémoires ne sont jamais qu'à demi sincères, si grand que soit le souci de la vérité: tout est toujours plus compliqué qu'on ne le dit. Peut-être même approche-t-on de plus près la vérité dans le roman.*[16]

[The most annoying thing is to have to present as successive steps states that occurred in confusing simultaneity. I am dialogical; everything in me fights and contradicts itself. Memoirs are only half sincere, no matter how great the concern is to tell the truth: everything is always more complicated than one supposes. Perhaps we even get closer to the truth in the novel.]

It is especially fascinating that Gide should have made such a comment just at the historical moment when writers were turning to the autobiographical novel for self-exploration. In protesting against the chronological imperative of autobiographical narrative, Gide was pointing to a synchronic or holistic interpretation of his life. Accuracy with respect to dates would only constrain his expression: *'Ma mémoire ne se trompe pas souvent de place; mais elle brouille les dates; je suis perdu si je m'astreins à de la chronologie'* ('My memory of a place does not often fail, but it confuses the dates. I am lost if I confine myself to chronology').

Considering himself 'dialogical', Gide introduces the element of self-scrutiny in his autobiography, as he focuses on moral tensions in his early life. In view of the controversial subject matter it conveyed to its time, Gide insists that his autobiography is not an apology (*défense*) but his story (*histoire*). It spans 26 years of his life from his years of childhood to the point of his homosexual adventures in North Africa. It ends abruptly with his mother's death and his engagement to his cousin Madeleine Rondeaux, whom he called Emmanuèle. In the course of that account, Gide undergoes self-castigation: 'let's say that I write by penitence' (*'mettons que c'est par pénitence que je l'écris'*). His puritanical restrictive background puts him in the situation of a confession, even as he blatantly relishes the exposure of sensual truth.

Certain reversals of precedents are apparent in this autobiography. Despite the fact that Gide starts his retrospective account with childhood, referring specifically to the ages of five to seven, he desanctifies the state of childhood. He warns the reader from the start that his childhood soul is not innocent, but rather prone to the pleasure principle and corruption:

A cet âge innocent où l'on voudrait que toute l'âme ne soit que transparence, tendresse et pureté, je ne revois en moi qu'ombre, laideur et sournoiserie.[17]

[At an innocent age when one would like to see transparency, tenderness and purity in the soul, I rediscover in myself only shadow, ugliness and deceptiveness.]

The word *sournoiserie* accentuates a kind of underhandedness or cunning, not normally associated with childhood. Subsequently, as the conversion factor is reversed into an admission of 'sin',

chronology made secondary and the need for an apology removed, the genre is developing its own polemic.

Outright manipulation of the genre occurs in Gertrude Stein's *The Autobiography of Alice B. Toklas* (1933). This author attempts to view herself objectively through the intermediary of 'the other', by creating a narrative persona. This drive toward objectivity within the formal genre seems to parallel the highly aesthetic means of objectification developed simultaneously in the autobiographical novel, as we shall see. As she becomes a practitioner of the genre, Stein recognises the same problems that Gide had observed regarding the element of psychological veracity in autobiography proper. Going beyond Gide, Stein seeks to eliminate the restrictions of the consciousness of chronological time by absorbing into her autobiography the impression of the continuous present. She purposefully dismisses the past as she rejects the notion of the historical continuity of a self. In losing its link with the retrospective, the autobiography concentrates on the writing self. Stein's autobiographies, even as she moves from 'the other' to the presumed self in *Everybody's Autobiography*, become self-critical. As she deals with the actual success of her previous autobiography, again her self is not isolated but relates outward to 'everybody', sharing the experience of a new identity. Commenting on her narrative, S. C. Neuman has observed that 'Stein writes autobiography that is both the genre and its criticism'[18] and that Stein 'transforms the genre into a profoundly impersonal one, a manifestation of the process of writing'. In fact, at this critical stage in the evolution of the genre, autobiographies become theoretically oriented as they expose their own concept of composition. At the time of the development of aesthetic autobiography, another cluster of writers adhering to autobiography proper were attempting to subvert the genre.

Although *The Autobiography of Alice B. Toklas* is basically a period piece, describing the modernist writers and artists in Paris before and during the war years, it pauses intermittently to capture portraits of Stein over a period of 30 years and ends with the startling admission that Stein actually wrote the autobiography. In this manner a transparently veiled autobiography has emerged which, however, describes Stein from the point of view of an observer without probing the inner self or offering anything near a complete portrait. This distancing from the self and the play within the strict genre contrasts with the intensity and artistry of autobiographical fiction.

Michel Leiris is another writer customarily brought into the discussion of the evolution of the genre. As the author of several autobiographies and preoccupied with the genre all his life, he continues to put autobiography proper into a polemical and highly self-conscious position. *L'Age d'homme* of 1939 (whose title was conceived in 1922) starts off in the recognisable category of a *récit d'enfance*, dealing with ages one to eleven, but soon departs from that strict chronology to describe the critical passage from childhood to virility by the processes of analogy, montage, collage and myth. He had borrowed some of those techniques from the Surrealist code of writing although he was to reject that application early in his career. Episodes from childhood, for example, are regrouped according to analogous incidents. Autobiography itself is envisaged in terms of the analogy of bullfighting. In his essay 'De la littérature considerée comme une tauromachie', which he added to the 1946 edition of *L'Age d'homme*, he draws a comparison between his activity as a writer of confessions and that of the torero. If the danger of the torero is physical annihilation, the writing of autobiography involves the psychological risk of exposing one's obsessions and destroying one's relationships because it is so totally dedicated to truth telling. Writers like Proust and Woolf were unwilling to run such risks and sought the ambiguous cover-up of fiction, as we shall see. But like Gide, Leiris draws a strict boundary between the genre of autobiography and the novel, stating that the autobiography or confession, as he calls it, is 'the negation of a novel'[19] ('*la négation d'un roman'*) because he does not allow his imagination to work on any of the facts. He forcefully subscribes to an autobiographical code of dealing with truths and shunning artifice in his writing at any expense:

> For to tell the whole truth and nothing but the truth is not all: he must confront it directly and tell it without artifice, without those great arias intended to make it acceptable, tremolos or catches in the voice, grace notes and gildings which would have no other result than to disguise it to whatever degree, even by merely attenuating its crudity, by making less noticeable what might be shocking about it.

Leiris's bull's horn runs the moral risk of social opprobrium, since his autobiography is overtly critical of his elite Western culture which has turned him into a misfit. No doubt under the

influence of Freud, Leiris uses his autobiography as a vehicle for self-analysis. He seems to be conducting a case study of a man controlled by the superego of his culture, and in particular by his classical education. He isolates certain symptoms of his condition such as ambivalent sexuality, obsessions with mythic female types, the fear of castration, a preoccupation with death. These disorders are presented in terms of dream, fantasy and myth conveyed in juxtaposition. The motive for such exposure is to effect a catharsis of his troubling afflictions or, to use the poet Baudelaire's expression, to lay his heart bare. Despite such claims, however, Germaine Brée has commented that Leiris made more of a maze than a way of the labyrinth of the self, having failed to reach a centre or to decode the life data he has amassed. As she puts it, Leiris is 'caught in the uncertainties of his passage through language'.[20]

From *L'Age d'homme*, written at the age of 34, Leiris extends his autobiography into *La Règle du jeu*, a four-volume work which he wrote over a period of 28 years – well into his seventies. His pun on *je* suggests the continuing search for the I and self-definition. The first section entitled *Biffures*, published nine years after *L'Age d'homme*, has recently been translated as *Scratches* to stress the fragmentary nature of the narrative as it digs further into disparate memories of his childhood and the origins of his language. Leiris himself explains the use of the French expression *bifurs* to suggest deviation in language caused by the culling of trappings of past experience. Such fragments do not culminate, as with the aesthetic writers, into the insight of an epiphany. Instead, they are reference points which derail the mind from its ordinary path, having the potential of shedding light on his identity although such illumination is never reached. Recreating aspects of his past through a recollection of words and their double meanings through wordplay, Leiris narrates a journey through language, atemporalising experience in the process.

But in this second attempt at autobiographical narrative, Leiris, like Sartre a bit later, has lost his faith in language and is self-critical. He asks:

> When I wrote *Manhood* did I reach the farthest limit of my capacities? Is the work I am writing now only a flabbier and more verbose rehashing of the attempt I once attempted, an undertaking one can perhaps manage only once in a lifetime?[21]

Here Leiris seems to contradict the truth claim of his earlier volume, which had so adamantly separated autobiography from fiction. He admits to inaccuracies, as his quest remains unfulfilled and ultimately he becomes sceptical about his project: 'indecision over the direction of my whole undertaking'.

This play with chronology and narrative that Leiris introduces into autobiography has been categorised by some, most notably Philippe Lejeune, as *l'ordre dialectique*. But it is Jean-Paul Sartre who most succinctly employs such structuring in his autobiography, *Les Mots* (1964). Sartre's narrative juxtaposes an account of his childhood (from the ages of four to eleven) and past self with his crisis at 50 or the 'present' self who is writing the autobiography. He denies that very youth as his 'imposture' and an 'old crumbling structure'. That is to say, the narrator first describes his own conversion to words and humane letters as an idealistic child and then disclaims that conversion in his adult years. From his youth in which he is a 'writer-knight', he moves to the jaded Existentialist of his mid-life crisis.

Calling himself a traitor, by setting the past and present in total conflict, Sartre continues in the line of those who seek to alter autobiography proper by dismissing the notion of unitary selfhood. He conveniently rejects a point of origin, by referring to the death of his father when he was one year old. He then recounts how this unfortunate event gives him the freedom to continuously create himself and eventually to deconstruct himself without the qualms of a superego guiding him in a uniform direction. Admitting his neurosis with respect to this split personality, he uses his autobiography for self-analysis, what Lejeune has called *'analyse totalement a-chronique'*.[22] The autobiography moves alternately between past and present, as it singles out evolving strains of thought but violates strict narrative continuity. And it is as much about the 30-year crisis which he has rejecting the bourgeois literary convictions of his youth as about the youth himself who was chronologically presented as having undergone a conversion between the ages of seven and nine to a humanistic faith in words.

An analogy unites the beginning and the end of the autobiographical narrative. As a 'traveller without a ticket', without paternal guidance, Sartre developed an instinct as a child to use words as a weapon to safeguard his free fare. If in the past he used the pen as a sword, later as an Existentialist and the writer of the

autobiography he has renounced the humanistic power of language
to give himself justification and cause:

> I've again become the traveller without a ticket that I was at age
> seven: the ticket collector has entered my compartment; he looks
> at me . . . he'll be satisfied with a valid excuse, any excuse . . .
> Unfortunately, I can't think of any; and besides I don't even feel
> like trying to find one.[23]

He may also be renouncing the very autobiography he has written
to define and circumscribe himself.

Like Gide, Sartre suggests that the truth about himself might be
more fully revealed in fiction. Although his career as a novelist is over
when he writes his autobiography, he specifically refers his readers
back to the Roquentin of his 1938 novel *La Nausée* as an accurate
depiction of himself: 'I was Roquentin; I used him to show, without
complacency, the texture of my life.' Here again was a gesture which
went totally counter to the aesthetic autobiographers, who had
shunned any outright identification with their fictional characters.

Sartre brings formal autobiography to a point of subversive function, totally inverting the conversion pattern and undermining the
significance of childhood. He attacks the deterministic causality
inherent in chronological narrative; 'the retrospective illusion has
been smashed to bits', he says characteristically.[24] If by comparison
at first Soyinka's *Aké: Years of Childhood* of 1981 seems anachronistic,
dealing with the first eleven years of a Nigerian boy's life, that
impression is soon dispelled when the reader recognises the cultural
impact of the work and the synchronic quality of the narrative.
However, despite the fact that this is truly a cultural autobiography
designed by Soyinka to instruct his fellow Yorubans into a culture
which is threatened by European influence, there is an intertextual
quality inherent in the narrative that situates it in the tradition of the
evolving genre. This could be due to the fact that this African writer
himself had been educated in the British university context from
which he must have absorbed certain elements that prevailed in the
development of the mode.

The incident of the neglected rose bush takes its place in the tradition
of spots of time traced back to Augustine's theft from the pear tree and
Rousseau's stealing of Mademoiselle Pontal's ribbon. But unlike
Augustine or even Rousseau, Soyinka recounts the event through his
highly sensual memory. The vividness with which the older Wole

describes this incident, 40 or so years after it had taken place, renders it 'present' and immediate:

> The fresh young petals lay wounded on the bed, caught among the thorns and branches. Even the leaves were broken, stamens were cut in half at the filament . . . I had physically assaulted Essay's roses.[25]

Soyinka demonstrates how as a guardian of his father Essay's rose bush, he wilfully neglects it. As in most autobiographies, a parental relationship is in question. But Soyinka is in outright rebellion against a father who stands for the acceptance of Christianity and Colonialism. Rather than point to an individual's crisis, his own field of vision is used as an index for the predicament of a society at large. There is no epiphany here because it is not a question of an individual insight or psychological idiosyncrasy.

Soyinka skilfully manipulates contrasts between the past and the present, as in describing the markets of the Nigerian village Aké through rich sensory images and then commenting that those rich smells are gone in the present moment of narration. Despite the erosion of the primitive element, he is able to recapture an element of Yoruban culture for his contemporary audience. If the chronology charts an elegy of a paradise gone, the synchronic vision amalgamates and restores the past in the collective consciousness of the present. More than recollect, Soyinka revives that richly sensual past in what Virginia Woolf might have called 'memory images'. For he is out to offer not merely his own autobiography, nor that of another individual, but that of the larger culture of which he feels part.

The evolution of autobiography in the Western world does proceed from the individual to the collective and cultural totality. Current criticism is devouring autobiographies from the perspective of a Taine all over again, for their sociological content – uncovering the culture of race, milieu and moment of which they are products. In the selected milestones featured in these past pages, it seems apparent that exterior events have been the motivation for the introspection of the authors. In contrast, in the chosen works of the autobiographical novelists in the pages to follow, the focus will be on the points dominated by the interior visions that use exterior events as accessories. Such interior visions were projected onto the fictional narrative and a hybrid genre was created coalescing life fact and artifact in a movement away from the gauge of extrinsic verification. The only standard in this avatar of life writing is art.

2

Theories of Autobiography

Theories of autobiography have proliferated since the 1970s. Most critical discussion has focused on formal autobiography and the fiction or truth within that form. Simple curiosity about people's lives may have first led critics into such theorising, but then more sophisticated questions of referentiality, mimesis and the issue of the ontology of the self began to dominate the inquiries. The question of autobiographical truths within the fictional form has certainly not been a concern of the critics thus far, and can represent an evolution in the study of the relationship between the self and the text.

In the very beginning there were those who were interested in the author for the author's sake. Readers attracted to the work of an author were motivated to seek out the life of the extraordinary or accomplished person, the better to understand the work. The critic Sainte-Beuve may have unwittingly begun the discussion with this orientation when back in the nineteenth century he proclaimed *'tel arbre, tel fruit'*. In other words, an understanding of the work could be reached through simple investigation of its source – the author. Such a causal relationship, deterministic as it could be perceived, would explain the derivation of the substance and character of the work of art. Expanding the view further, Hippolyte Taine had gone on to examine literary works as indices of certain societies at large, designating the value of a literary work in terms of what it said about the society from which it came. The concern was not so much with the individual sources as with the soil or culture that nurtured the work of art – a composite of individuals, if you will. Taine himself presented this theory and its praxis in his monumental work *Histoire de la littérature anglaise*. In his view such a comprehensive study of English literature would lead to an understanding of the psychology of the English nation and its people. Both of these Frenchmen were concerned with the subject matter of literary texts as revealing their sources.

Historically oriented critics of the twentieth century proceeded to study autobiography as a genre based on the notion of a pre-existing

ontological self. Georges Gusdorf's isolated article of 1956, 'Conditions and Limits of Autobiography', was a landmark piece in this regard, for in it he was claiming that autobiography was culture specific: 'a kind of apologetics of theodicy of the individual being'.[1] What has since been called 'classical autobiography theory' was established by this historical critic, who unequivocally maintained that autobiography was 'a solidly established literary genre' whose history could be traced in the 'masterpieces' of Western expression. Spanning the genre from Saint Augustine to Montaigne, Rousseau, Goethe, Mill, Newman and others, he discerned a common motivating concern of Western man in the awareness of the 'singularity of each individual life' even as that life reflected an historical and cultural totality. Nurtured in the climate of historiography with the works of Wilhelm Dilthey and Georg Misch in the background, Gusdorf assumed that the literary and artistic function of autobiography was secondary to its anthropological one. His became a strong case for autobiography as a truth-telling endeavour. The limits he referred to in the title of his article were those of time and space as they apply to Western culture in the post-Copernican era. Following Gusdorf, Roy Pascal expressed an even greater concern for the uniqueness of the self in his book *Design and Truth in Autobiography* (1960). Also asserting that autobiography is 'a distinct product of Western, post-Roman civilization',[2] he emphasised that the subject of such autobiographies was a sieve through which the outside world was processed. The selectivity inherent in the garnering of certain experiences constituted a greater truth than an objective historian's or biographer's account of a life of an era.

After Gusdorf and Pascal, historical treatment of the subject propagated and developed into a particular strand of autobiography criticism which was soon labelled as 'essentialist' or transcendental in reference to the notion of an autonomous pre-existing self from which the autobiography stemmed. Such criticism was interested in the authorial subject, either for itself or to explain the artistic work of the author.

It was inevitable that the historical view of autobiography as a culturally determined phenomenon dependent on certain notions of individualism should lead some critics to relate the genesis of the genre specifically to Romanticism and the invasive credo of subjectivity. After all, the Romantics had strengthened the links between the author and his work – the work being the manifestation of the author's genius. They had used the 'I' in its essentialist personal

sense. One could say that all their works were autobiographical regardless of genre classification. Karl Weintraub, a cultural historian, in his book *The Value of the Individual* (1978) saw it as a genre emerging as a corollary of Western culture's valorisation of the individual. Although he chronicled a history of individuality through the form from Saint Augustine to Goethe, he saw its most rapid growth since 1800. With a similar point of view but a bit later, Jerome Buckley in his book *The Turning Key* (1984) viewed autobiography as a manifestation of a subjective impulse since 1800. Buckley was actually saying that it grew as a form when a series of writers, especially the Victorians, felt compelled to search for their selves in efforts at self-scrutiny and self-revelation. Pursuing such a point in the same year as Buckley, A. O. J. Cockshut's book *The Art of Autobiography in Nineteenth and Twentieth Century England* found significance in the fact that autobiography was not really identified as a separate form until the early nineteenth century because it was not until then that the self-consciousness of the author and the individual point of view was expressed and became noticeable. In his view, autobiography is to be judged by the truth value which is the subjective truth of the author's view of his own life. Since author and subject are regarded as the same, a certain consistency between the style and the subject is necessary.

Further variations on the theme of autobiography as a dimension of individual or social *Zeitgeist* had been pursued earlier in terms of genre theory. The leading spokesman for a formal generic definition of autobiography was Philippe Lejeune. In *Le Pacte autobiographique* (1975) he presented a formula which satisfied certain conditions of chronological narration, mimesis and individualism:

> *Récit rétrospectif en prose qu'une personne réelle fait de sa propre existence, lorsqu'elle met l'accent sur sa vie individuelle en particulier sur l'histoire de sa personnalité.*[3]

[Retrospective prose narrative that a real person makes of his own existence, when he emphasises his individual life, especially the history of his personality].

Lejeune went out of his way to characterise the pact as a referential one, submittable to proofs of verification, which the reader would be brought in to ascertain. This carefully constructed autodiegetic contract established an identity between the author,

narrator and central character or protagonist. It stressed chronological narration and reference to the past. Lejeune was also intent on maintaining firm boundaries between autobiography and the novel. In contrast to all forms of fiction, he said, autobiography and for that matter biography, like social or historical discourse, offered information about an exterior reality. That information was not simply probable (*vraisemblable*) but actual (*resemblable*); he made this distinction between two French words to further his point about the factor of authenticity. The neighbouring genre of the *roman personnel*, for example, does not fulfil the conditions of the autobiographical pact and was to be considered under the rubric of *le pacte romanesque*, and hence divorced from questions of referentiality. Other adjacent genres, which he listed as memoirs, biography, the autobiographical poem, the journal, the self-portrait and the essay, were also excluded from the autobiographical pact.

If, on the one hand, Lejeune gained recognition for his definition and became a general frame of reference for further critical discussion, that very definition also became a subject for attack by assorted critics. What became particularly unconvincing for some was the inclusion of such moderns as Sartre and Leiris under the rubric of the pact. By simply stating that the invention of new structures of narrative by such moderns allowed for the evolution of the genre, Lejeune seemed to have weakened the strictness of his own classification. For example, for those who concentrated on the dialectics of Sartre's works, *Les Mots* was more than simply a 'variant of the seed of classical autobiography' ('*une variante du germe autobiographique classique*'). For others, when Lejeune placed Proust in a hazy region '*dans un espace ambigu*' between fiction and autobiography, noting a certain hint of identity between the narrator and protagonist, that ambiguity violated the definition.

But the identity of the author and speaker as a condition of autobiography was stressed by another critic at the time, Elizabeth Bruss, whose short and focused commentary *Autobiographical Acts* was published in 1976, a year after Lejeune's work. Like Lejeune, Bruss retained the traditional criterion of referentiality, but she went on to elaborate it into a set of conditions which the genre must fulfil. Describing the genre in terms of a function rather than form, she viewed autobiography as an evolving genre and specifically as an illocutionary act with an identifiable subject as source. Certain

conditions of veracity and sincerity had to be satisfied – claims for the truth value of the information and events reported in the text, and the sincerity of the autobiographer's assertions. In Bruss's view, autobiography retains a certain distinctiveness as a genre identified closely with biography. Her ultimate restriction on the genre was that 'some portions of the subject must concern the identity of the author'[4] even if fictional play intrudes, as in the case of Nabokov which she discusses at length. In fact, Bruss juxtaposed an autobiographical burlesque, *Lolita*, with an autobiography *per se*, *Speak Memory*, to demonstrate the way in which autobiography has evolved in the twentieth century but has retained its identity as a genre distinct from fiction. Limited as her commentary was to four heterogeneous writers of the English language – Bunyan, Boswell, De Quincey and Nabokov – it is questionable how she would have treated others in her definition.

Bruss was among those autobiography critics who insisted that autobiographers held the common assumption that events, objects or relationships described 'are there whether or not they are written about'. Despite the fact that she purported to define the genre by its activity or function, she made strong claims for the objective status of the events and autonomous existence of a pre-existing self: 'it remains in essence the record of a self with its own autonomous existence'.

A cluster of critics who are not genre critics *per se* made further attempts to delimit autobiography. In contrast to Lejeune and Bruss who insisted on a certain verifiability with the outside world, there were those critics who were interested in autobiography not simply because of its narrative re-presentation of a life but because of the light it throws on the intentional content of the work. Self-exploration would assume higher priority than simple representation. The commentary of William Spengemann in 1980 and Richard Coe in 1984, and more recently Linda Peterson in 1986 widened the view of autobiography along such lines. In *The Forms of Autobiography* William Spengemann presented autobiography as an evolving literary genre which proceeded from the historical to the philosophical and eventually to the poetic. As he charted its development from the formal paradigm of Saint Augustine's *Confessions*, he classified *The Prelude* of Wordsworth as a philosophical autobiography and *The Scarlet Letter* of Hawthorne as a poetic one. In including a confession, a poem and a romance as models of the form, he widened the boundaries of the genre, showing, for example, how *The Scarlet*

Letter enacted the writer's own psycho-drama. Spengemann's main premise is that autobiography, which began as a 'self-biographical mode', went on predictably to 'assume fictive forms in the modern era'[5] In his view, such a generic evolution was already accomplished a century ago.

Richard Coe's book *When the Grass was Taller*, as we have seen, has taken a thematic approach to the genre in defining a variant of auto-biography which is specifically connected to the recreation of the experience of childhood. Coe claims that what he calls 'the Child-hood' (but what would be no surprise to the French and their cat-egory of *récit d'enfance*) has only come into is own over the past 150 years. In this context, the criterion is inner, symbolic truth, often poetically expressed, rather than historical accuracy. But the form is construed as distinctly literary, 'intimately related to the novel'[6] because it is most often a narrative sequence reflecting the develop-ment of the writer's self to a certain degree of maturity. As illustra-tions of this species of autobiography culled from 600 well-known and lesser-known texts, Coe chooses *The Prelude* of Wordsworth and *A Portrait of the Artist as a Young Man* as two of the most carefully structured.

In contrast, Linda Peterson's specific treatment of Victorian auto-biography, in her book of that title, delimits the genre in terms of a common, closed hermeneutical orientation that had its inception in John Bunyan's *Grace Abounding to the Chief of Sinners*, its ascendancy at the beginning of the nineteenth century, and its demise at the beginning of the twentieth century. She argues that this form of introspective spiritual autobiography distinguished itself as a genre by its abiding interest in the interpretative act – the strategy of early biblical commentary. In her view, the tendency to treat the genre as a variant of the novel overlooks a major distinction between the two. That distinction is that the novel is concerned with narration, self-expression and representation, whereas autobiography deriving from biblical hermeneutics is concerned with self-interpretation. Since narrative emplotment is not a principal feature of this latter activity, Peterson draws firm lines between autobiography and the novel in the Victorian era.

But along with this development of a history of autobiography, with its basis in the essentialist notion of an independent entity which is the self, the philosophical attitudes at the source of Decon-struction had emerged and had provided the grounds for a debate about autobiography. Specifically, the challenge of the existence of

the author had arisen – unsettling autobiography and actually giving the discussion a theoretical character. Barthes' 'Death of the Author' (1968) and Foucault's 'What is an Author?' (1969) were two period pieces which had vast repercussions on assumptions of the authorial self and on the tenor of autobiography criticism.

Barthes' startling essay had much to do with autobiography unwittingly since it separated the personal dimensions of emotion and intention of the author from any text: 'writing is the destruction of every voice, of every point of origin'.[7] As opposed to the personal author whom classic critics had identified with the works was the impersonal scriptor who had no past and no 'passions, humours, feelings, impressions' and who in no way preceded or exceeded the text. It is to be remembered that the elimination of the personality of the author in no way implied a heightened self, as will be seen in what I term aesthetic autobiographies, because such artistry suggests an individuality of style which Barthes would have ideologically rejected. As for Foucault, he went on further to challenge the notion of the author in his essay by contending that biographical fact actually limits the texts. His is a quotable statement indeed: 'the author is the principle of thrift in the proliferation of meaning'.[8] Wittily, he answered the question of his own title by saying that the author had been a functional construct, for convenience's sake, to limit meaning. But let us remember that the issue here is still meaning. By allowing discourse to fill the gaps rendered by the presumed death of God, man and the author, these critics are transferring substance from person to signifiers in the text.

Furthermore, the *Tel quel* anthology of 1968, *Théorie d'ensemble*, under the influence of the *nouveau roman* had featured a chorus of critics who voiced the notion that a textual self was independent of any historic or referential one. As if it were also preparing the way for the discussion to follow, Jean Thibaudeau's article 'Le Roman comme autobiographie' distinguished that '*je textuel, non-subjectif*' from '*le moi de l'auteur*'[9] and went on to define the true autobiographical novel as the '*roman textuel*' and the product of a textual self. In contrast, he referred to the previous representational novels of Lukács's description as 'biographical' novels precisely because they emanated from what he considered to be a bygone authorial self and preconceptions about a problematic Western society.

Such '*Götzen-Dämmerung*' of the author – to borrow an expression of Nietzsche – was contagious and was the impetus for the

proliferation of autobiography criticism to follow. Nietzsche's 'Twilight of the Idols', proceeding beyond Wagner's *'Twilight of the Gods' (Götterdämmerung)*, set the stage for the undermining of the author's position in the work. The first critics of autobiography were merely chronicling the history of autobiography in the Western world. There had been the common assumption of a pre-existing ontological self in an objective world 'out there'. Attacking such premises, the Deconstructionists were positing a textual self and were stripping autobiographical discourse of referential truth even though they were associating other truths with the narratives. Assaulting what they called the traditionalists of classical autobiography theory and their descendants, the 'essentialists' as they called them, the Deconstructionists helped create a bibliography all through the 1970s.

A group of American critics who normally would have had no interest in autobiography were drawn into a debate precisely because their notions fed into the subject. Most prominently at first, Jeffrey Mehlman, Louis Renza, Paul de Man and Michael Sprinker attacked the notion of an autobiographical self which could be identified separately from the work of art and anterior to it. In his book *A Structural Study of Autobiography* (1974), Mehlman observed that the modern experiments in autobiography simply revealed 'the impossibility of becoming alive (bio) to oneself (auto) in the elusive realm that the French call *écriture (graphie)'*.[10] Subsequently, Louis Renza proclaimed the impossibility of self representation, stating: 'the autobiographical enterprise occludes the writer's own continuity with the "I" being conveyed through his narrative performance'.[11] He based his argument on his notion of the illusionary status of the concept of self and identity.

Perhaps the most quoted of essays of this vintage was that of Paul de Man whose 'Autobiography as De-facement' argued that the so-called autobiographical texts offer an illusion of reference rather than any referential truth. In his view autobiography did not even constitute a genre. Like his fellow Deconstructionists, he echoed the view that it was devoid of any authorial source or origin. Although steeped in Rousseau, de Man used the unlikely example of Wordsworth's *Essay on Epitaphs* to demonstrate what he regarded as an appeal and subsequent repeal of an already absent source. But it was perhaps Michael Sprinker who came out with the most drastic statement in the ominous subtitle of his article 'Fictions of the Self', which was 'The End of Autobiography'. He actually maintained

enough of a historical perspective to claim that the ontological self which had produced the classical autobiographies of the late eighteenth and nineteenth centuries had disappeared to annihilate the possibility of the form. His drastic statement summed up the position of the Deconstructionist critics: 'Autobiography and the concept of the author as sovereign subject over a discourse are products of the same *episteme*.'[12] He was connecting autobiography as a literary genre with an *episteme* based on the concepts of subject, self and author as 'independent sovereignties', which in his view were obsolete.

It becomes especially interesting that many of the leading Structuralist and Deconstructionist critics referred to Proust's *A la recherche du temps perdu* as evidence for their argument concerning fictive narrators assuming the position of the authorial self. It is a fact that a string of critics including Barthes, Sprinker, de Man, Mehlman and, most pointedly, Gérard Genette and David Ellison, adamantly denied the autobiographical element of Proust's *roman fleuve* on the grounds that the author could not be the persona who had not yet written the book. They reminded their readers that it is not until the last section of Proust's opus, in the great scene of the Guermantes library, that the narrator discovers his vocation as a writer. Therefore, as the narrative stops, the writer begins his task, or as autobiography ends, the writing begins. Barthes had singled out Proust as having gone out of his way to dissociate the writer from his characters 'by making of the narrator not he who has seen and felt nor even he who is writing, but he who is going to write',[13] hence, not the one who has already written: 'By a radical reversal, instead of putting his life into his novel, as is so often maintained, he made of his very life a work for which his own book was the model.'

Genette, in his early Structuralist analysis of the whole *oeuvre* in *Figures III*, bracketed any consideration of connection of the work with the life of the author. In that extended theoretical study, Genette read the work as composed of a series of rhetorical strategies, indifferent to any referent in the real world: '*l'indifférence à l'égard du référent, et donc l'irréductible irréalisme de la description proustienne*'.[14] Sprinker saw in the end of *Le Temps retrouvé* a demonstration of the fact that autobiography originates and ends in the act of writing, creating and destroying itself within the process of text production. David Ellison found no applicability of autobiography to Proust's work since he read the relationship between the narrator

and Albertine as a play of tropes which obliterate the subject entirely. De Man extracted a short passage from *Swann's Way* and drew vast conclusions from a 'rhetorical' reading:

> It can be shown that the systematic critique of the main categories of metaphysics undertaken by Nietzsche in his late work, the critique of the concepts of causality, of the subject, of identity, of referential and revealed truth, etc., occurs along the same pattern of deconstruction that was operative in Proust's text.[15]

The rich ambiguity of Proust's narrative and the complex relationship between the text and the author were bypassed and unexplored as his work simply became the target for an attack on autobiographical reading. The Deconstructionist positions ultimately moved into Postmodern criticism, with its spokesman Ihab Hassan making yet another dire pronouncement about autobiography, calling it 'an impossible – and deadly – form': 'Impossible: how can a life come alive to itself without ending in the infinite folds of its own hermeneutic circle?'[16]

In line with the probing of the position of the self or its absence, a critic like Michel Beaujour bypassed the task of delimiting autobiography as a genre whatsoever by defining an adjacent genre, the autoportrait. In his book *Miroirs d'encre* (1980), Beaujour distinguished between autobiography and the autoportrait by pointing out the absence of a continuous narrative in the latter. He contrasted the two approaches:

> *L'autobiographe, le mémorialiste veulent qu'on se souvienne d'eux pour leur vie, les actions grandes et petites qu'il narrent. Le mémorialiste est d'abord quelqu'un, un tel qui se raconte. L'autoportraitiste, en revanche, n'est rien autre que son texte.*[17]

[The autobiographer, the writer of memoirs, wants to be remembered for their life, their actions great and small which they narrate. The writer of memoirs is first somebody, someone who tells his story. On the contrary, the autoportraitist is only his text.]

In specifically dismissing Lejeune's criteria of chronological narrative, representational mimesis and the status of a personal self, Beaujour set out to establish a new category which included

Aesthetic Autobiography

works (not their authors) such as the *Essays* of Montaigne, the *Rêveries* of Rousseau, *Ecce Homo* of Nietzsche, and most notably *La Règle du jeu* of Michel Leiris. What he believes such self-portraits had in common was that they participated in a rhetorical tradition in direct contrast to a metaphysics of representation. The auto-portraitist does not set out on an arduous task of painting himself in terms, for example, of an occupational identity. Instead, he is a writer described by his *écriture* rather than by mimesis or representation.

Beaujour argued that the elements of analogy and impersonality derived from Aristotle's *Rhetoric* were exemplified through the *écriture* of the autoportrait. The paradoxical nature of such texts is that instead of defining the self, they illustrate the impossibility of painting the self except as a trace of a larger collective anthropological schema. With a range of examples from the medieval speculum to selected modern works, Beaujour chose Michel Leiris's *L'Age d'homme* and *La Règle du jeu* to demonstrate that Leiris's autoportrait was 'the discovery and revelation by an individual of the degree of his assimilation of the culture' ('*la découverte et la révélation par un individu "cultivé" du degré d'acculturation*').

But such positions represented only one facet of the discussion. Between the warring factions of transcendental and Deconstructionist formulations, certain conciliatory positions did emerge. It is a fact that there have arisen approaches toward autobiography that have viewed it less as a literary form, with concerns of genre or rhetorical strategies, than as a mode of cognition and perception. Such psychological and philosophical orientations have been apparent in the work of such critics as James Olney, Paul John Eakin, Avrom Fleishman and in the phenomenological legacy of Paul Ricoeur. In associating the words 'metaphor' (Olney), 'figures' (Fleishman) and 'fictions' (Eakin) with autobiographical writing, these critics have suggested that autobiographical truth is composed of certain configurations created by the phenomenological self. They have been concerned, therefore, with the mechanism of that mental activity. Distancing themselves from the notion of a static psychology of a non-changing self, these critics have viewed autobiography in terms of a perception theory based on the notion of a dynamic self which is experiential and operational.

In his early book *Metaphors of Self* (1972) Olney had regarded the autobiographer's mind as a metaphor-making mechanism with an impulse to order. Olney seems to have been sensing a developing

debate early on by saying: 'the most fruitful approach to the subject of autobiography, I believe, is to consider it neither as a formal nor as a historical matter'.[18] The view of self, substantive or otherwise, is irrelevant to its functional activity in autobiography. Autobiography in both prose and poetry presents the self in the process of becoming through the intermediary of metaphor. As illustrations, Olney gave a variety of writers such as Darwin, Mill, Montaigne and T. S. Eliot. Rather than attempt to determine an ontology of the self, Olney was developing what he called an 'ontology of autobiography' in the subtitle of a later article. This ontology was defined as 'the order of reality that an autobiography can make claim to'.[19] Olney was reaffirming that the self expresses itself through figurative constructs that transform its given past or historic 'bios' – its lifetime – into a 'bios of the second degree' – processed by the mind's creative forces: 'The bios of an autobiography, we may say, is what the "I" makes of it . . . neither the autos or the bios is there in the beginning.'

Olney was explaining that the creation of bios into what might be called its derivative results in an 'ontology' of autobiography which recreates the first degree level of narration and historicity into the realm of the phenomenological present by the very act of creative recollection. As such, past events are reinterpreted in the light of the autobiographer's 'present' consciousness and 'bear to one another a relationship of significance rather than of chronology'. Specific elements of lived 'reality' such as places, times and individuals are rendered universal, timeless and poetic in this mode. In eliminating a criterion of narrative or chronology of events and avoiding any generic restrictions, Olney focused on the method of what might be called autobiographical rather than what had been designated as strict autobiography in generic terms. He was also establishing means for dealing with a subtle topic operating within many autobiographies – the relationship between the past and the present self. An example he gives is Richard Wright's fusion of a 'twofold bios' of narration and commentary in the creative memory that shapes the historic past in *Black Boy*.

If Olney considered the metaphoric activity present in autobiography, Avrom Fleishman focused on actual figures of autobiography in his book of that title in 1983. There he sought to identify the various typology, myth, metaphor and symbol in a gamut of autobiographies, particularly those of nineteenth- and

twentieth-century England. Fleishman viewed autobiography as an activity, what he called 'self-life-writing' that includes fictional (George Eliot) as well as non-fictional forms (Mill). He views the self formed through that act of writing. But he was also concerned with the actual mechanism of the autobiographical activity, that is 'the dramatic action that takes place within and among metaphors'.[20] As Fleishman was interested in the general compositional qualities of the metaphoric language, the related thematic patterns prevalent in the works, he did not treat any particular artistic process.

With an orientation similar to that of Olney, Paul John Eakin argued further that autobiography is a psychological activity – an evolving process of self-creation and self-invention. He views the autobiographical act as a re-enactment of a certain drama of identity formation – 'not merely as the passive, transparent record of an already completed self but rather as an integral and often decisive phase of the drama of self-definition'.[21] As the title of his book *Fictions in Autobiography* readily suggests, Eakin is concerned with the degree of fiction or truth within formal autobiographies. Unlike the traditional view set forth by Rousseau and others that fiction threatens the success of autobiography, Eakin assumes from the start that autobiographical truth is composed of certain fictions. For he asserts that selfhood emerges along with the acquisition of language, and that it is a fictive structure in the narrative. Using twentieth-century autobiographers as his examples, he shows how such writers naturally incorporated fictions in the presentation of their lives in their efforts to arrive at biographical truth. It is precisely such intentionality which marks autobiography. Like Olney, Eakin affirms that the past as shaped by memory and the needs of the present consciousness can be regarded as factual. In the case of Henry James, for example, he shows how in *A Small Boy and Others* the author, motivated by the desire to regain his creative powers, rereads mundane facts of his boyhood as the early development of himself as an artist and thereby dissolves distinctions between the past and present self – thereby creating a self in this written act of recollection.

While stressing the interdependency of self and language and attempting to alleviate the tensions between the textual and essentialists factions of the debate on autobiography proper, Eakin has come forth in his book *Touching the World* (1992) re-

asserting the referential structures of narrative and chronology. In particular, he has concentrated on defending Philippe Lejeune's 'referential pact' by holding that autobiography is a prose form necessarily based on temporality. But Eakin regards autobiography as a refererential art in a new context. For he states that, like everything else, it should be assumed that reference has new conditions in the twentieth century, which do not necessarily presuppose 'simple models of unitary selfhood' that belong to a previous epistemology. He asks: 'Is narrative as a structure of reference to be understood as a period specific phenomenon, an outmoded literary convention that is to be identified as a vestige of a nineteenth-century historicist model of the subject?'[22] It is obvious that Eakin's rhetorical question assumes a phenomenological view of the self.

Such an assumption is part of the phenomenological hermeneutics of Paul Ricoeur, the philosopher-critic who concentrated on the representation of time in narrative. In the course of that scrutiny, he also unselfconsciously shed light on referential components of the autobiographical novel. Back in 1975 in *The Rule of Metaphor* Ricoeur had redefined the notion of referentiality in general in terms of reader reception:

> The suspension of reference in the sense defined by the norms of descriptive discourse is the negative condition of the appearance of a more fundamental mode of reference, whose explication is the task of interpretation.[23]

As the world of the text intersects with the world of the reader, it is refigured and as such redescribes a world rather than indicates a prior one. The world of the text is the reference, and it acquires a 'truth claim' in so far as it is validly received by the reader. Any world anterior to this refigured world (in a historical sense, for example) is bracketed in a manner similar to Husserl's phenomenological 'Epoché'.

Ricoeur proceeded in *Time and Narrative* to subsume autobiography in his premise that *all* narrative has the ultimate referent of temporality. Structurally, he saw a correlation between narrativity and the temporal character of human experience. He identified the self of self-knowledge, not as an independent and egotistical one, but one which was purged by the effects of narrative – hence, a textual self, once again, yet part of a hermeneutical

experience. In his view, a life is 'no more than a biological phenomenon as long as it is not interpreted. And in the interpretation fiction plays a considerable, mediating role'[24] Ricoeur gave new meaning to the old words of mimesis, reference and representation by replacing them with the new words of configuration and refiguration. Life, human experience, has what Ricoeur calls a 'pre-narrative quality'; in that condition it is a potential to be configured by narrative.

Notably Ricoeur had started off his four-part *Time and Narrative* with the analysis of Saint Augustine's *Confessions* without necessarily commenting on the genre *per se*. Instead, he examined the work in its presentation of a particular twofold experience of temporality, as an aporia between chronological time and eternity. This autobiography, which is not even categorised as such, is nonetheless perceived as referential in terms of being a model for an identifiable human experience. In Part III he went on to say that modern narrative fiction, in particular, provides for an understanding of the self; life examined is life narrated. The application of this premise to autobiography proper is useful in shifting referentiality from the 'outside world' to the textual one. The world of the text is the reference with the truth claim in so far as it configures life and is validly received by the reader. It is especially interesting that Ricoeur treats the fictional narratives of Proust and Woolf but also does not associate them with autobiography. Since he is not a literary critic, he analyses neither the workings of this process of configuration nor any particular genre. In his view these narratives are simply 'richer in information about time'[25] than historical narratives, which would include standard autobiographies and their more homogenous structures.

A far cry from this rarefied atmosphere in which autobiography can be engulfed and treated is a much more tangible realm of sociological interests in which autobiography studies have been drawn. The historical treatment of the subject has been supplanted of late by gender and ethnic orientations to the genre – as representative of certain collectivities reflecting multicultural diversity. In this context, revisionism of the concept of selfhood continues, this time with the view of the self as a cultural construct instead of a private subjectivity. The terms 'the Other' and 'Difference' are among those most commonly used in this critical discourse on autobiography, which is out to code female difference or cultural otherness in the texts and redefine the theory of autobiographies in the process.

Special-interest groups have moved into the field in their focus on the marginal, ethnic or gender literature. Is slave narrative a species of autobiography? asks John Sekora.[26] Such critics all appear to have the same interest of what could simply be called Rousseau-bashing. For example, in her consideration of women writers' autobiographies, Julia Watson states:

> But the 'I' enunciated in no case manifests the self-dramatizing egoism and obsessive self reference of the Rousseauean autobiography which is understood by most critics as prototypical for the genre.[27]

Watson redefines the 'I' in women's life writings as 'mediated by the agency of a significant other(s) and originates as an Other to itself'.

In this latest stage of autobiography criticism, which verges on sociology, little or no attention has been paid to an aspect of the self which surpasses the personal or the cultural because it is precisely the aesthetic one. What is transparent is the fact that the Deconstructionist theorists of autobiography are not contesting the old-fashioned mimetic assumptions and premises of such sociological groups, precisely because they share certain ideological orientations with them. Much of the attack on autobiography has really been an attack on individualism and aesthetics – attempts to undermine the individualistic, independent self as the referential factor.

For the most part, however, the literary critics in their continuous and adventurous unearthing of new collective species of autobiography and cultural reference systems have not come to terms with the autobiographical novel as a genre with its own autonomous structures and concerns. But this has been the case even with critics prior to them. It should be noted that one of the very first genre critics, who was also concerned with cultural ramifications of literature, contributed to the ambiguity of the term 'autobiography' by placing it under the broad rubric of fiction. Treating autobiography unselfconsciously and rather awkwardly in a few pages of *Anatomy of Criticism*, Frye saw it actually merging with the novel by a 'series of insensible gradations',[28] calling it the confession before Rousseau and fictional autobiography thereafter. One of its features was that it was 'intellectualized in content'. By this he meant that the confession

form, as he called it, had certain ideological interests in aesthetics, politics or religion enhancing a life, that did not serve merely as social data as they did in the novel. A strange definition indeed, in the light of the much more specific delimitations that followed. But it was Lejeune who seemed to have picked up the subject almost two decades later only to dismiss the realm of autobiographical fiction as a vast *'espace ambigu'* and a challenge for future critical study.

The only critic who thereafter specifically took a position regarding the autobiographical novel and the degree of referential truth therein has been the Hungarian Comparatist Mihály Szegedy-Maszák. In examining mid-twentieth-century Hungarian autobiographical novels as constituting a hybrid genre in the postmodern context, he concludes that it is the *Rezeptionästhetik* critic rather than the narratologist who is best fitted to judge the referential factor. In such novels, though subject matter may be historically verifiable, certain semantic levels and time manipulation distance the world of the text from the world of the narrator. He points to cases in Hungarian novels where the autobiographical self is divided between its narrative and experiential functions – which are reminiscent of Proust. He also observes that such novels incorporate experiences that occur during composition.

The current book returns to a group of twentieth-century writers to fill a gap in autobiography criticism. This mixed genre has not been part of the ongoing debate. As has been seen, representative studies have necessarily been selective in choosing a group of autobiographical writers to deal with and to demonstrate the various theses. The lengthy subtitles of such studies have qualified investigations in this overwhelming field. My primary interest in autobiography is not as a psychological revelation of authorship, nor in the disappearance of the author in the text, nor in the truth or fictional factor in autobiography 'strictly speaking', but rather in the transformation of autobiographical data into literary *écriture* – pursuing and catching that dimension in certain works to which I would apply the term 'aesthetic autobiography'. My own examination of the aesthetic devices involved in the unfolding of a 'non-narcissistic reflexivity',[29] as Ricoeur would have termed it, targets a certain area of life-writing whose aesthetic expression has a universal dimension for creative writers everywhere and perhaps even forever.

3

A Theory of Aesthetic Autobiography

Il cherche son âme, il l'inspecte, il la tente, l'apprend.
[He looks into his soul, he inspects it, he challenges it, learns it.]
Arthur Rimbaud

Autobiographical fiction has been regarded as a blurry hybrid genre not easily depicted or delimited. Using the four key writers Proust, Joyce, Virginia Woolf and Anaïs Nin as models, I have developed a theory of aesthetic autobiography. For a common aesthetics is apparent in the process by which such writers of the first half of the twentieth century transformed lived data into fictionalised discourse. Such novelists are in striking contrast to their predecessors of the nineteenth century who drew their material from 'the outside world'. For we recall that the greatest fiction of Dostoevsky, Flaubert, Hawthorne, Stendhal, Austen, Trollope, Henry James and others came out of circumstances outside the authors' own lives. Historical events or daily incidents even reported in newspaper articles, what the French might call *faits divers*, were the materials which nourished the great novels of the nineteenth century. When Flaubert came out with the resounding statement, '*Madame Bovary, c'est moi*', the implication was that he had chosen that strange person, actually from a newspaper story, and absorbed her into his own thoughts as he worked her into his consciousness as well as his fiction. Writers like Flaubert were appropriating material from other people's lives.

What a far cry from some novelists of the early twentieth century who construed major 'events' from the minor occurrences of their *own* personal lives! Such novelists, three of whom can be grouped in a historic cluster and the fourth who follows in their wake, drew out of their *moi* or self the ingredients to project on to the 'many', with which others can identify. When we reach innovators of early modernism, we find an exploitation of those inner resources rather

43

than what had previously been in fiction the exploration of the outer world.

In the process of the fictionalisation of autobiographical data by such moderns, an aesthetics of artistic transmutation emerged. For it was not simply a case of reflection of personal life material in the fiction. An autobiographical style developed in this period of modernism which went well beyond the circumstantial identification of the author in the work. In discerning the threshold of artistic transformation beyond the search for biographical authenticity, insights can be gained into the creative process.

The term 'aesthetic' qualifies the specific kind of autobiography I am identifying. If we are also to distinguish the literal autobiography from the aesthetic one, we move readily from fact to fiction surpassing elements of confession and embellishment which are a part of the original form. As already seen, the standard autobiographies 'strictly speaking' of the Western world such as those of Cellini, Rousseau and Gosse convey an intentionality which is both overt and indulgent. It is fascinating, no doubt, to witness Rousseau's insistence on 'telling nothing but the truth', Cellini's embellishment of the Renaissance scene, Gosse's candour in revealing the true relationship with his father. And with their own intentionality, cultural historians have read Cellini for Renaissance sociology, Rousseau for seeds of the French revolution, Gosse for crisis facets of Victorianism. These readings have followed the approach of the nineteenth-century cultural critic Hippolyte Taine who had asserted:

Un grand poème, un beau roman, les confessions d'un homme supérieur, sont plus instructifs qu'un monceau d'historiens et d'histoires.[1]

[A great poem, a fine novel, the confessions of a superior man, are more instructive than a heap of historians and their histories.]

Such works are therefore perceived together in an historical chain through their cultural and personal referentiality. Or as Sainte-Beuve had said: *'Je puis goûter une oeuvre, mais il m'est difficile de la juger indépendamment de la connaissance de l'homme même*[2] ('I can taste a work, but it is difficult for me to judge it independently of the knowledge of the man himself'). In this light, the individual personality of each writer remains transparent and inseparable from the work.

On the other hand, what I call the aesthetic autobiographies emerging in the early twentieth century reclothe personal facts in

poetic relations, in a re-presentation of the person, not of the person-ality. Actually, both the poet-critic T. S. Eliot and the psychologist Jung had inadvertently recognised this fact in the early twentieth century. For Eliot had warned in his 1917 well-known essay 'Tradition and the Individual Talent':

> The more perfect the artist, the more completely separate in him will be the man who suffers and the mind which creates; the more perfectly will the mind digest and transmute the passions which are its material.[3]

To be sure, the key to such a process is transmutation; such Eliotic 'depersonalisation' occurs in the transfer from the personal to the universal, in the movement from the subject to the object which anchors the subjectivity. Similarly, Jung's notion of the 'supra-personal' was also descriptive of a process whereby the personal is raised to the level of the mythic or universal. For in criticising Freud's biographical approach Jung wrote in 1922:

> Indeed, the special significance of a true work of art resides in the fact that it has escaped from the limitations of the personal and has soared beyond the personal concerns of its creator.[4]

Likewise, some of the novelists of this era were shunning the vest-iges of lyrical Romanticism and dealing with the subjective factor in a new way. They found themselves in the tricky position of experi-menting with and innovating a new form – that of autobiographical fiction – while attacking the personal elements that could be cat-egorically associated with it. After all, in his Continental context, Proust was countering the Positivistic biographism of a critic such as Sainte-Beuve who had said '*tel arbre, tel fruit*'. In his polemical work of literary criticism *Contre Sainte-Beuve* (written between 1908 and 1909) Proust challenged Sainte-Beuve with the fact that many close to an author appreciate his literary qualities less than those who have had no contact with the biographical data or the personal-ity. Proust seemed to have been providing the gauge for the autobio-graphical novel of his own time by declaring that the 'I' of the novel was a different and deeper one from the personal self that produced it: '*Ce moi-là, si nous voulons essayer de le comprendre, c'est au fond de nous-même.*'[5] Of course, his predecessor the poet Rimbaud had been ahead of his time in proclaiming back in 1871: '*Je est un autre*' – that

the poet, in seeking for his quintessential self, which he would use in his writing as 'the other', had the arduous task of draining away all the 'poisons' of egotism:*'il épuise en lui tous les poisons, pour n'en garder que les quintessences'*.[6] Such poisons would be the incidental externalities of individual personality.

With objectives similar to Proust, Joyce sought to surpass what he called 'the lyrical form'. The resounding statement from *A Portrait of the Artist as a Young Man* best expresses his view of the artist's position as being detached from the art: 'within or behind or beyond or above his handiwork, invisible, refined out of existence, indifferent, paring his fingernails'.[7] Woolf, seeing vast possibilities in a new form of fiction, worked specifically to avoid drowning in the personal or what she called 'the damned egotistical self'.[8] Much later, but still in the same vein, Nin in her theoretical work *The Novel of the Future* was to deplore the biographical method which had been in the meantime ironically imposed on Proust by some of the critics. She defined the true autobiographical method of re-creation in her fiction as going beyond any individual referent to the magical composite:

> A composite may become something more than one artist, writer, more than one person – a unit. A composite is no longer the original. It is something else . . . How much is lost by retranslating such composites and redistributing each trait where it belongs is exemplified in the biography of Proust by George D. Painter.[9]

Despite certain cultural barriers between them, these independently minded writers had a common concern for the insufficiency of the conventional genre of the novel to contain the artistic transformation of their life materials. They were suggesting, therefore, inadvertently in unison, that the bounds of fiction had to be transformed precisely because of the new demands of autobiographical writing. It will be seen how in their diaries, letters and notes they voiced their common preoccupation with the dynamics between the vita and the artistic refabrication. For example, Joyce and his brother Stanislaus have a correspondence about the element of autobiography in *A Portrait*, drawing lines between fact and fiction. Vanessa Bell writes to her sister Virginia that Mrs Ramsay in *To the Lighthouse* is indeed a striking transcription of their mother. This may have been so, but the lighthouse image made that transcription suggest much more. Proust's well-known letter to Jacques de Lacretelle

disclaims any one-to-one identification between characters and real persons. And Nin, both in her diary and *The Novel of the Future*, speaks of transplants from the real to the fictive and the transposition into 'the other'.

After all, the 1920s was not only a time of the burgeoning of modernism, but also the time when André Breton and the Surrealists were attacking the novel altogether as an unacceptable form for the imagination. Breton's *Nadja* was the non-novel, as he mixed his own autobiography with a fictional creation. This rejection of the novel as an adequate form for the representation of life is reflected as well in the search for new narrative forms. It is manifest in Joyce's passing from the lyrical to the dramatic on to the epical, in Woolf's naming of the elegy as an appropriate form for *To the Lighthouse*[10] and eventually in Nin's creation of the 'poetic novel' as the novel of the future.

From her earlier British perspective, Woolf had considered the English novel, the conventional realism as practiced by the Edwardians, to be antiquated and not a work of art. In her 1927 essay 'The Art of Fiction' she noted: 'surely, the definition of life is too arbitrary and has to be expanded'.[11] In her study and commentary on painter and art critic Roger Fry, she brought up a critical question about the English public which she and Fry had assuredly shared back in 1910: 'Why were they all engrossed in childish problems of photographic representation?'[12] We can understand, then, why she introduced and qualified the word 'symbolism' with respect to *To the Lighthouse*. Her exposure to the visual arts through her sister Vanessa Bell, her brother-in-law Clive Bell, and that friend Roger Fry, all of whom were advocating Post-Impressionist aesthetics, made her especially aware of the need of certain parallels in fiction.

This common evolution of aesthetics, which was occurring in the treatment of life ingredients by writers and artists of this era, is more significant than any overt recognition of one by the other. For these writers were *not* in any complicity regarding their aesthetics. Actually, it is a curious fact that Proust, Joyce and Woolf did not even engage in any intercommunication. Joyce happened to attend the funeral of Proust, having met him once six months previously in Paris. That encounter of 18 May 1922 at the English novelist Sydney Shiff's supper party has become legendary, as Richard Ellmann reports the anecdotes which show the writers' indifference to each other.[13] Apparently, according to a variety of sources from Margaret

Anderson to Frank Budgen, both writers admitted that they did not want to know each others' works. The social milieux of the two writers were so different: Proust talked about duchesses and Joyce was interested in chambermaids; Proust worked by night isolated in a cork-lined room, Joyce worked by day, constantly interrupted in his temporary dwellings all over Europe. Actually, Joyce, living a life of exile, did not communicate with other writers of his own stature, partly also because of his superiority complex. Woolf's case had yet another angle to it. She confined herself in and related to an artistic milieu, that of Bloomsbury, which was distinctly British and insular. She half-heartedly read her Irish contemporary Joyce. At other points, she made some attempts to extend outward to the French, reading Rimbaud or having a version of the 'Time Passes' section of *To the Lighthouse* translated into French by Charles Mauron. Her diaries, letters and essays indicate that she was gradually reading Proust, as the volumes appeared. Specifically in April 1925 she did note that she was deeply 'embedded' in Proust.[14] But there is no evidence of her being capable of fully probing the intricacies of his fiction.

The later writer Anaïs Nin, who was linguistically closer to Proust, read and quoted him constantly. There are more than a hundred references to Proust in her diaries and commentaries, including her most forceful statement in her diary regarding her indebtedness to the French author: 'My self is like the self of Proust: an instrument to connect life and myth.'[15] It was Nin who made the most theoretical statements in retrospect in *The Novel of the Future* that has a bearing on autobiographical fiction. She declared that the modern novel was to go further in the direction first outlined by Proust, Joyce and Woolf, and that the dissection of the human psyche that these authors performed would later be recomposed in yet new psychic realities in the poetic novel: 'What remains to be created is a new synthesis to include all the newly discovered dimensions.'[16]

However, the true basis of the evolution of an autobiographical style among these writers and others of their era is that they had inadvertently accepted a common 'aesthetic attitude' towards life. But again there was no coterie which developed a codified system of aesthetics, as there had been earlier with the Symbolists in France or even the Aesthetes in England. And of course, the autobiographical aesthetics which developed had a very different basis from the attitude of the Aesthetes of the 1890s, who considered life facts vulgar

and whose life-style therefore imitated art. Let us remember Villiers de l'Isle-Adam's striking statement: 'As for living, let our servants do that for us.' On the contrary, the autobiographical novelists drew first from their personal everyday life, cultivating perceptions selectively which could then be transposed into their fiction. A primary facet of their art can be said therefore to be an activity of perception. Then comes the leap to what is literary. In the passage from self-observation to self-recreation, life facts were transferred to structures dictated by concepts of aesthetics.

For example, although these writers shunned the subjective factor in its facile expression, they went out of their way to exploit the process of memory, even in objectifying its contents. Drawing from this source, they were unconsciously discovering new pathways into this mental process as they looked back over their lives to extract raw ingredients for their fiction. Studies have linked Proust to Bergson and Freud. On the one hand, Proust's indebtedness to Bergson is clear cut and acknowledged. As a 20-year-old student, Proust had listened to lectures by the great master at the Sorbonne. Bergson had made a crucial distinction between the chronological memory of events and the inordinate duration of moments outside their chronological measurement. Proust highlighted such notions of the privileged moment with his narrative of remembrances. On the other hand, if Freud is credited with the discovery of screen memory, Proust might have arrived at that same concept unconsciously and independently and for different purposes. Freud was giving it the psychological definition of being the memory of a trivial event, most often from childhood, which can hide an emotionally significant realisation and have a pathological significance. His contemporary Proust was expressing his version of the concept through fictional incidents, which must have simply been mimicking personal life experiences but which he exploited for aesthetic purposes.

Perhaps even more arresting is the fact that current twentieth-century psychological studies have defined categories of memory which were intuitively or experientially sensed by these novelists and used in their fiction. A collection of essays in David Rubin's anthology *Autobiographical Memory* sums up some of these categories. If the physiological study of memory views the process in terms of chemical changes at the synapses of neurons, the more general studies in this volume classify different types of memory, which can actually be located in the fiction of these novelists. That is to say, the

novelists themselves were transferring certain experiential elements of the memory process into artistic structures in their fiction.

For example, the description of what has been called 'generic memory' can provide guidelines for the truth factor of autobiographical fiction. The psychologist William Brewer has defined this form of general memory as an amalgamation of special personal memories into a generic image of common or repeated experiences.[17] Such a 'self-schema' is not a duplicate of actual daily events and, hence, the criterion is one of truth, not accuracy. This designation is appropriate to the study of aesthetic autobiographies – which often seem to be proceeding from such schematised experiences or in fact simulating them in a conscious or even unconscious effort to depersonalise them.

Another form of memory which is mimicked in the fiction is called 'flashbulb memory'. Such memories are more specific, intense and immediate, report psychologists Roger Brown and James Kulik, since they are 'memories for the circumstances in which one first learned of a very surprising and consequential (or emotionally arousing) event'.[18] Epiphanies, pervasive in this fiction as awakenings or insights through a stimulus of the senses, seem to have characteristics of this particular form.

In addition, effects caused by auditory, olfactory and visual memories are reproduced in the fiction. An 'engram' has been defined as hearing a tune which leaves a trace that can last until we die. What better definition for Proust's motif of the Vinteuil sonata? Also, visual memories are said to be strong components of personal memories of seemingly trivial events. Virginia Woolf's memory of her young brother's aborted trip to the lighthouse is visually powerful and elaborated upon in the fiction.

It is interesting and almost coincidental that all four authors under consideration manifested certain obsessions about close family members which were not simply reflected but 'recreated' in the fiction. Certain techniques actually derived from these authors' intent of recapturing these deceased personalities yet maintaining a distance from them in the fiction in order to avoid the personal. Such relationships were objectified and magnified in the fiction creating archetype, universality, social stereotype and mythic dimension.

Proust's close attachment to his mother, for example, was recast into the sequence of the *'drame du baiser'* in *Combray* and transferred to the grandmother figure in *A l'ombre des jeunes filles en fleurs* and *Le*

Côté de Guermantes. Joyce's guilt with respect to his dying mother's religious wishes is objectified in image and sequence in the background of *Ulysses*; his disrespect for his drunken and dissolute father is transferred to images and persons in the short stories and in *A Portrait*, after which the preoccupation with the father becomes the thematic line of *Ulysses*. Joyce himself had admitted that his irresponsible father was the source for hundreds of characters; both mother and father become national archetypes in the fiction. How far from the singly identifiable father figure in Edmund Gosse's *Father and Son*! As for Virginia Woolf, she blatantly stated in her memoirs 'A Sketch of the Past' that she was obsessed by the premature death of her mother, and that it was not until she recreated telescopically her mother in the 'universal' Mrs Ramsay figure of *To the Lighthouse* that she was liberated from that painful obsession. In so doing, she transformed personal grief into metaphysical statement. Finally, Nin's diaries, specifically *Linotte*, are instigated by the search for her father who had abandoned her family in Europe when she was an eleven-year-old child. Throughout her life, she harboured a feeling of betrayal by her father. The 'missing' father figure re-emerges throughout the fiction, as in *Winter of Artifice*, *Ladders to Fire*, and *Children of the Albatross*. The search is often camouflaged in relationships, as for instance when she seeks in the husband figure the father. In *A Spy in the House of Love* Sabina splits her sexuality into the passionate love for a young aviator and the comfort of the protective benefits that the husband figure provides her.

Such data concerning relationships of mother–son, father–son, mother–daughter and father–daughter not only provide for psychological and biographical interpretation of these works; they also offer significant raw materials which can be analysed in terms of an aesthetic process of 're-creation', which is of a different nature than simple referentiality.

As in the standard autobiographies, 'that great Cathedral space which was childhood', as Woolf calls it in 'A Sketch of the Past', or the traumatic passageways of adolescence, are featured in these novels. But beyond the standard biographies, these perspectives become the source for the fictionalising process. For Proust and Woolf, childhood contains elements of an idyllic experience (although recent critics of Woolf have pointed to sexual abuses by her half-brothers). Such a view is recast in some of their fiction, as the perspective of the child marks both *Combray* and *To the Lighthouse*. On the other hand, in the case of Joyce, childhood is marked

by repression by his society and his elders – expressed by the author as a 'grave of childhood' in *A Portrait*. So, too, in Nin, anxiety is attached to the early period of her life, as expressed overtly in her childhood diary *Linotte*. But instead of narrating, as does autobiography proper, isolated incidents as single 'crisis experiences' or turning points with psychological implications, these authors create from them representative scenes. 'Scene making', as Virginia Woolf called it, or 'symbol making', as Anaïs Nin would say, figures in these novels to transform such real incidents into aesthetic ones. Woolf recaptures the past through the recollection and recreation of single framing scenes. She goes so far as to ask in 'A Sketch of the Past': 'Is this liability to scenes or concrete pictures the origin of my writing impulse?'[19] Joyce and Proust may have asked themselves similar questions, since after all Joyce recreated his mother's deathbed in *Ulysses* and Proust focused on a scene of 'goodnight kiss' in the first section of *Combray*. Nin then went further to reproduce a dream scene of a shipwrecked boat in *House of Incest* and *Seduction of the Minotaur*. In recreating such scenes in their fiction, the authors manipulate their recollected experience.

This selectivity with which the past is retrieved and refashioned marks the creative process. It is as if these authors read life backwards 'novelistically', attaching drama and object to character. In the construction of such scenes, a certain universality of situation is created. The denial of the child's wish to go to the lighthouse in Woolf's novel or the pandying incident in Joyce's *A Portrait* suggests the repression of a paternalistic society and the general regret of the injured innocence of childhood. In contrast, when Rousseau has a little servant girl unjustly accused of stealing in *The Confessions*, the scene is at the service of a generalising social principle instead of being an artistic product.

In terms of content, the fictional autobiographers seem to represent and extenuate the ending of childhood. Proust separates the Combray section from the rest of his long work as a paradise gone and overshadowed by the corruptions that permeate the rest of the volumes – from *A l'ombre des jeunes filles en fleurs* on. In fact, this latter title is an ironic undercutting of such innocence since the *'jeunes filles'* are ambiguously girls and hardly innocent! The Swann motif within the *Combray* section is already a hint of the outside world that is to overwhelm the innocence. Joyce marks a turning point from childhood in the scene in Cork, when at the age of twelve the son senses a total alienation from his father, and the atmosphere of

the Cork scene suggests the total decay of that relationship. Woolf, who in her autobiographical sketch links the death of her mother with the end of childhood at the age of thirteen, had already made an analogy for this transition in the passage from the first to the second part of *To the Lighthouse*. Similarly Nin, who in her diary *Linotte* connects the end of her childhood with the departure of her father and the end of the illusion that he would return, creates a climatic correlative for that loss in *Winter of Artifice*. Most striking is a specific scene recalled by the patient to the psychiatrist in the third section of that work, the patient confessing: 'The world of our childhood closed with his departure.'[20] In all cases, the end of childhood represents a traumatic experience for these authors who seek to recast it in the artistic locale of their fiction.

As with family relationships, place becomes a prominent and obsessive factor in this fiction. These authors, who identified themselves strongly with certain locales, then proceeded to transpose these locales into their fiction into what the critic Georges Poulet has called '*le lieu privilégié*' or '*privileged place*' in his analysis of Proustian space. The manipulation of place, its dislocation and amplification is another aspect of artistic transmutation in the novels. All the writers draw specifically from known and rather unexceptional locales of their childhood and adolescence and recreate these locales in different ways. As will be seen, Proust multiplies individual places into a fictional composite so that, for instance, Combray or Balbec is more than simply Illiers or Cabourg. A multiplication factor is highly prevalent in Proust's work, wherein various châteaux or churches and their respective locales contribute to the production of the fictional ones. Transposition, transplanting and transformation occur with respect to place, as we shall see. Joyce offers yet another approach which, however, still involves transformation. For if the various streets and places in Joyce's Dublin are realistic and carry their real names, they are symbolic at the same time. It is the very dissection of Dublin in the consciousness of the characters that recreates the Dublin of the fiction. As for Woolf, like Proust she transports 'real' place, giving it a new name (even if it is a real one as with the Hebrides). In her novel Woolf transposes St Ives to the faraway Scottish island in the Hebrides in order to remove the novel from any overt autobiographical reading and to intensify the feeling of remoteness associated with the lighthouse image. Both Proust and Woolf attach a sense of distance to place – identifying it with the unreachable. In the case of Nin, it is not even a question of transformation of place, but the creation of interior

places. Her 'cities of the interior' suggest that the place inhabits her rather than that she inhabits the place. If Golconda is fashioned after a Mexican city, the languor and heat of such a city is internalised and an aesthetic place is created as a locus for an evolving consciousness. It will be seen, therefore, how all four authors proceed from the reality of places to create 'magical composites' – to use Nin's expression from *The Novel of the Future* – which are equal to more than the sum of their parts.

The mythopoetic factor in the transformation of autobiography into fiction can also be located in the intervention of artifacts and artists appearing regularly in the narrative. A variety of material objects or what Proust called *sine materia* in *Un Amour de Swann*, change their status from real to 'aesthetic' objects. For such objects serve as anchors or receptacles of subjectivity. For example, in Proust's work the objects are sensual in nature and proceed from the well-known madeleine to the cattleya, the steeples of Martinville, the trees of Hudimesnil, the musical phrase of Vinteuil's sonata, the uneven paving stones of Venice, and the Botticelli painting. Just as the process of involuntary memory is lodged in the madeleine, the imaginative process of 'falling in love' (likened to artistic illusion) is linked to the cattleya of Odette. In Joyce's *Stephen Hero*, the Ballast Office clock loses its realistic import to become the ultimate material object, from which the theory of epiphany is derived. The fact that the Ballast clock was a standard of time for every Dubliner of Joyce's day suggests that Joyce went out of his way to locate the everyday object as the source for the extraordinary and for aesthetic sensation. Other everyday objects accrue significance such as the lemon soap and brass bells of *Ulysses*, the wading girl, the pool and cup of tea in *Ulysses* and the Wellington monument in 'The Dead'. Just as the madeleine triggers Marcel's memory process, so do the wine and gorgonzola cheese in Davy Byrne's pub trigger Bloom's meditations upon his past life with Molly. In Woolf, comparable to the Ballast Office clock in Joyce, the lighthouse serves as the most dominant object of the subjective factor; Big Ben in *Mrs Dalloway* also functions as one. And in Nin, the house of Louveciennes is transformed into the 'house of incest', lodging the intricate facets of the artist's selfhood.

Hence, the attention to detail that has so often been associated with the modern novel may be associated with this process regarding the object. Such details may be in part the real remnants of life memories brought into new artistic perspectives and given new

meanings. The writers themselves seemed to have been conscious of this process. In her diary, Nin referred to Proust's 'passion for every detail of his life' by which he 're-creates a flower, a leaf, a cathedral spire, a sunset, a meal'[21], to give each object of recollection a significance. Similarly, in her diary Woolf said of Proust that 'he searches out these butterfly shades to the last grain'.[22] She also singled out Joyce, in her essay 'Modern Fiction', as one of the 'new' novelists of her time who was 'attempting to come closer to life', and she urged modern writers to follow his example: 'Let us record the atoms as they fall upon the mind in the order in which they fall, let us trace the pattern, however disconnected and incoherent in appearance, which each sight or incident scores upon the consciousness.'[23] Woolf had referred in 1919 to Joyce's exploitation of the particular and the minute in the episodes of *Ulysses* which were appearing in serial form in *The Little Review* in New York. Cognisant of this perspective in Joyce's writings, despite her later dislike of the crudity of his subject matter, she went on to expostulate: 'Let us not take it for granted that life exists more fully in what is commonly thought big than in what is commonly thought small.'

This type of autobiographical fiction involves such transformations of the quotidian. These writers fashioned in-depth perceptions occurring in the course of their everyday lives into literary images and scenes. If Proust sought the deeper self *beneath* the everyday one in the context of the selective process of the privileged moment of recollection, the more plebeian Joyce exploited the everyday by immersing himself *within* it. He dramatised and stylised such material in the continuity of the 22-hour day of *Ulysses*, which is the artistic product of the recasting of the quotidian. Woolf, in her more rarified prose, sought to simulate the everyday. She heightened the trivial, for instance in the climactic and protracted scene in *To the Lighthouse* of the *boeuf en daube* dinner. Like Joyce, she structured *Mrs Dalloway* in the framework of the daily. In her two major novels, she appropriated memories of daily experiences that could well have been associated with her own past into an artistic atmosphere, which situates the everyday in a new symbolic context. And then, there is Nin who, as the symbolic ragpicker, gathers the shreds and fragments of everyday life (as her story of that metaphor suggests most vividly) and transposes those bits and pieces into artistic situations and images. These novelists' obsession with the matter of everyday life shows once again their preoccupation with autobiographical material, on the one hand, and their transformation of that material into their art, on the other.

It is also notable that certain references to art and artists communicate an explicit aesthetics within the novels that can be viewed architectonically. The artist figure prominently appears in *A la recherche du temps perdu* through Marcel's self scrutiny as a writer in *Le Temps retrouvé*; it emerges overtly in the Stephen Dedalus figure in *A Portrait*. In fact, both works provide a specific scene of artistic awakening and self-analysis in an apparently accidental manner: the scene at the Guermantes matinée and the scene at the Bull, respectively. The figure of Lily Briscoe in *To the Lighthouse* is the artist transposing in her painting the life scene before her, as she shuns representation and draws into her art the abstraction of the Post-Impressionists of Woolf's own time. The various personae of Nin contain the artistic personality, as Sabina, Lillian and Djuna are artists of some nature. Even the ragpicker is a metaphor for one. Specific references to artists are multiplied in Proust's work as reflected in the writer Bergotte, the composer Vinteuil and the painter Elstir. And it is actually a description of Elstir's art as 'a sort of metamorphosis of represented things' ('*une sorte de métamorphose des choses représentées*'[24]) that serves as a guide to the artistic process in all the works.

This common notion of art as a transforming process in all the works makes it difficult to accept the contention made by some critics that the aesthetic theory within the text should be dissociated from the author's own. For there are even specifically theories of autobiography enunciated in the texts, as in the discussion of Shakespeare's life and work in *Ulysses* and in the narrator's reflection on his life (just narrated) as becoming the subject of his future novel in *Le Temps retrouvé*. For example, Proust's narrator speaks of 're-reading life backwardly', Joyce's 'artist' aspires to 'recreate life out of life', Woolf's painter seeks in her art 'an equivalent for life', Nin's ragpicker sings a song of transformation: 'nothing is lost but it changes'. Such theories correspond to the very process of composition as they constitute the metafiction of the texts. The texts seem to implement the very theories that are expressed.

The perspective which the actual artist figures project seems to reflect the aesthetic orientation of the works themselves. When Proust's narrator comments that the mirage-like effect of the steeples of Martinville gives him an exquisite feeling of pleasure – which he then transposes on to a page of writing – the visual effect has become an intermediary to the aesthetic. The impression rather than the reflection is what is registered. The constant metamorphoses that take place in the minds of the characters create the

power of illusion that is germane to the artist. In Proust's novel, the contemplation of the Duchesses of Guermantes is an illustration of this phenomenon. Seen for the first time from near, the Duchess loses her distant aristocratic aura. Disillusioned by the sight of her 'real' ruddy complexion and ugly nose, Proust's narrator prefers to distance her from himself again and regain the artistic illusion of her presence. The same distancing occurs with respect to the Persian church in Balbec. Similarly Woolf's Lily Briscoe can only complete the abstract painting of Mrs Ramsay and son when, years later, Mrs Ramsay has died and her son is distanced in his journey to the lighthouse. Simultaneously, that son, James, prefers the lighthouse from a far to the one close up, 'stark and physical'. This process of telescoping throughout the novels reflects the process by which the writers view their past, from afar. Optics of distancing and falsification are elements of artistic perception which seem to heighten the self-referential factor.

The aesthetic self which is created in these novels is shared by both characters and personae. It is interesting that Proust is said to have split himself between the 'social' side of Swann and the 'artistic' side of the narrator. He is, of course, absorbed into other characters as well who bear certain characteristics similar to his own. Similarly, Joyce positions himself between the Jewish citizen Bloom and the artist figure Dedalus, and in fact has their personalities fuse in a kind of transmigration. Their fraternity in the closing chapters of *Ulysses* suggests the mingling of the material and the spiritual. Woolf moves from Mrs Dalloway to Lily Briscoe, also vacillating between her 'social' and artistic side, even to the point of projecting an androgynous self in *Orlando*. As for Nin, she is in and out of her various personae from Sabina to Lillian to Djuna, unable to transfix herself in any one of them because of her multifaceted self. Nin used Marcel Duchamp's 1912 painting of the *Nude Descending the Staircase* as a model for this concept of multiple selves attempting to move in unison. In her own novelettes, Nin split the 'I' into multiple personae. On the one hand, in the works of these four authors, there is the proliferation of the self into selves through characterisation; on the other hand, there is the creation of a composite aesthetic self emerging from that multiplicity to create a totality.

In both revealing and concealing facets of their own autobiographical selves, these writers create evolving personalities through their drafts and early versions of their works. To some extent, each of the novelists creates a continuity of character through a *roman*

fleuve manner. For example, the rather amorphous Stephen Hero develops into the more distinctive and mythic Stephen Dedalus of *A Portrait of the Artist as a Young Man*, which itself had a previous story version ten years before called 'A Portrait of the Artist'. The figure then continues to evolve into the Stephen–Telemachus figure of *Ulysses*, which is a direct carry-over from *A Portrait of the Artist as a Young Man*. In the case of Woolf, the Mrs Dalloway figure is a haunting presence as it first appears in a peripheral way in *The Voyage Out*, then eight years later in a germinal story 'Mrs Dalloway in Bond Street', thereafter surfacing as a title character in the novel *Mrs Dalloway* in which a much more complex personality appears. Giving that personality an *alter ego* who commits suicide, Woolf preserves the character, which is then included in eight other stories written after the novel.

As with Proust and Nin, there were of course, more technically written *romans fleuves*, due perhaps to their more conscious recognition of the notion of multiple selves and the fluidity of human character. Proust's entire process of *remaniment*, the French word for reworking the narrative through many drafts, involved the evolution of characters and the final naming of them as well as the distancing of them from any recognisable sources. Proust had such concerns up to the time of his death in 1922, when he was actively deleting sections of his work. The case of the narrator involves the development of the artist persona in *A la recherche du temps perdu* from the early rather simplistic 'autobiographical' character Jean Santeuil, and the subsequent removal of the name 'Marcel' from the text so as to dissociate the persona, at least overtly, from the author. Under the influence of Proust, Nin had originally intended to publish specifically her novelettes in the form of a *roman fleuve*. But she explains in the preface to *Cities of the Interior* that she was discouraged from doing so by her publishers, who said that the American public would not appreciate that form of extended fiction. Instead, the works came out individually until 1959 when 'the continuity was established' in the publication of *Cities of the Interior* as a single volume.

Nin had been drawn toward the notion of a *roman fleuve* precisely because she had not wanted to circumscribe any character definitely; evolving characters corresponded to her notion of the evolving self. But actually all these writers were proliferating and continuously modifying their characters for the same reason. They were distancing themselves from the autobiographical personalities by putting them in constant flux and evolution so as not to transfix

them in a single version of character which could then be identified. This approach reveals another distinction with formal autobiographies which seek to circumscribe the very author's character.

Whereas the standard autobiographies, as has been seen, are dependent on the chronological factor for narrative progression, these works undermine chronological time through the frequent intervention of subjective time, a concept that Bergson had uncovered in his philosophy. Shifts between 'chairos' and 'kronos' occur constantly in the fiction, so that chronological time is indeed transformed. Epiphanies become common phenomena where sections of time are extended to yield insights. Woolf's notion of 'moments of being' are parallel to Joyce's concept of epiphanies. The examples are obsessive, such as the matinée at the Guermantes in Proust, Stephen Dedalus's vision at the Bull and Lily Briscoe's vision in completing the painting. Proust's notion of involuntary memory transports the narrator over large blocks of time, bringing the past to the present moment of narration. The 'recapturing' of time at the end of the novel is a triumph over chronological time. Often processes of tunnelling and telescoping are used by the writers with respect to the representation of the past and the breakdown of time barriers. Joyce became famous for bringing a lifetime into the time span of a single day. Woolf imitated this orientation in *Mrs Dalloway* but then proceeded to manipulate time further in *To the Lighthouse*. There she shifted between a concentration of time in a single afternoon and evening to a ten-year span. Nin's novels are often timeless in a mythic setting of perpetual present.

Reminders of chronological time, however, amidst the subjective wanderings of involuntary memory, epiphanies and 'moments of being', endow these subjective states with contours of reality, immediacy, place, history and authenticity. It is especially interesting in this regard that Proust, Woolf and Joyce each have instances in their work in which they create what could be called a 'chronometer' or gauge of chronological time. In Proust's Combray the steeple of Saint-Hilaire, which dominates the entire village (fashioned after Saint-Jacques of Illiers), is viewed by Marcel as indicating the various hours of the day by the amount of sunlight hitting it. In fact, Proust creates a 'steeple day', a typical day in the life of Combray, as he charts the steeple's tonality. The perspective, however, with which he views the steeple is through involuntary memory which has been set in motion by the tasting of the madeleine, offered to him by his mother in their Paris apartment, years away from the day in question. Through the mingling of the subjective factor

(memory) with the objective (steeple time), Proust breaks down the distance of real chronological time in retrieving the past.

Similarly, the Ballast clock in *Ulysses* and Big Ben in *Mrs Dalloway* serve as reminders of the 'real' in days which otherwise take place in the confines of subjective time. In Woolf's work, which was originally entitled 'The Hours', Big Ben strikes to bring Mrs Dalloway back to the immediacy of the present from her vagaries about the past. In the earlier Joyce work *Stephen Hero*, the Ballast clock was identified as the source of the concept of epiphany; in *Ulysses* it serves to promote the concept of 'parallax', which suggests the relativity of time, depending on perspective. Furthermore, historical time, that of the First World War, enters specifically and significantly into the works of Proust and Woolf. The Great War ages and deteriorates Proust's characters – marking the end of the era of the Faubourg St. Germain in *Le Temps retrouvé*, and closes the Edwardian era, ushering in the darkness of modernism in Woolf's *To the Lighthouse*. In both instances, the war period is condensed and viewed in terms of its effect as a catalytic process of change.

Such transmutation of time, place, object and character are the results of the particular techniques that each of these authors employed in their artistic transformation of life. Although all apply the alchemy of art to life facts, each of the authors seems to stress a particular aspect of transformation which contributes to the total theory that is derived from their juxtaposition.

For Proust, misrepresentation seems to be the fundamental motive for the art, as a defence against total divulgence of his life. It was a principle which led to the multiplication factor. Proust conglomerated experiences and examples into compounds which made for his art – avoiding any transparency with respect to life, yet harbouring the accumulation of life elements in fictional composites.

Joyce, on the other hand, physically distanced and exiled for most of his life from his background, wanted most to retrieve it even in attacking it. In the stylisation of Dublin and its citizens, he transformed the quotidian. His art recycled such ingredients into thematic pattern and the objectification of myth.

Woolf, perhaps most fearful of drowning in her personal emotions, due to her highly vulnerable sensitivity, used analogy and substitution to transform her life ingredients. Ever on the verge of madness, she tried to control and fight off her obsessions by transferring them into the abstractions and creative ambiguity of her fiction.

Finally Nin, in her desire to proliferate and expand her sense of self, created poetic symbol to transfix life facts in poetic metaphors and mythic personalities. She transplanted the externalities of her life into a richer world of the interior and transfigured them through her power of artistic alchemy. She seized upon Proust's notion of the composite and developed it further in relation to her theory of multiple selfhood.

It is a striking paradox that these very writers who made the most effort to camouflage their life facts through artistry have been most persistently probed – their fiction being reduced to biography through one branch of scholarly activity. With their multiple obsessions, these writers have provided rich life data for Freudian and post-Freudian critics – especially since childhood was a major subject of their fiction. But it is a fact that Freud himself had recognised quite early the limitations of his own method, stating in his paper on 'The Moses of Michelangelo' (1914):

> I may say at once that I am no connoisseur in art, but simply a layman. I have often observed that the subject matter of works of art has a stronger attraction for me than their formal and technical qualities, though to the artist their value lies first and foremost in the latter. I am unable rightly to appreciate many of the methods used and the effects obtained in art.[25]

Freud's cause-and-effect theory does bypass the artistic, which he rightly perceived as method involving form and technique.

The writers of aesthetic autobiography went beyond the psychological to the artistic, to what Carl Jung appropriately termed 'the golden gleam of artistic creation'.[26] Although the individual psychologies of these writers are intriguing and can be regarded as components for their fiction, ultimately those components are matter which is transformed. The distinctions between such writers is less significant than the common methods which emerge from the amalgamation of their works. In reading these writers as they are juxtaposed, one realises the convergence on the aesthetic level of the fundamental devices that turn their autobiographical memories into fictional cohesions. Ever close to the life material, they construed literary methods to distance themselves from it. This genre of fictional autobiography was creating techniques of artistry used for the simultaneous revealing and concealing of the self. And within this mode there lies the heart of the creative process whereby the truths of fact were becoming truths of fiction.

4

The Art of Misrepresentation in Marcel Proust

Marcel Proust, who for so many years was noted for his portrayal of a vanishing aristocratic society, has become in recent years the fodder of demonstration for explosive theories on textual manoeuvres that go beyond the mimetic procedures of the social climate he was previously credited with delineating. Proust himself, who was presumed to be the universal observer, has virtually been made to disappear from his own writings. He has been separated from the narrator of *A la recherche du temps perdu* who is depicted as someone 'who is going to write' and therefore not the writer who has written. Among critics who deny self-referentiality in Proust's work is Roland Barthes, who has concluded that Proust's *Recherche* was the model for his life. Ironically, some biographers, who hold the contrary view, confront the relative paucity of Proust's life material, and have actually derived certain biographical facts from the fiction. As for Proust himself, when asked whether there were keys to his art, he repeatedly denied any outright correspondence. Instead, as a great dissembler, he teased the reader – on the one hand suggesting familiar sources, on the other hand camouflaging any identifiable reality by an intricate art of misrepresentation.

Proust stated at the beginning of his career that 'a book is the product of a different self from the one which we manifest in our habits, in society, in our vices' (*'qu'un livre est le produit d'un autre moi que celui que nous manifestons dans nos habitudes, dans la société, dans nos vices'*[1]). In this often-quoted excerpt from *Contre Sainte-Beuve*, Proust was distinguishing an everyday self from a deeper self or *le moi profond*, possibly forewarning future critics that his own work could never be fully understood by a simple reference to his life. He was attacking his predecessor Sainte-Beuve for initiating biographical criticism, which he, Proust, deemed

simplistic and reductive. In a letter of 1908 to his literary school-friend Robert Dreyfus, Proust spoke of 'the suprasensible reality of art', dismissing realistic or representational novels as anecdotal and contingent – 'art being too superior to life, as we judge it through the intellect and describe it in conversation, to be satisfied with copying it'.[2] Years later in 1920, as if to continue his argument about self-reference in fiction, the Proust who had completed most of his writing referred to his own narrator as the one who 'says "I" and who is not always me' (*'qui dit "je" et qui n'est pas toujours moi'*[3]). In differentiating the 'I' of the *Recherche* from the 'me', he had sought to eliminate the personal 'I' from his fiction. In 1921, André Gide, his publisher and fellow-writer, had quoted Proust as saying that a writer could write anything 'as long as he did not say "I" ' (*'à condition de ne jamais dire: Je'*).[4] But, in practice, Proust had not actually eliminated the 'I'; rather, he had depersonalised it. Gide, nonetheless, saying 'it doesn't suit me' (*'ce qui ne fait pas mon affaire'*), was shocked at what he considered to be an admission of deception. For unlike Proust, Gide was creating transparent auto-biography, blatantly flaunting himself both in the strict form and in the novel.

In contrast to the candour that was emerging in the genre of auto-biography proper, it is obvious that Proust was conscious of manip-ulating whatever personal element there may be in his fiction, in the process creating an aesthetics of deception for the autobiographical novel. Since there are so many drafts or *esquisses* and reworkings or *remaniments* of his long novel, one can witness the slow and crafty genesis of his art with respect to the transformation of his life facts. As the first of a cluster of autobiographical writers who are to be discussed in this book, he actually seems to have been more in line with his predecessor Mallarmé than with his contemporary, Gide. Mallarmé's 'Crise de vers' of 1885 had concluded that the pure work of art implied *'la disparition élocutoire du poète'*.[5] This meant that the personal or lyrical voice of the poet was to be depersonalised within the text. Proust, turning to prose, seems to have adapted this notion to narrative through the fictional devices of transposition. If Mallarmé had sought the pure flower absent from all bouquets, Proust was abstracting the particulars of his surroundings and reconstituting them into artifacts.

It is true that Proust's own life was rather uneventful. Yet it seemed to proceed in two stages – from his immersion in life expe-rience to a period of isolation and concentration on art. Readers

most readily picture Proust as the frail, asthmatic writer who worked through the night in the sound-proof cork-lined room of 102 Boulevard Haussmann after the death of his mother in 1905. Surprisingly, that creative period constituted only the last third of his life. His earlier acceptance into certain upper-crust circles and salon society of the Third Republic gave him material for his art for which he eventually chose the name *Guermantes*. Aside from his early excursions to Illiers and Normandy, and later trips to Venice, Cabourg and the South of France, and a few other places, Proust confined himself to his stationary existence in Paris. Yet it was from those very trips that he drew material for his opus and catalysed it into art. The source for the significant and renowned *'drame du baiser'* of *Combray* is so negligible that some even dispute its reality. Proust's biographer Painter has found the source in a scene in 'real life' not at Illiers but at Auteuil when young Marcel (some say aged seven) had been prevented from having a good-night kiss from his mother because of the presence of a medical colleague of Proust's father. But it still is uncertain whether this incident actually occurred. What is true is the underlying sentiment of such a scene – the very strong attachment that Proust had to his mother. Exploiting the use of involuntary memory, Proust must have sought to recollect any minute incident to expand and deepen it in his art form.

The most traditional approach to Proust's work by the original biographical group of critics was to regard the *Recherche* as depicting the growth of the artist's soul, its apprenticeship to art, much like *A Portrait of the Artist as a Young Man* has been interpreted for Joyce. Unlike Joyce, however, whose artistic calling was immediately followed by his departure from a society which was incompatible with it, Proust created an art which opened the doors of a society. The final volume, *Le Temps retrouvé*, can be read as mirroring this progress, as the narrator has an illumination of his vocation in the setting of a social milieu – the library of the Princesse de Guermantes. By contrast, the earlier volumes have been regarded as harbouring the passage from childhood to adolescence; the movement from Combray to Balbec parallels the shift from Illiers to Cabourg. The highlight of Proust's early years was, of course, the Easter and summer visits to the house of his paternal aunt Elisabeth Amiot and her husband Jules in Illiers – depicted in the idyllic section of Combray. The death of his aunt in 1886 ended his vacations in Illiers and that innocent period of his youth. Proust's mark on

that little village in the vicinity of Chartres was so great that even today the road signs read 'Illiers-Combray'. But Cabourg became the scene from the 1880s on, when Proust began to suffer from asthma and was advised to go to the Normandy coast for that condition. The Grand Hotel of Cabourg, where Proust was a frequent guest, an *'habitué'*, has since turned Proust's actual room into a museum piece. The hotel, of course, is clearly identified in *A l'ombre des jeunes filles en fleurs*. The passage from innocence to experience has been linked to the transition between the two places, Illiers and Cabourg, in Proust's formative years.

According to autobiographical readings, both the narrator and Swann have been associated with Proust on the grounds that there are blatant parallels between Proust the social riser and Proust the artist. But Proust himself would have found any outright identifications between characters and sources as highly simplistic because of his stress on his artistic invention in the creation of character. On this very subject, he made the following statement to Jacques de Lacretelle in his dedication of a copy of *Du côté de chez Swann*:

Il n'y a pas de clefs pour les personnages de ce livre; ou bien il y en a huit ou dix pour un seul . . . Je vous le répète, les personnages sont entièrement inventés, et il n'y a aucune clef.[6]

[There are no keys for the characters of this book or else there are eight or ten for a single one . . . I repeat this to you, the characters are entirely invented and there is no key.]

Although the purpose of this statement was to deflect from any outright identification with notorious personages of his era such as Robert de Montesquiou, it was also intended to set the record straight regarding Proust himself. He was in the process of channelling his complex self into several striking personalities, as will be seen. And his art involved fusing the many into one or confusing the one with the other. For example, the narrator's grief over his grandmother's death – an arresting moment in the text in the second part of *Le Côté de Guermantes* – reflects Proust's own inconsolable sorrow over his mother's passing. For that was the strongest tie he ever had. Although Proust's grandmother is said to have accompanied him in 1892 to the Hôtel des Roches Noires in Trouville, she died in 1895 and thereafter it was his mother who accompanied him to Normandy, and specifically to Cabourg, ever anxious about her

son's health problems. Proust's mother died in 1905 – the year of her trip with Marcel to Beg-Meil. But memories of both mother and grandmother were associated with the Normandy region as a whole. It was especially Cabourg, as Proust admitted in a letter to Madame Catusse, that kept alive for him the memory of his mother, although in the text he positions his grandmother arriving at the Balbec station and standing on the grand staircase of the Grand Hotel.

The fusion of mother and grandmother in the fiction illustrates how certain instances of misrepresentation in terms of literal facts contribute to the process of enlargement and amplification in Proust's art as a whole. It is true that Proust had been close to both his grandmother, Adèle Weil, and his mother, Jeanne Proust, throughout his youth. Both women were highly educated and literary, and they nurtured the young Proust in his readings and accompanied him on various trips. Although at the age of 24 in 1895 he lost his grandmother, it was ten years later on 26 September 1905 that he sustained the most traumatic loss of his life – the death of his mother. Until her death he had lived with her, and she had been over-protective of him to the last days of her life. The multitude of letters between son and mother are evidence of that excessively strong tie. And after her death, the statements about his mother in letters to friends show how that grief would stay with him forever. The day after her passing, Proust wrote to Madame de Noailles: 'She takes away my life with her'.[7] And then to his friend Robert de Montesquiou, Proust is most eloquent about his profound loss:

> My life has now forever lost its only purpose, its only sweetness, its only love, its only consolation. I have lost her whose unceasing vigilance brought me in peace and tenderness the only honey of my life . . . I have been steeped in every sorrow, I have lost her, I have seen her suffer.[8]

One biographer of Proust, Richard Hayman, has gone as far as to say that 'Proust's search for lost time was partly the search for a dead mother.'[9] Not only did Proust begin the seeds of his great opus right after his mother's death, but the germinal essay on Sainte-Beuve had in its provisional title 'Souvenir d'une matinée', which contained from the start a scene of the mother coming to the narrator's bedside and their conversation about aesthetics. It does

seem significant that the whole notion of involuntary memory is raised with the mention of the mother both at the beginning of the work in *Du côté de chez Swann* and at the very end of the work in the last pages of *Le Temps retrouvé*. There the narrator-turned-writer recollects the incident of the imperilled good-night kiss as a source of inspiration for the work about to be written. Indirectly, Proust seems to be cultivating his memory for artistic purposes at a time when he is using it to resurrect his dead mother. But unlike Virginia Woolf who, as we shall see, created a central mother figure and maintained that centrality in transforming it into an objective symbol, Proust diffused such concentration by focusing more specifically on the grandmother figure and her dramatic death and by allowing the mother to disappear from notice, behind the scenes as it were, soon after the train ride back from Venice in *Albertine disparue*. She is only mentioned thereafter in *Le Temps retrouvé* as a reminiscence to be resurrected by the memory process of the artist.

Such diffusion and substitution might have been prompted by Proust's constant desire to cloud any outright transparency in his fiction – to prevent the identification of his attachment to his mother so as to avoid another means of identifying the narrator with him. At the same time, he succeeded in amplifying the more abstract emotion of attachment to a maternal figure by doubling the maternal identity and thereby enlarging the ramifications of the very strong sentiment. The prolonged death scene of the grandmother which occurs in *Le Côté de Guermantes II*, is the only one of its kind in the novel, except for that of the artist Bergotte – other deaths (those of Swann, Albertine, Saint-Loup) being reported. The medical symptoms it reports correspond to those of Proust's mother dying from uremia; in particular, the impression of rejuvenation at the moment of the death '*l'apparence d'une jeune fille*'[10] – parallels Proust's description of his dead mother's face in the letter to Madame de Noailles: 'death restored to her the youthfulness of the days before her sorrows'.[11] Paradoxically, in Proust's novel, in the context of recaptured subjective time, the mother of the narrator never really dies – an artistic effect which again dispels such life fact orientation.

In this and many other instances, Proust was creating an art of multiplication with respect to the representation of person or place. This approach coincides with the narrator's statements on places in *Le Temps retrouvé*. Just as many persons could contribute to the

creation of one character, so many churches can contribute to the depiction of one church in the fiction:

> *Et plus qu'au peintre, à l'écrivain, pour obtenir du volume et de la consistance, de la genéralité, de la réalité littéraire, comme il lui faut beaucoup d'églises vues pour en peindre une seule, il lui faut aussi beaucoup d'êtres pour un seul sentiment.*[12]

[And more than the painter, the writer, in order to obtain substance and consistency, universality and literary reality, as he might need to have seen many churches to depict a single one, so he needs many beings to convey a single sentiment.]

Here is one of the many points at which the aesthetics of the narrator and that of Proust converge. In this light, it seems limiting to follow the approach of Proust's biographer Painter who sought to identify place and person according to recognisable sites and persons which Proust knew. Many maps of Illiers have been drawn tracing Swann's Way and Guermantes Way, and tourists go each May to this countryside and outline the walks. But at the same time critics have continuously objected to such a production of equivalences.

Léon Pierre-Quint, the earliest biographer of Proust, who had vivid recollections of the writer, whom he knew personally, nonetheless realised from the start that it was a deeper reality, irreducible to life facts, that Proust had transcribed in his fiction. As if echoing Proust's own statement on the subject of his sources, Pierre-Quint stated in his book *Marcel Proust*:

> *Il n'y a jamais de clef véritable dans les romans de Marcel Proust. L'auteur cherche simplement dans diverses réalités, dans plusieurs pays, dans plusieurs personnages des traits choisis avec lesquels il recrée un seul pays fictif, Combray, un seul personnage, Swann, une seule sonate, celle de Vinteuil.*[13]

[There are never any real keys to Marcel Proust's novels. The author simply searches in diverse realities, in several countries, in several characters for the chosen features with which he creates a single fictitious country, Combray, a single character, Swann, a single sonata, Vinteuil's.]

Similarly, André Ferré commented some time ago: 'We cannot assign to places a fixed place in the atlas.'[14] And later, Herni Bonnet blatantly criticised Painter's desire for verifiability by saying: 'We were shocked also by Painter's mania for seeking and finding everywhere the keys or the sources.'[15] Even a local poet deeply familiar with the Cabourg region, Bernard Coulon, has shown in his guidebook *Promenades en Normandie* that Proust 'describes across landscapes an essentially interior universe' ('*décrire au travers de paysages un univers essentiellement intérieur*'[16]).

Yet again, it was Proust himself who first suggested how to use any source work that was found. It is a fact that, under the influence of Ruskin and following the English critic's death in 1900, Proust embarked on a series of 'pilgrimages' to explore the churches memorialised by Ruskin in Italy and in France. Through the concentrated study and translation of Ruskin, Proust, the critic in his twenties, recognised a concrete connection between objective places and thoughts. In speaking of Ruskin's quality of vision, he seems to have been formulating his own:

> *L'objet auquel s'applique une pensée comme celle de Ruskin et dont elle est inséparable n'est pas immatériel, il est répandu çà et là sur la surface de la terre. Il faut aller le chercher là où il se trouve, à Pise, à Florence, à Venise . . .* [17]

[The object to which a thought is applied as in the case of Ruskin and from which it is inseparable is not immaterial; it is spread here and there on the surface of the earth. One has to go and find it where it happens to be – in Pisa, in Florence, in Venice . . .]

In this comment, Proust was demonstrating that the rudiments of the ideas which art incorporates are found in retrievable reality and then built upon. To fully understand Ruskin's work, Proust visited Venice twice in 1900, in April with his mother and in October alone. He applied his observations of that city to the study of the writer. The same can be done with Proust's own work. Certain actual locales can be identified, and then it can be observed how places are enlarged and disoriented in the art form by Proust's imagination and sensibility. Indeed, Georges Poulet was suggesting this approach in assigning the term '*le lieu privilégié*' to Proust's treatment of place. For it is precisely the dislocation, adumbration, multiplication and mystification that marks Proust's aesthetic process as a

form of re-creation of persona and place through composite constructs.

As in the case of numerous novelists after him, Proust seems to incarnate in his work, which includes his many drafts and revisions, the guidelines for its interpretation, so that the very work contains the key to itself. Throughout Proust's long *'roman fleuve'* there are aesthetic theories regarding displacement and transmutation uttered either by the narrator-writer to be or certain artist figures. Some of these comments seem strikingly close to those set forth in Proust's early critical work, *Contre Sainte-Beuve*, where Proust was already airing certain aspects of his own artistic method. After all, Proust had originally conceived *Contre Sainte-Beuve* as a hybrid work of fiction, autobiography and criticism. By 1909 the essay was overwhelmed by narrative sections and Proust was calling it, despite its title, a 'real novel'. He made this explicit statement in a letter to Alfred Vallette, the head of *Mercure de France*, hoping to get it published in serial form:

> The book does indeed end with a long conversation about Sainte-Beuve and about aesthetics and once people have finished the book they will see that the whole novel is simply the implementation of the artistic principles expressed in this final part, a sort of preface if you like placed at the end.[18]

It was natural, then, that Proust's developing aesthetics should be intimately connected to the genesis of his grand novel, as he actually transformed sections of *Contre Sainte-Beuve* into the first and last sections of the novel and continued the intermingling of aesthetics and fiction, experimented on in the germinal essay, in the larger scheme of the novel. In particular, the last volume, *Le Temps retrouvé*, although published posthumously, clarified the aesthetics of the novel itself. This should not be surprising given the fact that manuscript studies have revealed that the novel and its aesthetics were integrally conceived and related from the beginning since the last part of the last volume *Le Temps Retrouvé* and the first chapter 'Combray' of *Du côté de chez Swann* were written at the same time in the years 1909–11. Certainly Proust's letter of 1919 to the literary critic Paul Souday confirms this point.[19] In analysing the many drafts of the work in progress, Bernard Brun has perceived a set of narrative fragments, united as motifs, which get linked organically through what he refers to as a turmoil of representation: *'mise en abîme de la*

représentation'. In his view, then, the final text is an 'accidental res-
idue' of the play of displacements, transformations, additions and
deletions which appear in the drafts. Brun has shown how Proust
gradually transferred his aesthetics to the end of the novel. Moreover, it is obvious that this aesthetics permeated the novel from the
beginning to the end. Such genetic criticism readily links Proust's
aesthetics to the narrator's.

But it is even more pertinent that the very aesthetics discussed
in the last section, named by Proust *Matinée chez la Princesse de
Guermantes*, pertains specifically to the nature of autobiographical
fiction and the relationship between art and life. It is appropriate,
therefore, that the theories can be examined first before isolating the
practice of such theories in the earlier sections of the novel. We recall
that it is in the library of the Princesse de Guermantes that the narrator has an epiphany or insight about his vocation as an artist. At this
climactic moment of social acceptance and artistic calling, the artist's function is designated. It is to re-create the true life (*'recréer la
vraie vie'*[20]), to rejuvenate the impressions (*'rajeunir les impressions'*),
to recompose life (*'recomposer exactement la vie'*). The vantage point
of the burgeoning artist in the *Recherche* is strikingly similar to that
of the artist positioned by Joyce in *A Portrait of the Artist as a Young
Man*. Both works trace the evolution of a boy into a creative writer
whose very subject matter is his life. Through his narrator, Proust is
identifying two levels of experience: the mundane and the artistic.
Unlike the quotidian of Joyce, the mundane of Proust becomes what
the French call *'les mondanités'* – the world of social experience
derived from the salons of the upper levels of French society. In contrast, Proust perceives the artist as a skindiver, probing beneath the
surface of everyday experiences to find the denominator of real life.
In order to reach this deeper level of experience, the writer must
'undo' (*défaire*) the surface traits of habit, self-love, passion and even
intelligence by which the world delimits him:

> *Ce travail de l'artiste, de chercher à apercevoir sous de la matière, sous de
> l'expérience, sous des mots quelque chose de différent, c'est exactement le
> travail inverse de celui que, à chaque minute, quand nous vivons
> détourné de nous-même, l'amour-propre, la passion, l'intelligence, et
> l'habitude aussi accomplissent en nous, quand elles amassent au-dessus
> de nos impressions vraies, pour nous les cacher entièrement, les
> nomenclatures, les buts pratiques que nous appelons faussement la vie.*[21]

[This work of the artist, to seek to discover beneath a certain matter, beneath a certain experience, beneath certain words, something different, is the exact reverse of the work which at each moment that when we live unconscious of ourselves lets self-love, passion, intelligence and habit also take place in us, when these qualities gather the names and practical purposes that we call falsely life above our real impressions, in order to hide the latter from us entirely.]

This statement in *Le Temps retrouvé* coincides both in meaning and language with the earlier one in *Contre Sainte-Beuve* which speaks of the distinction between the writer and the worldly man (*'l'homme du monde'*). These parallel assertions support the view that *Contre Sainte-Beuve* can be considered an *avant-texte* of the *Recherche* and, moreover, that the narrator's voice in *Le Temps retrouvé* can be associated with the author's.

The narrator of *Le Temps retrouvé* clearly reiterates the statements of *Contre Sainte-Beuve* regarding the artist's relationship to a 'deeper' reality. Autobiographical fiction is specifically the object of the narrator's thoughts since he views his past life as providing the ingredients for his becoming an artist and those ingredients will be the material for his fiction: *'Et je compris que tous ces matériaux de l'oeuvre littéraire, c'était ma vie passée.'*[22] But he realises that this past life will be differentiated from the true life crystallised in the creative process that is literature: *'La vraie vie, la vie enfin découverte et éclaircie, la seule vie par conséquent pleinement vécue, c'est la littérature'* ('The true life, the life discovered and illuminated, consequently the only life fully lived is literature'). That is to say, the artist multiplies the particulars of his mundane experiences and reincarnates them into a generalised, universal form. This process enables the artist to free himself from himself: 'Only through art can we leave ourselves behind' (*'Par l'art seulement nous pouvons sortir de nous'*).

In using the words *déchiffrer* (unravel) and *traduire* (translate), the narrator is pointing to interpretation as the means of recreating the past experienced life artistically. The artist, here identified as the autobiographical novelist, reads his life backwardly (*'à rebours'*) and is the translator of its hieroglyphic. By removing the ordinary and the habitual from life experiences, the artist reconstitutes that life:

Il me fallait rendre aux moindres signes qui m'entouraient (Guermantes, Albertine, Gilberte, Saint-Loup, Balbec, etc.) leurs sens que l'habitude leur avait fait perdre pour moi.[23]

[I had to return to the smallest signs which surrounded me (Guermantes, Albertine, Gilberte, Saint-Loup, Balbec, etc.) their meaning which habit had made them lose for me.]

An analogy can be drawn from this statement. The fictional narrator, in speaking of fictional characters and places, corresponds to the author and his 'real' persons and places. Without this analogy, critics like Gilles Deleuze can be led to a purely semiotic interpretation of Proust, reading the novel as a system of signs – of society, love and art. From an autobiographical standpoint, however, the creation of the fictional signs has involved a metamorphosis of the material reality into an aesthetic one.

In referring to art in this last volume, the narrator is speaking specifically of the autobiographical novel and its new form. He distinguishes this form from 'literature of description' or representational literature since autobiographical fiction involves artistic recreation. He views the structure of such an autobiographical novel in terms of a certain repetition or recurrence of motif which defines a life: '*Car une oeuvre, même de confession directe, est pour le moins intercalée entre plusieurs épisodes de la vie de l'auteur*'[24] ('Because even a directly confessional work is at the least interwoven between several episodes of the life of the author').

Art must mimic the fact that a series of analogous incidents can occur in life. Several women, for example, can create a similar emotion for a man. Likewise, for Proust himself it would not be a question of spelling out the particular persons, male or female, who provoke the particular emotion but of conveying the very emotion which might have been produced by a multiplicity of partners. Individual instances of homosexuality will be generalised and broadened into theme and metaphor in *Sodome et Gomorrhe*, as we shall see. Whereas the individuality of any relationship is a personal factor, the phenomenon produced over time depersonalises the experience and incorporates it into paradigms for art. This perspective appears throughout the narrative of the *Recherche*. For example, Albertine and Gilberte are interchangeable since it is the similar emotion or mental effect that they produce which is permanent, not their individual identities. Furthermore, their effects are comparable

to that produced by Odette de Crécy on the character Swann. Analogous conclusions can be drawn from the use of any life sources in the work. The possibility of such substitutions adds a 'disinterested' element to the work of art, as it moves its concerns from the personal (the identities or sources) to the general. A multiplicity of episodes, places and individuals contribute to the creation of fictional ones. A composite image, sentiment, place or character constitutes the synthesis of the artistic product, which is fashioned by the recurrence of motifs.

Such a theory of transposition and substitution applies most readily to the Martinville and Hudimesnil epiphanies, which resemble each other, though they are separated by several books of the *Recherche*. We recall that there are two instances of mirage-like misrepresentation which occur to the narrator at different stages of his life. In fact, the particular illusion which occurs in both instances is so similar that it establishes a link between the geographically separated Combray and Balbec, which are atmospherically and thematically so different. What is even more interesting is that the apparent sources for the two places, Illiers and Cabourg, respectively, can be traced to 'real' phenomena which could create such effects.

The aesthetic of misrepresentation is highlighted in these instances affecting the perception of place. Proust is obsessed by mirages, a word he uses frequently in his writings. The first example of such a mirage is the well-known sequence on the steeples of Martinville in *Du côté de chez Swann*. In that scene, the narrator recounts a little carriage trip he took as a young boy in the vicinity of Combray. During that trip he is arrested by an image of rising steeples before him:

'*Seuls, s'élevant du niveau de la plaine et comme perdus en rase campagne, montaient vers le ciel les deux clochers de Martinville. Bientôt nous en vîmes trois: venant se placer en face d'eux par une volte hardie, un clocher retardataire, celui de Vieuxvicq, les avait rejoints.*'[25]

['Alone, arising on the level of the plain and as if lost in the bare countryside, arose toward the sky the two steeples of Martinville. Soon we saw three of them; the latest steeple, that of Vieuxvicq, having boldly shoved itself in front of them, joined them.]

This juxtaposition of distant steeples creates a sense of artistic 'pleasure' which the narrator feels compelled to record in actual writing. His response becomes a document of his emerging sensitivity as a creative writer of his childhood in Combray. We note that he is recording a misrepresentation rather than a representation. The impression is to be repeated in a later incident in adolescence in Balbec and therefore becomes a recurring motif of artistic perception.

Guided by Proust's own statement in a *Figaro* article of 1907 'Impressions de route en automobile', which was later reproduced as 'En mémoire des églises assassinées' in the collection *Pastiches et mélanges*, certain literary-minded critics have identified Caen rather than Illiers as the source for the apparition of Martinville. In that article, Proust was combining impressions of several actual automobile trips he had taken in Normandy in the region of Lisieux and Caen during which he had encountered a multitude of steeples rising from the numerous churches in his path. In one instance, he noted that three steeples were appearing before him, a vision which he likened to three birds poised on the plain. In a footnote, Proust admitted that such descriptions actually passed into the *Recherche*. Hence, critics such as Henri Bonnet have regarded the Martinville epiphany as a simple phenomenon of transposition: from that of 1907 near Caen. Proust could have been entranced by the multitude of churches in that city, such as Saint-Etienne, l'Abbaye-aux-Dames, l'Eglise Saint-Pierre. One can go further, however, and note that the controlling factor in any transposition for Proust is the theoretical claim he had made that the impression of place rather than the place itself is what the artist transfers into art. This point was also made in the preface that Proust wrote for his translation of Ruskin's *Sesame and Lilies*:

Cette apparence avec laquelle ils nous charment et nous déçoivent et au-delà de laquelle nous voudrions aller, c'est l'essence même de cette chose en quelque sorte sans épaisseur – mirage arrêté sur une toile – qu'est une vision.[26]

[This semblance with which they charm us and deceive us and beyond which we would like to proceed, is the very essence of that unsubstantial thing – a mirage caught on a canvas – that is a vision.]

As with places for the painter, so the vision of the churches, wherever they were, must have been for the agnostic Proust a purely aesthetic experience which found its way into his art.

Even if Proust actually saw three steeples on a specific trip to Caen in 1907, it is more likely that the fictional image of the three steeples derives from the mirage-like effect in the environs of Illiers – an image probably going back to earlier primal memories of childhood. In such a case the latter apparition could be interpreted as a screen memory reinforcing the first. Ultimately, the Martinville apparition is a case of amalgamation and substitution – a technique which Proust uses repeatedly in his fiction. It involves a certain dimension of authenticity and others of transposition. If, on the one hand, a case can be made for the transposition of steeples from Caen to Illiers, from one side of France to another, an equal case can be made for the multiplication of steeples in Illiers itself. A traveller going to Illiers and tracing the car journey described in *Du côté de chez Swann* can experience a mirage-like effect in the vista around the solitary church of Vieuxvicq, a village adjacent to Illiers. It seems most likely that Proust intentionally confused the two images, both experienced, to create the composite of Martinville. Such a fusion camouflages the identification of any single 'real' locale. Manipulating, therefore, the external sites, he communicates the internal sensations provoked by those sites, and he transports those steeples into a fictional world.

It is not surprising that Proust continues this process of substitution and transfer to yet another fictional locale – that of Balbec. The trees of Hudimesnil in the Balbec landscape which are visible in *A l'ombre des jeunes filles en fleurs* have similar effects to the steeples of Martinville earlier in the novel. A continuity of artistic perception is established between the two analogous scenes. The latter is that of a summer afternoon ride in the environs of Balbec. This is during the time of the narrator's first visit to Balbec when he stayed at the Grand Hotel on the Normandy coast. The scene is especially prominent because the narrator is in the company of his grandmother's influential friend, Madame de Villeparisis, an acquaintance who will be the link with the aristocratic world and take him a step closer to the Guermantes way.

Proust explicitly establishes the link between the two epiphanies as he first describes the Hudimesnil apparition:

Nous descendîmes sur Hudimesnil; tout d'un coup je fus rempli de ce bonheur profond que je n'avais pas souvent ressenti depuis Combray, un

bonheur analogue à celui que m'avaient donné, entre autres, les clochers
de Martinville . . . Je venais d'apercevoir . . . trois arbres qui devaient
servir d'entrée à une allée couverte et formaient un dessin que je ne
voyais pas pour la première fois.[27]

[We came upon Hudimesnil; all of a sudden I was filled with that
deep happiness that I had seldom felt since Combray, a happiness
analogous to that which the steeples of Martinville had given me
...I had just perceived . . . three trees which were to serve as an
entrance to a covered path and formed a pattern which, it seemed
to me, I had seen before.]

It is as if the narrator is experiencing a *déjà vu*, associating the view
of the three trees with that of the three churches. Realistically speaking, the hills behind Cabourg, the raw material for Balbec, are
strewn with trees overlooking the Normandy coast. From the
perspective of those hills, the sea is seen between the branches of the
trees – a physical phenomenon which is an apt source for the refrain
of this section: '*la mer entre les feuillages des arbres*' ('the vision of the
sea between the foliage of the trees'). What makes Proust single out
three trees from among the multitude is to connect one level of artistic pleasure with another in rites of passage from childhood to
youth. What happens to the narrator could have happened to Proust
himself: a heightened artistic experience created by the power of
suggestion which the present has in its evocation of the past. The
apparition of the trees summons what Proust would call '*la vraie
vie*', or true life. The mundane experiences which may have
occurred between these two epiphanies are rendered as insignificant
as the time which has passed.

The contradictory elements of vagueness and precision drawn
from Proust's description of certain landscapes in his fiction seem to
reflect the combinations that often occur in dreamscapes or memory,
paradoxically clouded and clarified by certain distances. In addition, the thematic recurrence of certain images create a musical
refrain or *reprise* through the novel. In yet another instance, a certain
plasticity of image describing Combray is connected to Balbec. For
example, the colour of the sky above the place du Calvaire in
Combray, described as a reflection of the setting sun on the
windows of the house and a purple band in the depth of the woods,
seems to be transposed and taken up again in *A l'ombre des jeunes
filles en fleurs* in the red colours of sunset saturating the desert-like

beach of Balbec, described as a band of red sky over the sea. Proust makes poetry out of such fictional scenes when they recur as motifs throughout the novel.

It is fascinating to observe the construction of the two major places in the *Recherche*: Combray and Balbec. Each is a world of its own; each has very real roots in specific locales in France. But it is the very passage from the real to the fictional which sheds light on Proust's creative process. Whereas Combray gives the impression of a child's domain of innocence, Balbec is that of a mysterious faraway land with associations of Sodom and Gomorrah.

In the creation of these fictional places, Proust uses a combination of sources. For some, Combray contained characteristics of both Illiers, the site of his vacations in the 1870s, and Auteuil, Proust's birthplace outside Paris, whose backyard, some have argued, resembles the description more than the minute and enclosed garden outside of his Aunt Amiot's home in Illiers, still standing today. On the other hand, that very house and its rooms are very similar to the description of the house of Combray in the novel, with Proust's little room on the second floor and the kitchen and dining-room downstairs. The town itself remains like a stage-setting today, with its quaint train station opening on to the tree-lined Avenue de la Gare which leads on to the rue de Chartres and on to the square of the church of Saint-Jacques which dominates the small village. Around the corner is the modest house of the Amiots. However, what might be more interesting is the derivation of the name Combray as a combination of two sources: a little village fourteen kilometres west of Illiers is called Combres, and another small village near Cabourg is called Combres-sur-Mer. Other names from the region become assimilated and modified in the early section of the novel, such as *Méséglise* for *Méréglise* and *Mirougrain* for *Monjouvain*. Proust's actual memories of Illiers would have dated from before the age of thirteen, since thereafter he was taken to inland resorts of Normandy for reasons of health. In fact, the faultiness of such memory may have created a certain artistic topography which is symbolic in this early section of the *Recherche*.

The two opposing ways in the novel, Swann's way and Guermantes way, have been said to correspond to Méséglise and Saint-Eman or Villebon respectively – two villages in the vicinity of Illiers. On the way towards these places it is true that the scenery begins to change near Saint-Eman, positioned at the source of the river Loir which, combined with the river Thironne, has been

viewed as the equivalent of the river Vivonne in the novel. That fictional river, which in reality is a rather thin, insignificant stream, acquires, as we know, a certain suggestiveness in the novel of something extraterrestrial and mysterious. The castle of Guermantes alluded to in the novel is actually more like the further Villebon than the more modest one of Saint-Eman connected to the Goussencourts, to which it is more frequently likened. Reconstituting real places, Proust superimposes upon them new significances.

Actually, Proust went to great pains in selecting the particular name Guermantes for his fictional aristocratic family and château. He was obviously drawn to the resonant quality of the name, which he called 'pretty' (*'joli'*) in 1909. He had first met François Vicomte de Pâris on 12 June 1908 at a ball given by the Princess of Polignac. The next month Proust, seeking (unsuccessfully) to develop a friendship, suggested seeing Pâris again in the country at the Château de Guermantes.[28] This actual château near Lagny, in Seine-et-Marne, had been inherited by François de Pâris's aunt, the Baronne de Lareinty, née Puységur. Proust had been particularly interested in the Vicomte because of his association with the Guermantes name, but, being rebuffed by him at their first meeting, Proust called him a 'strange creature who inspires affection without being able to establish friendship'[29] and hesitated about using that name. On the other hand, since Proust had earlier been a welcome guest at Madeleine Lemaire's country house Réveillon, also in Seine-et-Marne, he had used that name in *Jean Santeuil* and thereby linked his hostess with the aristocracy instead of with her true bourgeois standing. In eventually replacing Réveillon with Guermantes, he associated the later name with the impression of distance and inaccessibility that the Vicomte de Pâris had left with him.

Before actually using the name in the *Recherche*, however, Proust asked numerous questions about its origins. Unlike Joyce, who wrote letters to his brother asking questions about the authenticity of a location, Proust wrote letters to his aristocratic friend Georges de Lauris in 1909 asking him if Guermantes was really actively connected to a family or whether it could be considered 'extinct'. He was seeking a certain anonymity with respect to the name – to prevent any identification of known persons with it:

Do you happen to know whether *Guermantes*, which must have been the name of some people as well as of a place, was then already in the Pâris family, or rather, to put it in a more seemly

way, whether the name of Comte or Marquis de Guermantes was a title used by relations of the Pâris family, and whether it's entirely extinct and available to an author?[30]

In that same year, in the early draft of 1909, he called it the Château du Poitou, giving it yet another location. Not receiving a response from Georges de Lauris about this matter, by 1911 Proust answered his own question and opted for the extinctness of the real name Guermantes. But Proust's cautious nature and perennial desire for camouflage seems to have made him ultimately transport the recognisable château to another part of France near Illiers and to confuse it with two other existing châteaux in that region. The result of this intricate case of transposition is that a rich ambiguity surrounds the château of Guermantes in the novel, never traceable in literary pilgrimages to that region of Illiers-Combray. Like Virginia Woolf with her lighthouse, Proust takes a real place and transports it to another faraway place, associating it with distance and remoteness. But unlike Woolf, yet for the same purpose of dissemblance and mythification, Proust keeps the original name and reconstitutes it so as to sever it from its original connections, diffusing any distinct referentiality with respect to it.

It is well known that the early volume of *Du côté de chez Swann* stressed the opposition of the two ways by positioning them in opposite directions and describing them as having two different topographies and totally different flora. The Guermantes Way, we recall, was predominated by a river landscape, whereas Swann's Way consisted of open fields and plains. The Guermantes Way, in keeping with its association with the aristocracy, was coloured by esoteric water lilies and darker, rarer flowers, whereas Swann's Way was fragranced by the more common pink hawthorns. As a matter of fact, the narrator himself would more easily embark on walks through Swann's Way. Any change in weather, for example, would discourage a walk toward the Guermantes Way, where several châteaux housed the distant aristocracy. The narrator comments that the two ways are so distinct that they correspond to two different sides of the brain or poetically to two different afternoons:

Et cette démarcation était rendue plus absolue encore parce que cette habitude que nous avions de n'aller jamais vers les deux côtés un même jour, dans une seule promenade, mais une fois du côté de Méséglise, une fois du côté de Guermantes, les enfermait pour ainsi dire l'un de l'autre,

inconnaissables l'un à l'autre, dans les vases clos et sans communication entre eux, d'après-midi différents.[31]

[And this demarcation was rendered even more absolute because this habit that we had of never going in the two directions on the same day, in the course of a single walk, whether in the Méséglise Way or the Guermantes Way, confining them, so to speak, far from each other, unknowable to each other, in non-communicating vessels, on different afternoons.]

The depiction of the Guermantes Way in the first volume of the *Recherche* had been one of inaccessibility and immense distance. However, towards the end of the work, just prior to the Great War, when the narrator revisits Combray where the married Gilberte is living at her father's house in Tansonville, the perspective has changed. A certain reality of place is suggested in the description of the Vivonne river as 'slim and ugly bordering the towing-path' (*'mince et laide au bord du chemin de halage'*[32]) or of its source as a sort of square watering-place full of rising bubbles (*'une espèce de lavoir carré où montaient des bulles'*). These descriptions are more in line with the actual view of the river Loir near Saint-Eman. Furthermore, distances are suddenly envisaged as shorter; in a quarter of an hour one could be at the Guermantes. In this atmosphere of depoetisation, as the scene comes closer to its presumed source, there emerges Gilberte's apparently astounding statement:

'Si vous voulez, nous pourrons tout de même sortir un après-midi et nous pourrons alors aller à Guermantes, en prenant par Méséglise, c'est la plus jolie façon,' phrase qui en bouleversant toutes les idées de mon enfance m'apprit que les deux côtés n'étaient pas aussi inconciliables que j'avais cru.

['If you want, we could nevertheless go out one afternoon and we could go to Guermantes, by way of Méséglise, that is the prettiest way to go' – a statement that upset all my childhood notions, made me aware that the two 'ways' were not as unreconcilable as I had believed.]

This statement appears to subvert the narrator's earlier childhood convictions that the two ways did not connect:

Alors, 'prendre par Guermantes' pour aller à Méséglise, ou le contraire m'eût semblé une expression aussi dénuée de sens que prendre par l'est pour aller à l'ouest.[33]

[So, to 'take Guermantes Way' to go to Méséglise or the contrary would have seemed to me an expression as devoid of meaning as to go east to get to the west.]

Gilberte's statement – that they could take one way to get to the other – awakens the narrator to insights which culminate in the artistic epiphany at the very end of the novel, in the 'Matinée de Guermantes'. It is significant, too, that Gilberte's observation has realistic grounds in the setting around the actual Illiers. For in tracing equivalents for the opposing ways, one finds an actual point of intersection between the two ways around a town called Amo. It can be observed that Méréglise, the actual town upon which Méséglise seems to be modelled, is not as diametrically opposed to the equivalent of Saint-Eman or the Guermantes Way. In fact, there is a circular route around Illiers which can connect the equivalents of Saint-Eman and Tansonville. Proust seems to be returning to a certain referentiality at the end of the novel entirely for purposes of correspondence. The real may surface as dreams are realised. Studies of the drafts reveal that Proust had considered adding Gilberte's statement to the first section (to be spoken by someone else, of course); this would have created a discrepancy from the start. Instead, the conciliation of the contrary ways by the end of the novel suggests that the narrator's art and life are one, which they were not in the beginning.

For in gaining access to society, in the very salon of the Guermantes, the narrator succeeds in becoming an artist. The fact that Swann's descendant, Gilberte, successfully breaks social barriers by marrying a Guermantes, Robert de Saint-Loup, is another indication of the union of the two ways, and it is therefore appropriate that Gilberte should be the one to make the observation. Furthermore, the fact that the very name of the aristocrat, Saint-Loup, is taken from an actual village in the Illiers region gives clues to the eventual unification.

This rapprochement of what is considered to be distant and inaccessible can be compared to similar effects in Virginia Woolf's *To the Lighthouse*. In both cases, bad weather is an incidental obstacle to reaching the ultimate points. What was considered an unattainable

ideal for Proust is projected on to his characters; the ultimate acceptance of Marcel into the Guermantes salon suggesting Proust's own
fulfilment of his life-long desire to attain social distinction. Analogously, as we shall see, what was postponed for the Ramsay family becomes realised for them years later, as Virginia Woolf comes to
terms with the death of her mother and the fictional family reaches
the lighthouse. Both novelists manipulate perspective – of distancing and then eradicating that distance, as certain aspirations are
realised by their characters and by projection by themselves.

Proust's artistic method of transforming place is seen from yet
another point of view in the exploration and symbolisation of the
'two ways'. There is an overt misrepresentation of the two ways
which has not yet been noted by the biographical critics who have
been intent on establishing equivalents. In the text itself, the two
ways are demarcated as emanating from two different doors. The
path to the Guermantes Way is out the back door through the
garden gate (to the rue de l'Oiseau-Fléché) whereas the path to
Swann's Way is out the front door to the rue du Saint Esprit. A visit
to Illiers reveals that the route to what has been considered the
equivalent of Guermantes, Villebon, originates from the front door
and passes through the village. The question then remains as to why
Proust switched directions in his text. Did he simply forget the
geography, since his childhood recollections date only up to the age
of thirteen, after which his visits to Illiers became rare? Or did
Proust simply want to add another element of ambiguity which
would prevent any exact verification with real places? Unlike Joyce,
who verified the accuracy of places transcribed in his fiction, Proust
manipulated places for artistic purposes. The overt misrepresentation of direction in this case seems intentional and not accidental,
since it lends itself to the theme of the convergence of the two ways.

Whereas the inaccuracies regarding the actual direction of the two
ways have not been discussed by the biographers, the substitution
of the fictional Gilbert the Bad for the Virgin in the Saint-Hilaire/
Saint-Jacques chapel has been noted. Painter has explained that the
eleventh-century church of Saint-Jacques at Illiers is less ancient
than the fictional Saint-Hilaire and that a certain Geoffroy d'Illiers
dating from before William the Conqueror may have been the
source for the creation of Gilbert the Bad:

Even the presence of Gilbert the Bad is not far to seek . . . It was
their first ancestor Geoffroy d'Illiers, builder of the castle of

Illiers, who suggested the desperate life and horrible end of Gilbert the Bad.[34]

The well-known scene in which Proust puts the formidable Duchess of Guermantes in the Chapel of Gilbert the Bad lends a distant and inaccessible aura to the figure. Proust was constructing an awesome ancestry for his Duchess by also associating her with the medieval legendary Geneviève de Brabant, who presumably was blessed by Saint-Hilaire, the fictional name he had assigned to the Illiers church. In the scene, the narrator suddenly sees the Duchess at close quarters and is disappointed by the imperfections of her face. In subsequently restoring the distanced and idealised image of the Duchess and her ancestry that he had carried throughout his childhood, he reclaims the idealised world which he judges to be more substantial than the real one. Analogously, at the very end of the novel, the narrator, in returning to Combray and finding the *'mince Vivonne'*, clings to his literary career which will restore the previous image of the Guermantes Way – idealised forever. Proust is demonstrating that the subjective factor, whether working through art or memory, enlarges experience. The church of Saint-Jacques is as ordinary as the Ballast clock for Joyce or the Godrevy lighthouse for Virginia Woolf, but in each case the particular structures serve the writers as catalysts for their imagination, setting up a trigger for powers of association which produce the fictions.

Amalgamation is another element of Proust's creative process which transforms the 'real' and identifiable place into the imaginary and fictive. In 1987 both the mayor of Cabourg, Michel Moles, and the local writer and poet Bernard Coulon agreed that Balbec, although specifically associated with the seaside town of Cabourg, which Proust visited seven times in the period from 1907 to 1914, incorporates the entire Normandy region as a whole superimposed by other allusions and transformed by Proust's imagination. Actually, the specific name Balbec could have been drawn from a town in the region of Cabourg, Beg-Meil, which Proust is said to have visited with his grandmother in 1895. The oriental flavour assigned to this imaginary region as a whole may well have been affected by Proust's reading of *1001 Nights*. Balbec has the same kind of effect as Araby had for Joyce – evoking the faraway, the exotic and the distant. In the case of Proust, that atmosphere is coupled with yet another allusion, the haunting one of Sodom and Gomorrah, which eventually dominates the description of the region (in the narrator's

second visit to the resort) as it transforms the white sandy coast into the impression of an arid desert. But in the latter association, there is the element of reality which affects this characterisation since it can be virtually witnessed that the sandy coast visually appears as arid as a desert. Certain characters then are scrutinised, such as the Baron de Charlus and Morel, corresponding to this suggestive setting.

The search for the 'Persian Church', *l'église persane de Balbec'*, as the narrator calls it, has captivated many of Proust's biographical critics, especially since the church is the focal point of the narrator's vision in *A l'ombre des jeunes filles en fleurs*. Proust's notion of multiplicity – that many 'real' churches contribute to the making of a fictional church – certainly applies in this case. Literal minded critics have identified the church of Dives-sur-Mer, a structure dating from the time of William the Conqueror in a quiet town adjacent to Cabourg, as the source, although there is actually another church in Cabourg, and others in other parts of France, which might have contributed to the making of the fictional one. What can be confirmed is that the little town of Dives-sur-Mer is adjacent to Cabourg. The Dives village station is where Proust would have arrived on his visits to Cabourg. Although a four-to-five-hour train ride from Paris at that time, the trip could take as long as 22 hours, as Proust once wrote to Madame Catusse.[35] He would then have taken a coach or tram across a little bridge to Cabourg and down the avenue de la Mer to the Grand Hotel. During his visits, however, he must have explored the very old town of Dives, with its old church dating from the eleventh century. Going there today, winding one's way through the narrow streets of the town, one comes upon this old church which looks like an ancient fortress with mouldering old walls; it appears massive in contrast to what remains of this tiny, medieval town. In the text, the narrator's mention of the stained glass window which portrays fishermen finding a cross from the legend of Christ the Saviour – 'the miraculous Christ the mystery of which was told in a stained glass window in the church a few paces away from me' (*'le Christ miraculeux dont un vitrail de cette église qui était à quelques mètres de moi racontait la découverte'*[36]) – does correspond to the little Dives church which actually has such a window. Proust obviously found material from this church to exploit in his fiction.

On the other hand, certain discrepancies eliminate the possibility of a simple or single source and widen the associations. The characterisation of the church as Persian prevents the reader from

establishing a strict equivalence to the little Dives church. On his Ruskinian tour of churches in Normandy, Proust had mentioned his attraction to the church of Bayeux, which for him had an oriental flavour. He had in fact written to the art historian Emile Mâle that he was 'charmed by the oriental figures in the Bayeux cathedral'[37] – intrigued therefore by the presence of orientalism in the romanesque setting. It is striking that in that same letter Proust had listed Dives along with Bayeux as places he had visited. The 'contamination' of Dives by this perceived orientalism can be explained by this juxtaposition of impressions – a process similar to the case of the steeples of Martinville.

As for the narrator, he had already constructed the image of the church through his dreams back in Paris:

> *Tant que je m'étais contenté d'apercevoir du fond de mon lit de Paris l'église persane de Balbec au milieu des flocons de la tempête, aucune objection à ce voyage n'avait été faite par mon corps.*[38]

[As long as I was happy to discover in the depths of my bed in Paris the Persian church of Balbec in the middle of the snowflakes of a storm, my body made no objections to this trip.]

Proust goes out of his way to locate the church in Balbec-le-vieux or in Balbec-en-terre, instead of in Balbec-plage ; that is to say, he correspondingly situates it in Dives proper rather than in Dives-sur-Mer where the old church actually stands. This variation adds another element of ambiguity about any direct association compounded by a discrepancy on the level of the text itself. There the narrator is disappointed not to find what he had poetically imagined: the sea in front of the church he had dreamt about and the foam of the waves at the base of the cupola. Instead, he confronts the harsh reality of the church in the drab village with its standard café and train station, its square and the branch of a savings bank. The name of the church is first overrun by the 'reality' of the witnessed scene, having lost the magical quality of the dream or imaginings. The signifier of the Persian church of Balbec at first loses its significance as it becomes defined by its realistic surroundings. Proust confronts the reader with a double process of misrepresentation on the textual and extra-textual levels; the image of the church is dislocated from the dream and destroyed by the referential reality. As in the case of the Duchess of Guermantes, in this instance the dream is greater

than the reality which encroaches upon the magical quality of the name. But peering into the notion that the very word 'Balbec' has created in him, the narrator frees the drab places and objects and moves them in the very same way he had moved the church in his dream. He liberates the surroundings as well as the church from the stereotype images that the standard meaning of Balbec conjures for the ordinary observer and has those images, evermore separated from their ordinary connection, join the imagined church.

In Proust's transformation of place there are two stages, as evidenced in this reference to Balbec. Having already created Balbec as a composite of actual towns in the Normandy region, the most equivalent being Cabourg, Proust has his narrator contrast the fictionally 'real' Balbec to the imagined one or 'other Balbec'. The 'other' in many instances corresponds to the 'pure fiction'. Here, it is the one that the little boy narrator dreamed of, after hearing Swann mention it back in Combray. It is the one he had anticipated, often thinking of the departure of the 1:22 train. Allowing the name, with its oriental charm, to absorb the image, sets the purely imagined place prior to the fictionally real place; that is to say, the thoughts and associations of the place precede its existence in the novel. Joyce treats place in a similar way in his story 'Araby'. Both Balbec and Araby, when actually reached, are disappointing, for they fail to live up to the illusions and impressions that have been made of them. In the case of Balbec, in taking the fictional to the second degree – the fiction within the fiction – Proust has undermined the referentiality of place with all its ramifications, for he has enlarged that original locus beyond its spatial and environmental restrictions to be compatible with the product of his imagination.

The intricate passage about Balbec in *A l'ombre des jeunes filles en fleurs* delineates the artistic process which mystifies a place as it removes it from the contingencies of its realistic locale. Such mystification and demystification of places and persons recur throughout the novel. After all, the process of naming was for Proust a means of artistic recomposition, analogous to reincarnation. As already seen, the case of the evolution of the Guermantes name is most exemplary. It is also interesting that it was not until the 1914 version of the *Recherche* that such names as Balbec, Saint-Loup, Charlus, were invented, taking the place of less colourful ones such as Querqueville, Montaigy and Guercy. Balbec could have come from a combination of two towns in Normandy, Bolbec and Beg-Meil; Saint-Loup from a little town near Illiers – all

the more fascinating since Saint-Loup was eventually destined to unite with the girl from Tansonville in Illiers/Combray.

What is true of the treatment of place in Proust is also true of that of persons. Proust himself had stated that there were no exclusive keys to the identification of his characters. In a letter to Jacques de Lacretelle he sounded a warning: 'It is the weakness of books that they can become, even though they were spontaneously conceived, *romans à clef* after the fact' ('*C'est la déchéance des livres de devenir, si spontanément qu'ils avaient été conçus, des romans à clefs, après coup*'[39]). Not heeding such a warning, critics like Painter sought to identify the multiple sources for Proust's characters. However, others such as Bonnet preferred to observe how Proust altered his characters from the said models of Charles Haas (for Swann), Robert de Montesquiou (for the Baron de Charlus) or Alfred Agostinelli (for Albertine). Still others, such as Barthes, have sought to abolish all sources saying: 'Proust himself despite the apparently psychological character of what he called his analyses, was visibly concerned with the task of inexorably blurring, by an extreme subtlization, the relation between the writer and his characters.'[40]

Notwithstanding the tendency to eliminate Proust as the source, one of the most intriguing questions is the projection of Proust's own identity on to the multiple persona of Jean Santeuil, Marcel, the narrator of the *Recherche* and even Swann. As in other instances of autobiographical fiction to come, elements of bifurcation and transformation can be detected. The narrator, as if speaking for Proust, had made the point in the text of *Le Temps retrouvé* that a distinction is to be made between the multiple selves, that die successively in us, and a more durable one that holds the parts together. It is interesting that Anaïs Nin, years later in the twentieth century under the influence of Proust, was to adopt the notion of the multiple selves defined by various relationships and thereby reject the notion of any prevailing self. In Proust's case, however, the permanent self might have been reserved for the artistic composite or aesthetic self that is other than the 'quotidian' self.

It has been seen how Proust's work was the point of departure for theories concerning the fictive 'I' and the elimination of the authorial source. Some have even argued that the draft work of *Jean Santeuil* contains much more autobiographical material than the *Recherche* with its first-person narrator. David Ellison's article of 1980 saw autobiography in Proust as 'the textual differential movement by which the "I" is separated from itself and thrust . . . into the

alienating representations of the narrative's all-encompassing, self-obliterating rule'.[41] Although it can easily be seen how the fictive 'I' is distinguished from the personal one, it has been tempting for some, nonetheless, to associate the author with Marcel by virtue of the first name. But then again, it has remained an enigma as to why the name 'Marcel' is actually used only twice in the novel, and by Albertine for that matter. Had Proust, in objectifying the evolution of an impersonal author, merely forgotten to delete the name in the two sections? It would appear that as Proust moved along, he became less and less dependent on the writer as a live person. Any correspondence with his own self would be by analogy, as in the case of the aesthetic theories which the narrator expounds upon.

It is as if Proust diffuses any outright identification with the narrator by suggesting connections with the character Swann. Aside from the narrator himself, the two most prominent figures, artistically speaking, in the *Recherche* are Swann and Albertine. In fact, the narrator goes out of his way in *Le Temps retrouvé* to make this point in reviewing the genesis of the work that he is about to embark upon. He cites Albertine as the 'inspiration' or the muse of his work and Swann as the 'begetter' of the course of his life and hence the course of the novel. In reference to Albertine, he notes that had he not come to know her, his ideas would never have been developed. He reasons further: 'so that even my presence at this very moment with the Prince de Guermantes, where suddenly the idea for my work came to me . . . came to me at the same time also from Swann' ('*de sorte que ma présence même en ce moment chez le prince de Guermantes, où venait de me venir brusquement l'idée de mon oeuvre . . . me venait aussi de Swann*'[42]). It was, after all, Swann who had first spoken of Balbec in the narrator's childhood, inspiring him to go there, and it was at Balbec that the connection with the Guermantes was made.

Even as the narrator gives prominence to these two figures, the fabrication of these two fictional characters can be observed in terms of facts affecting Proust himself. For a long time now, Alfred Agostinelli has been identified with Albertine, and Alfred's relationship with Proust has been traced as far back as 1909 when the two first met. Similarly, Charles Haas has been most readily linked to Swann; Proust had probably met Haas in Madame Straus's salon around 1890, and thereafter Haas had been one of his major connections with the aristocracy. Both fictional characters have an invasive presence through the many volumes, creating a network of interconnections.

When the first volume of the *Recherche* began to appear, Madame Straus, the hostess of both Proust and Haas, fondly dubbed the character Swann/Haas. She seems to have had every reason to do so, especially since in a later volume Proust seems to have slipped and actually mentioned Haas by name. Swann resembled, at least from exterior appearance, the social climber Charles Haas, who as the son of a Jewish stockbroker had made his way into some of the most sought-after salons of his day, even becoming a member of the Jockey Club. Proust was obviously struck by Haas's extraordinary rise to social prominence. Emphatically, however, Proust in a letter to Madame Straus of June 1914, responding to her enthusiasm about his characters in general, tells her that she will indeed see more of his characters in later volumes but denies the Swann/Haas identification (that she has made) or for that matter any other sources: 'although it isn't Haas and in it there are no keys or portraits' ('*Quoique ce ne soit pas Haas et qu'il n'y ait nulle part clefs ni portraits*'[43]).

Ironically, in eliminating Haas as the source, Proust was leaving the way open for himself as one, for the identification of Swann with Proust seems more likely in psychological terms. One of Proust's early critics, André Maurois, has stated:

> It is far more important to realize that Swann was mainly a projection of Proust himself, as should be perfectly obvious from the passages in the *Notebooks* where Swann, as a young man, is presented as the hero of those selfsame episodes which were afterwards fathered on the narrator.[44]

Other critics have simply concluded that Proust actually divided himself into two characters: one having his Jewish identity and the other his Christian background.

It seems obvious that the identification of Proust with Swann as the Jew expresses Proust's own view of himself as an outsider, an alien, in a closed French society, which presumably discriminated against him. In the case of Proust, there are letters which express his feeling of being an outsider, and the aristocrat Montesquiou's rejection of him could have been on social-ethnic grounds. Proust's general sense of alienation as an artist could have also been expressed in the 'Judaism' of Swann. A comparison can be made with Joyce's Leopold Bloom, who though from a totally different class and environment, nonetheless could be said to express Joyce's own alienation from his homeland. Both Joyce and Proust felt alien in their own

society and the Jewish persona in both cases catches that distance they feel. Furthermore, as if for embellishment or play, the very name 'Swann', sounding like the most common symbols used by the Symbolists for the alienated artist, suggests Symbolist escapist tendencies, which reflect Proust's own abnormal behaviour and periods of seclusion in his cork-lined room of artistic creativity.

The fact of the matter is, however, that despite his ethnic background, which might have stood in the way of his crossing social barriers at that particular historical moment, Charles Haas, as has been noted, was a successful social climber. In this respect he was unlike Proust, who ultimately retreated to his art after a period of introductions in the 1890s into social circles of high standing. Presenting Swann as writing a paper on Vermeer (which becomes specifically interrupted during the love affair with Odette) is to suggest that he is some kind of aesthete. This type of aesthete in high social circles was perhaps a person that Proust would have wanted to be but basically wasn't because art pulled him in different directions. Furthermore, the marked heterosexuality of Swann the womaniser (often carrying on several affairs at once) is in stark contrast to the homosexuality of Proust, which though still publicly unacknowledged by him at the time of writing the first volume, surfaced later. Regarding these differences, two conclusions may be drawn. Either Swann was a person that Proust might have wished to have been; many writers, Henry James for instance, have created such 'would-be' characters. Or Proust was creating an identification by analogy, making for example Swann's secret heterosexual affairs analogous to his closeted homosexuality, and the apparent aestheticism of Swann analogous to his more serious art.

A case for such an analogy can be made by likening the fictional Verdurin salon to Madeleine Lemaire's bourgeois, artistic salon which Proust frequented in 1894. At one of Lemaire's musical soirées, Proust may have met his prospective companion, the musician Reynaldo Hahn. It has been said that Reynaldo introduced Proust to the music of Saint-Saens, and that Proust was thereafter captivated by the principal theme of the first movement of the Saint-Saens Sonata in D minor for Piano and Violin. Proust is said to have asked Reynaldo to play the melody repeatedly, in much the same way that Swann listens to the 'Vinteuil' sonata. As can be expected, there are several other sources for the fictional sonata. The creation of the character Odette in this context may have been Proust's hidden way at that time of expressing his strong attachment to

Reynaldo – covering up a homosexual affair by a heterosexual one. This would therefore be another instance of the technique of intentional misrepresentation – blurring the sources by substitution but conveying the sentiment in the fiction.

However, despite the parallels or analogies that can be drawn between Proust and Swann, the character itself is eventually dehumanised and dissociated from any source, as it is turned into a sign in *Le Temps retrouvé*. This is where the aesthetic transformation ultimately leads. The narrator's final view of Swann, in retrospect after his death, is as a 'slender stalk' which had supported the development of the narrator's life. As such, the character Swann is transformed totally into an aesthetic factor. Specifically, it is the material 'plot' factor which links Swann's Way to Guermantes way, as Swann is indirectly the link to the Guermantes via Balbec. Furthermore, it is Swann's daughter, who married into the aristocracy, who makes the ultimate pronouncement about the two ways really being one. In this light and through this image, the identification of Swann with Haas or Proust or any other person for that matter is deconstructed at the end as the figure moves into the structural element of narrative and provides the artificially contrived links which construct the novel.

The transformation of Alfred Agostinelli, Proust's chauffeur and homosexual lover from 1909–13, into the androgynous Albertine is perhaps more intriguing than the case of Swann, and sheds additional light on Proust's artistic process. Much has been made by recent genetic criticism of the creation of the Albertine character, although parallels between Alfred and Albertine have been traced for a long time. The discovery in the Mauriac typescripts of Proust's works in 1987 has revealed that just before his death in 1922 the author had changed the title of the volume called *La Fugitive* to *Albertine disparue*. Although this change emphasised the lead character's name, it actually shortened the section on the character, deleting, in particular, the long search for Albertine's sexual orientation. Some critics have even argued that in the shorter version Proust, when contemplating the publication of the section, was actually distancing himself more from the repercussions of the lead character. On the other hand, whereas this figure had appeared originally under the name of Maria as the chieftain of the band of young girls, it was first altered to Albertine back in 1913, in a notebook at the height of Proust's relationship with Agostinelli, when in fact Agostinelli had become Proust's personal secretary and was actually typing the second part of the novel. Most important is the

fact that Philip Kolb brought out in his publication of the telling letter of Proust to Agostinelli of 30 May 1914 that the very words
Agostinelli cited in the letter are those of Albertine to the narrator
after her flight from him. This points to the ever-growing association of Albertine with Agostinelli despite the earlier rendition of
the Maria figure.

Among the parallels that have been drawn between Agostinelli
and the fictional Albertine is of course the analogous manner of
death that the two undergo and the particular tragedy of young
deaths. Proust had obviously associated Agostinelli with youth;
Agostinelli was seventeen years younger than he and was aged 21–26
during their relationship. It can be recalled that Proust was writing
his letter to Agostinelli on the very day he received a telegram telling him of Agostinelli's death. Proust was embittered that he had
actually financed a plane to satisfy Alfred's desire to fly. He had
been reluctant to do so in the first place, fearing a possible accident.
Reality had confirmed that fear; on his second attempt to fly, Alfred,
at the age of 26, crashed his plane into the Mediterranean off the
coast of Monaco and died. In a letter to Monsieur Straus of June 1914,
Proust expressed his profound regret and sense of responsibility for
this catastrophe: 'Alas, today I have the sorrow of thinking that if he
had not met me, and had not earned so much money from me, he
could not have afforded to learn to fly.' In the same letter, Proust
communicated his great attachment to and esteem for his companion:
'Agostinelli was an extraordinary being, possessing perhaps the
greatest intelligence I have ever known! . . . he and his wife became
an integral part of my existence.'[45]

In the novel, the narrator has been abandoned by Albertine and
has been writing numerous letters and telegrams beckoning to her
to return. At one time, he threatens to cancel buying for her a Rolls
Royce which she has requested. Not long afterwards, he is given
word that Albertine has fallen from a horse and has died in
Touraine. Like the author, the narrator is devastated by such an accident and loss, likening the loss to the earlier one of his grandmother,
and attesting to Albertine's total invasion of his consciousness.

But again, despite these most flagrant parallels, there are strong
differences between the character and the possible source. The most
obvious one is that Albertine is presumably a young girl and considered to be unintelligent. Many critics have noted that Proust's
own reticence with respect to revealing his own homosexuality
made it convenient to hide the narrator's lover in the form of a girl.

After all, it was not until Gide's journal of l4 May 1921 that Proust was reported as saying that 'he had never loved women but spiritually and that he had never known love but with men' ('*Il dit n'avoir jamais aimé les femmes que spirituellement et n'avoir jamais connu l'amour qu'avec des hommes*'[46]). Of course, Gide and others had been convinced of such a sexual preference in Proust long before the straightforward admission. If indeed '*les jeunes filles en fleurs*' is a euphemism for a band of young boys, the homosexual element was attempting to emerge but remained to some extent ambiguous. Yet Proust added sarcasm to his qualification of '*en fleurs*' since the band is hardly innocent or female. It is another instance of misrepresentation in Proust's art. In making Albertine less intelligent than Alfred and in changing the sex of the beloved, Proust was again intentionally distancing the model from the character.

Actually, the misrepresentation of '*les jeunes filles*' seems a flagrant effort to reveal and conceal simultaneously. The band of young girls is first perceived by the narrator from a distance, as a flashing comet along the esplanade of the sandy coast. Using again the perspective of mirage, Proust can allow another illusion to occur given the fact that the narrator first views the band of young girls from the mountain tops of Elstir's studio. Such an image suggests his desire to blur the individual and to envisage the collective band. The very name Albertine, a feminised masculine name (like Gilberte) highlights the intended sexual ambiguity, which is further corroborated by the constant reference to the character's lesbianism and her numerous affairs with other members of the band, even linking her to the evasive Mademoiselle Vinteuil. The narrator is constantly seeking to know Albertine's secret, something he probes after her death and about which he becomes jealous, even though she no longer exists.

Proust once again has constructed an analogy with respect to his own inclinations. For the behaviour of the narrator and the 'girls' might very well reflect his own predicaments with his male lovers. But in suggesting such an analogy in his fiction, he has dehumanised a character again. Although he refers to Albertine's female body at various instances, particularly when the narrator is gazing at her sleeping in *La Prisonnière*, Proust has hardly created a fleshy character or what E. M. Forster would call a 'round character'. In this light, Albertine may have been a draft of a character struggling to emerge. Proust might well have been caught in the ambivalence of sexual transformation. Could he have been sketching Albertine in

preparation for fleshing her out – which he never did. For Albertine's supreme quality is evasiveness; she is a fleeting specimen, racing on bicycles, a permanent fugitive who lacks the pulse of a real, vibrant female. Although she is engaged in play, she lacks the flirtatiousness of Odette de Crécy, for example. This absence of conventional femininity, which could be attributed to her youth, nonetheless continues to render the character an abstraction. The narrator in fact admits that she, like Gilberte and others, is only significant in terms of the effect she has on the narrator's mental state.

In Proust's work, the object of love is always an elusive figure who plays havoc with a male character's emotions. In this light, any other girl could be substituted for Albertine, or for that matter any young boy could also be her equivalent. Whether the object is male or female makes no difference. Although the immediate sources for such characters may be identifiable, those identifications are negligible since they ultimately serve a functional purpose. Proust creates a series of Others to act upon the Subject whose psychology is that of the artist.

By infiltrating his novel with this concept of substitution, Proust is producing an open-ended character who exists by virtue of her mysterious allusiveness and suggestion. The narrator proceeds from the Albertine affair to a generalisation at the end: 'for we are not as faithful to the being we have loved most as we are to ourself' (*'car à l'être que nous avons le plus aimé nous ne sommes pas si fidèle qu'à nous-même'*[47]). He concludes that he can only love himself in others and that is why he can constantly reinvent love through a series of substitutions that reflect his own being. Proust may also be suggesting certain similarities between homosexual and heterosexual love by making his characters interchangeable. The generalising factor, present in both the longer and the abridged versions, removes Albertine from any obvious source yet makes her all the more provocative in terms of the author's own proclivities and orientation. Using analogy and image, Proust offers the most blatant and creative form of misrepresentation.

Whereas critics have considered the Albertine cycle of the novel the most autobiographical part of the work, they have regarded the *Sodome et Gomorrhe* sections woven between the Albertine ones as the most novelistic and have thereby minimised its autobiographical and artistic components. If *Sodome et Gomorrhe* is centred on the revelation of the Baron de Charlus's explicit homosexuality with *'l'inversion sexuelle'* as its theme, it can be viewed

also as Proust's effort to objectify and generalise his own hidden inclinations, without the necessity of actually connecting the Baron de Charlus to himself in any way, or even for that matter with a more obvious model, Robert de Montesquiou. Clearly, from the start Proust had wanted to give a portrait of homosexuality through the creation of the Baron de Charlus, having explicitly written to the *Mercure de France* in 1909 that 'one of the principal characters is a homosexual' (*'un des principaux personnages est un homosexuel'*[48]). His autobiographical impulse was to suggest his own orientation through 'the other', even though he felt such a subject was 'shameful' (*'impudique'*). His craft enabled him to objectify his homosexuality through the provocative reference to 'the cities of the plain'.

It is in the very title *Sodom and Gomorrah*, chosen during the war years, that Proust's artistic process can further be probed. Here transposition and association are at work. In his notebooks of 1909 Proust envisaged the Guermantes as being connected to the region of Poitou, a particular province of France formed of dry plains consisting of clay soil and rock. The impression of this particular arid landscape obviously suggested to him the aridity of the twin 'sinful' cities of the Bible. Through the return to the biblical archetype he objectified the individual instances of homosexuality both in the novel and in his private life on to a universal level. His own experiences had multiplied after the close liaison he had with Reynaldo Hahn back in 1894. Proust even went to the point of investing in Le Cuziat's male brothel in Paris in 1917, which has been likened to that of Jupien in the *Le Temps retrouvé*. And in the novel, of course, homosexual characters were many, including Charlus, Jupien, Morel, Saint-Loup, Albertine and Andrée. Notably Proust protested to Robert de Montesquiou that his character Saint-Loup was not to be associated with the Marquis Boni de Castellane nor with any other real-life personality.

The particular effort of artistic camouflaging was therefore most at work in this section of the novel. For Proust introduces not only a theme but a technique along with it: that of enlargement. It is in this section that Proust expands the notion of love by introducing the facets of homosexual love, despite the fact that he veils his exposé through critique and ridicule. The clue to this technique of enlargement is found in that draft version of 'La Race des tantes' (*tantes* being slang for pederasts) where he describes the *'invertis'*:

*Et par une transposition inconsciente ils rapportent si bien à leur désir
bizarre, tout ce qui dans la littérature, dans l'art, dans la vie a depuis
tant de siècles élargi comme un fleuve la notion de l'amour . . .*[49]

[And by an unconscious transposition, they relate so well to their
bizarre desire everything that in literature, in art, in life, has for so
many centuries enlarged like the river the notion of love . . .]

The entire notion of a *roman fleuve* was connected to the enlargement
of a principal theme of sexual inversion, regarded as 'shameful' in
1909 but pursued in one character after another through the long
narrative until it reached a universal landscape of multiplicity and
density in *Sodome et Gomorrhe*. The critic Léon Pierre-Quint inter-
prets this particular section of the novel as corroborating the larger
context of unfilled desires in the rest of the novel 'because no one
better than the Sodomists could make us understand the degree to
which all desires are unrequited' ('*car personne mieux que les
sodomistes ne pourrait nous faire comprendre la presque impossibilité de
tous les désirs*'[50]). One can say that Proust had arrived at an objective
correlative of his own sexual autobiography.

Distancing, therefore, was a necessary technique used by Proust
which in turn created aesthetic realities. When the narrator uses the
analogy of the telescope rather than the microscope to describe his first
perceptions and early writings, this is an aesthetic which applies to
Proust's view of his work as well. For Proust's tendency is to circum-
vent the particular, as for example in describing the love affair of
Swann and Odette at the very beginning of his work. The metaphor of
the cattleya, in suggesting the love-making, removes the actual and
concrete from the reader's view, and the physical relationships become
dematerialised through the artistic analogy. The same kind of distancing applies to the psychology of the characters. The narrator, for one, is
the observer; his love affairs begin with his observations: Gilberte and
Albertine from Elstir's studio. When the narrator ultimately captivates
his Albertine, he often watches her asleep – which prevents interaction
with her. If love is perhaps 'marred' by such distances, art requires it –
as in the case of Elstir's landscapes, little Marcel's Martinville vision, little Marcel's view of the Duchess of Guermantes, young Marcel's
dreams of Balbec. The entire process of memory and recall, which
spans blocks of time through 'telescopic vision' nonetheless requires
that distance, since the past is the primary subject of the projected text.
In a similar manner to that of the narrator *vis-à-vis* Combray, Proust is

distanced from Illiers but guards the illusion of its delight; the perspective of distance, hence, creates the misrepresentation, which in turn
creates the art. In terms of psychobiography, it is the psychological
perspective of the author, which seeks to distance tangible reality
through language, that creates this artistic technique.

For ultimately, the perspective of the narrator is that of the artist. As
a writer so interested in method, Proust created a series of artist-
characters. In several instances, particularly with respect to scenery,
Proust sought analogies between the writer's and the artist's act of
representation. From the composer Vinteuil, to the dramatist
Bergotte, to the actress Berma, and to the painter Elstir, there is a
thread of commentary relating to the artist and even to Proust himself. Critics have sought sources for these artists, seeing César Franck,
Saint-Saens, Debussy or Fauré in Vinteuil, Monet and Turner in Elstir,
and Anatole France in Bergotte. The Comparatist Diane Leonard, for
one, has focused on the sources for Proust's visual distortions and has
classified Proust as a Post-Impressionist, using the term coined by
Roger Fry – as we shall see in the context of Virginia Woolf's writings.

Regardless of classification according to artistic school, a more generalised theory of representation can be drawn from a consideration
of this company of artists in Proust's work. This theory, in turn, is pertinent to the optic of autobiography in Proust's work. A key passage
is that of the painter Elstir's rendition of the Balbec countryside, as
commented upon by the narrator in his first visit to Elstir's studio:

> Et l'atelier d'Elstir m'apparut comme le laboratoire d'une sorte de nouvelle
> création du monde . . . Naturellement, ce qu'il avait dans son atelier, ce
> n'était guère que des marines prises ici, à Balbec. Mais j'y pouvais discerner
> que le charme de chacune consistait en une sorte de métamorphose des
> choses représentées, analogue à celle qu'en poésie on nomme métaphore.[51]

[And the studio of Elstir appeared to me as the laboratory of a sort of
new creation of the world . . . Naturally, what he had in his studio
were merely seascapes taken here in Balbec. But I could discern that
the charm of each one consisted in a sort of metamorphosis of represented things, analogous to what in poetry one calls metaphor.]

Artistic perception, therefore, becomes a kind of re-reading of the universe in the transformation of 'represented' things – what Proust himself seems to have been doing in his novel. An example, given in the
context of this citation, is the elimination of any demarcation between

land and sea in Elstir's seascapes – an effect which is described as a metaphor in the painting of the port of Carquethuit. Referring to that painting, the narrator explains that Elstir was actually copying *'véritables mirages'* – a concept which appears oxymoronic. But it is true that the coast of Cabourg lends itself to mirages. One can witness the setting sun on that Normandy coast having the effect of extending the sky into the sea. Parts of the sky actually seem like sea, and the horizon which normally separates sea and sky appears to be eliminated. Hence, the artistic perspective seems to be drawn from an actual one of a distorted seascape which Proust transfers to the artist figure in his novel.

Beyond the transparency of certain artist figures in Proust's work, the fundamental analogy is established between the artist and the narrator. For the primary characterisation is that of the aesthetic self which is the common denominator in the proliferation of characters and incidents. It is the perspective of the writer which is defined as the many selves converge into the one that has the aesthetic perceptions.

In *Le Temps retrouvé* when the artistic technique outlined by the narrator and the aesthetic technique discerned by the reader meet, the aesthetics is revealed. An aesthetic pact between the author and the reader is created whereby the reader, having gone through the process of the novel, arrives at the same aesthetic theories that the narrator announces at the end of the book that the reader has just read.

It was appropriate that the self-conscious and self-centred Proust should construe an artistic process based on distancing. In an effort to dissemble the personal elements of his life, Proust created an art of subterfuge, yet to some extent was omnipresent in the major characters. He manipulated his materials regarding place and person, creating artistic composites of locale or character. His fictionalisation involved a conglomeration of real life components into the richness of aesthetic ambiguity. He resorted to elements of substitution, analogy and abstraction in his art, which by virtue of the technique of musical motif reiterated themes throughout the *roman fleuve*. The very 'river' of the *roman fleuve* can be seen as a metaphor in Proust for the enlargement process which occurs when a theme, often drawn initially from life experience, is taken and expanded upon in all its ramifications throughout the novel. But most strikingly, Proust manipulated the very genre of the autobiographical novel in order to convey his aesthetics regarding life and art. The projected 'product' at the end of the *Recherche* contained the aesthetics of autobiography that had governed Proust's own recreation of life into fiction.

5

The Stylised Quotidian in James Joyce

For most biographical critics, James Joyce's life has been intimately tied to his fiction. Characters in *Dubliners* have been identified with real-life counterparts. Associations have been drawn between Michael Furey of 'The Dead' and both Michael Feeney and Michael Bodkin, the first loves in Galway of Nora Barnacle, who became Joyce's wife. More and more parallels have been drawn between Nora and Molly Bloom, even to the point of refashioning the real-life woman after the fictional one. Some critics have continued to read *A Portrait of the Artist as a Young Man* as pure biography up to the time of Joyce's departure from Ireland in 1902 despite the objections to such literal interpretation, the most forceful being that of Joyce's brother, Stanislaus, who may have been his most discerning critic. Joyce himself argued late in his life to his French friend Louis Gillet that his work and life were completely interwoven: *'quand votre art et votre vie ne font qu'un, quand ils s'enchevêtrent dans le même tissu . . . '.*[1] Earlier his devoted brother Stanislaus seemed to have been analytical about the nature of his autobiographical work. For in his record of Joyce's life to the year 1904, *My Brother's Keeper*, Stanislaus remarked that actually Joyce 'exploited the minute, unpromising material of his immediate experience'.[2] We can observe how, over and over again, Joyce stylised the quotidian from his recollection of the everyday drab world of Dublin.

The parallels may indeed be interesting between the life and the work, but they circumscribe the texts instead of highlighting the way Joyce expanded outward, like Proust, from the limited experiences and locale he drew from. For Joyce it was one wife and one city. And having moved at least 20 times within Dublin during his childhood because of his father's financial instability, he knew that city well. Later as Joyce travelled as a vagabond writer from Trieste to Rome, Zurich and Paris, rejecting Ireland, his main intent remained that of memorialising Dublin, the city in which he lived

100

until the age of 20 and visited three times later only briefly until his self-imposed exile became permanent. With the playwright Ibsen as his model, Joyce had written a university essay 'Drama and Life', in which he stated: 'Even the most commonplace, the deadest among the living, may play a part in a great drama'.[3] Like Ibsen, Joyce was to heighten Naturalistic detail onto a dramatic plane of symbolic art.

If, on the one hand, the autobiographical ingredient was very much a part of Joyce's artistry, it was consciously recast in a mode of depersonalisation, objectification and mythification. To have stayed on the personal level would have been Romantic and lyrical for him, a tendency he rejected from his university years onwards, as he strove toward epic proportions and dramatic intensity. Again, his brother who had been following his life most closely, observed his passage from autobiography into fiction. In his diary notation of 2 February 1904, Stanislaus recalls that *Stephen Hero*, the title he had suggested for the first version of *A Portrait*, was to be 'almost autobiographical':

> Jim told me his idea for the novel. It is to be almost autobiograph-
> ical . . . He is putting a large number of his acquaintances into it,
> and those Jesuits whom he has known.[4]

In a subsequent note of 29 March 1904, commenting on several chapters he had read of *Stephen Hero*, Stanislaus described the style of that narrative as 'altogether original' and a 'lying autobiography'. In a later comment on *A Portrait*, Stanislaus emphasised the distinction he perceived between his brother and the evolving persona of Stephen Dedalus:

> My brother was not the weak, shirking infant who figures in *A
> Portrait of the Artist*. He has drawn, it is true, very largely upon his
> own life and his own experience . . . But *A Portrait of the Artist* is
> not an autobiography; it is an artistic creation. As I had something
> to say to its reshaping, I can affirm this without hesitation.[5]

Such successive comments made by his brother suggest that as Joyce had taken many incidents from his everyday experience, he had also altered and refashioned them. Instead of a formal diary, as with Woolf and Nin, Joyce assembled a collection of raw life materials primarily in the years 1900 to 1903 in a book of what he called 'epiphanies'. He defined the term 'epiphany' while using some in

Stephen Hero as 'a sudden spiritual manifestation, whether in the vulgarity of speech or of gesture or in a memorable phase of the mind itself'.[6] His brother Stanislaus likened the collection to the sketchbook of an artist. These fragments of life experience, 40 of which are preserved, whether they were a recorded vulgar overheard conversation or a trivial incident, were some of the clay from which he proceeded to mould his fiction.

By extracting items from what is called 'the catalogue of Dublin's street furniture', Joyce transforms the ordinary and everyday into the aesthetic. The derivation of a theory of epiphany from the Dublin Ballast Office clock is curiously illustrative of this process. One of Dublin's old landmarks, the Ballast clock was known for the accuracy of its time-keeping. Many a Dubliner would walk to the clock and set his watch by it, and therefore it was actually a focal point for the inhabitants of that city. Originally situated on Westmoreland Street, the Ballast Office housed the administrative offices of the Port Authority that had directed the activities at the port of Dublin. The clock, protruding from the building, was round and black with gold roman numerals on its face. On an official building, at the very centre of the city, the clock effectively incarnated the authoritative power of chronological time. Visitors today realise that the original building has been destroyed and rebuilt, and that the clock has been set into the brick building around the corner, now facing the river Liffey instead of Westmoreland Street. However, what Joyce was suggesting through this very clock was that, from ordinary confines and objective reality, there is the possibility of subjective expansion through the sense of sight, which can create an intensity of focus and revelation. This notion and reference are actually declared in *Stephen Hero*:

> He told Cranly that the clock of the Ballast Office was capable of an epiphany. Cranly questioned the inscrutable dial of the Ballast Office with his no less inscrutable countenance.

It is interesting that the function of the 'real' Ballast clock is similar to that of the fictional steeples of Martinville (having been derived from some identifiable steeples) which had created an aesthetic experience for Proust. As in Proust, an ordinary apparition or object is capable of producing a profound insight.

'Reshaping' was the method Joyce used to transform his crude, raw material, which included his own vision of himself as the artist

grounded in the streets of an urban site. Theoretical discussions on the role of the artist in his work are found in both *A Portrait* and *Ulysses* and seem to reflect Joyce's own debate regarding his own presence in his work. Joyce's persona Stephen in the 'Scylla and Charybdis' section of *Ulysses* remarks that the artist 'weaves and unweaves his image'. In the scene in the National Library, Stephen discourses on the very subject of autobiographical writing, and in reference to Shakespeare he insists on the identification of that author with his work. Joyce then has Stephen in a position of being opposed by contrary views. A friend, George Russell, in particular protests that readers should not 'peep and pry' into the poet's drinking habits and debts because the artistic creation of King Lear remains immortal and removed from such concerns:

> I mean when we read the poetry of *King Lear* what is it to us how the poet lived? As for living, our servants can do that for us, Villiers de l'Isle has said.[7]

Joyce himself would have been antagonistic to such a statement made by Villiers de l'Isle Adam, the well-known aesthete who had believed in the superiority of art over life. Actually, Shakespeare was an interesting reference point here, since his work was a case in which supreme poetry and the crude popular medium were interwoven. And Joyce's own aesthetics ran counter to aestheticism, since for him living and creating were inseparable.

The question of the personality of the artist had been more directly addressed in the well-known passage from *A Portrait* where the Stephen persona spoke of three forms of expression: the lyrical, the epical and the dramatic. By 'lyrical' he meant a primitive self-expression; by 'epical', however, the 'narrative is no longer personal'; as for the ultimate dramatic phase, life is purified in the aesthetic image and reprojected as the personality of the artist is 'refined out of existence'. As a young man, Joyce himself had praised his favourite dramatist, Ibsen, for his 'lofty and impersonal power'.[8] In his own work, Joyce actually went through an evolution of style which progressively distanced and depersonalised the self, creating an artist-human archetype with vestiges of personal attributes. It has been observed that in the progress from *Stephen Hero* to *A Portrait*, for example, Joyce reached a certain level of depersonalisation, even though the stream-of-consciousness 'I' was featured in the narrative of the latter rather than the former. A

French critic of Joyce commented that when Joyce wrote *A Portrait*, he had already possessed that double consciousness of watching oneself live: '*cette conscience double, cette conscience du vivant qui se regarde vivre*'.[9] Actually, one can say that Joyce views himself from two perspectives, virtually weaving and unweaving his image. In *Stephen Hero* and *A Portrait* he is seen in exiling himself from his fatherland, whereas in 'The Dead' and *Ulysses* he is imaged as what he would have been had he forgone exile and remained in Ireland. In the later work, the situation becomes hypothetical and further removed from mimetic correlation. But, in fact, it is the condition of being spiritually rather than physically exiled.

It is also interesting, of course, to trace, along with Joyce's own personality, the three key family members: his mother Mary Joyce, his father John Joyce, and his wife Nora Barnacle, in the evolution of his fiction. Joyce's mother seems to have the primary role in the early *Stephen Hero*; her death is omitted in the chronology of narrated incidents in *A Portrait* but then is recalled in two reveries about her actual death in *Ulysses* – as we shall see. On the other hand, Joyce's father is featured most prominently in *A Portrait*, particularly with respect to his financial demise poignantly captured in the visit to Cork. He becomes a background presence in *Ulysses*, a silhouette roaming the streets of Dublin and attending a funeral. Meanwhile, in Joyce's most substantial story, 'The Dead', both parents are noticeably omitted, as Nora moves into the centre through the figure of Gretta Conroy. When we come to *Ulysses*, it is as if Nora, in terms of Molly, has replaced Joyce's mother, and the new 'everyman' character Bloom has replaced the father – as a transfer has been made to surrogate personalities and mythical schemes.

It is clear that the life facts which haunted Joyce become woven into his later work: the request of his dying mother for him to pray at her deathbed and the search for a father figure to replace his own drunken and irresponsible one. By the time Joyce reached *Ulysses* he had used the artistic process of selection to single out the most traumatic aspects of his life and rework them in thematic and even mythic terms. There is a certain kind of intellectual workmanship evident in Joyce's multiple transpositions of similar themes which differs from the musicality of Proust's recurring motifs. Like Proust, however, Joyce succeeds in transcending whatever referentiality exists in the work. If Proust had denigrated the quotidian self, seeking the profound one in the artistic process, Joyce stylised the everyday, transforming the ordinary into the mythic as a fitting

stereotype of modern man in search of an identity. That is to say, he projects the specific search for the father figure and the guilt *vis-à-vis* an abandoned religion and culture onto a fabricated figure, Stephen Dedalus.

The various themes woven into Joyce's works stem from his own life in Dublin, but the itinerary through the recognisable streets and places take on extra personal dimensions. As far as place is concerned, Joyce retained all the real names of streets and places in his exclusive treatment of Ireland, and most especially Dublin. A traveller today can readily identify the places in his fiction. Unlike Woolf, Nin and Proust, Joyce did not camouflage any of the locales, but his cunning craft gave them a stylised aura. Sydney Parade Station, North Richmond Street, Eccles Street, Stephen's Green, Merrion Square, the Bull, the Pigeon House, Usher's Island, and countless more, are actual recognisable places, yet they become tinted by the power of association in Joyce's fiction. Joyce expands the cross-section of Dublin to the universe at large, as suggested by the little limerick in the opening section of *A Portrait*, which moves from County Kildare to the world. What is happening in the microcosm of a little place becomes applicable to the macrocosm. As such, the attention to 'microscopic' detail in Joyce's work, as it might be the particular behaviour of little people in relatively insignificant places, is at the source of the transformation process. For proceeding from the 'insignificant' characters in *Dubliners* who inhabit these drab, real Dublin streets and frequent the dead alleys or corners, Joyce transforms the ordinary and everyday into the aesthetic.

In some instances, the process of naming – Clongowes, Clane, Cork – has the same conceptual effect as in the case of Proust with Combray and Balbec, although the Proustian names are of course fabricated. Such places become artistic signs, as the critic Giles Deleuze has noted in Proust. As we shall see, Clongowes, the name of the real Jesuit boarding school in County Kildare that Joyce attended reluctantly as a young boy, loses its objective designation because in *A Portrait* it becomes a negatively suggestive sign for the constrictions which he sustained in his childhood. In alluding to another phase of his development, Joyce created a masterful story from the tantalising impression of the name *Araby*, which he had apparently heard in his boyhood. In the story, the young boy states: 'the syllables of the word *Araby* were called to me through the silence in which my soul luxuriated and cast an Eastern enchantment over me'.[10] As Joyce's biographer Richard Ellmann has

documented, an actual oriental bazaar by that name took place in Dublin in 1894, when Joyce was twelve years of age. A decade later, in writing the story for *Dubliners*, Joyce, in recollection, gave the festival its delayed interpretation by expounding its mystery. Joyce associates the word with the period when the family moved to the blind, dead-end alley of North Richmond Street across from the Christian Brothers' School which the Joyce boys had attended for a brief period. That area, even in these days, remains isolated, as if it were cut off from the rest of the city. It actually looks like an artificial stage set, which Joyce might have envisioned as an objective correlative of his soul.

With this very real backdrop, Joyce makes the name 'Araby' harbour a crisis of his youth. The well-known story involves a shy young boy's sudden disappointment at arriving too late at a bazaar. A reason for his tardiness is that his drunken uncle, his surrogate father, returns home late to give him the money he needs to go to the fair. The boy had escaped from the deadening atmosphere of North Richmond Street but was saddened at his inability to satisfy his dreams of romance. He is unable to purchase a gift for the object of his infatuation, the sister of his friend Mangan. By association, therefore, Joyce projects onto the name of 'Araby' a negative assessment of the Dublin environment: the disillusionment with the Church and the alienation from a father figure. A similar negative aura is projected onto the city of Cork, which appears in *A Portrait* and becomes more of a state of mind than an actual objective place. Joyce's trip to Cork with his father in 1894 marked the end of his childhood, for he painfully witnessed the degradation of his father who was in the process of losing his properties and drinking with his cronies. The name 'Cork', by association again, moves from a denotative to a connotative meaning, suggesting degeneration. As in standard autobiographies, the end of childhood is perceived as a turning-point, here heightened by a crisis incident and a certain awakening of awareness. But in this example of the progression through three places – from Clongowes to Araby and on to Cork – the crisis is elaborated through the thematic and symbolic means of place names.

The themes of alienation from father, fatherland and religion, originating in Joyce's early years, are of course pervasive throughout his works and are transfixed repeatedly in patterns and symbolic predicaments. In *Dubliners* Joyce focuses on Dublin as 'the center of paralysis and frustration', as apparent in such stories as

'The Sisters', 'Eveline', 'Araby', and 'Clay'. The fifteen stories which comprise *Dubliners* have been considered Naturalistic insofar as they depict the sordid state of Dublin daily life. After all, Joyce had intended to bring Dublin 'onto the map' to surpass Paris and London which had been exposed by chief novelists before him. But one wonders whether there has ever been a more extensive dissection of place for artistic purposes. For Joyce was aware that he was trying to derive greater significance in his scrutiny of his city. He wrote in 1905 to a prospective English publisher Grant Richards: 'the expression "Dubliner" seems to me to have some meaning and I doubt whether the same can be said for such words as "Londoner" and "Parisian" '.[11] And it soon became apparent that these minimalist stories, eventually to culminate in the elaboration of 'The Dead', were objectifying a mood or atmosphere which had implications beyond the referentiality of places or persons.

On the other hand, the element of veracity in these stories was something that Joyce could not do without. This requirement is seen, for example, in a well-known letter that Joyce wrote from Trieste in 1905 to his brother Stanislaus.[12] Joyce asked his brother to verify facts included in four of his stories. Some very mundane questions are asked: 'Can a priest be buried in a habit?' – for 'The Sisters'. 'Are Aungier Street and Wicklow in the Royal Exchange Ward?' and 'Can a municipal election take place in October?' – for 'Ivy Day in the Committee Room'. 'Are the police at Sydney Parade of the D Division?' and 'Would the city ambulance be called out to Sydney Parade for an accident?' Also, 'Would an accident at Sidney Parade be treated at Vincent's Hospital' – for 'A Painful Case'. Stanislaus promptly and dutifully responded with the facts.[13] Joyce had a pretty good memory. He was told that a priest would be buried in a habit if he belonged to an order that wears a habit; that a municipal election might take place in October but would be more likely to take place in January; that indeed Aungier Street was in the Royal Exchange Ward; and that, though unlikely, an ambulance could be taken out to Sydney Parade. In a later letter to Stanislaus of 13 November 1906,[14] Joyce himself verifies for the story 'Clay' that the 'Dublin by Lamplight Laundry' truly existed at Ballsbridge.

These responses do suggest that Joyce, while writing these stories from 1904–7 in a self-imposed exile abroad, was immersed in recollections of his native city. Indeed, such authenticity with regard to place was a necessary ingredient in exposing what he considered to be the ills of Ireland. In addition to identifiable places, Joyce

depicted everyday people of the middle or lower classes, such as maids, clerks, clergymen, travelling salesmen, who would characteristically be seen roaming those recognisable streets at the turn of the century. Many were ill-educated and pathetic. Stagnant, frustrated and fixed, these characters have no possibility of flight from their constrained life which is ruled by a degenerate church and state – often encapsulated in father figures. Recent Bakhtinian approaches to these stories, such as R. B. Kershner's *Joyce, Bakhtin, and Popular Literature*, have read a dialogism in these narratives between the lowly protagonist or youth, the resistant consciousness, and the voice of 'the Other' which is the collective communal voice of the dominant, authoritative discourse of father, church and state. In this view, the narrative is infused with the dominant discourse of popular speech or that of past popular fiction. But if such material has been deemed significant as sociological fact, as Naturalist interpretations have had it in the past, it can also be examined as artistic ingredient.

On the surface Joyce was dissecting a society in what resembles Naturalistic analysis, identifying categories of the population according to age groups as well as occupations. Starting with the boy narrator 'I' in the first three stories of the collection, 'The Sisters', 'Araby' and 'An Encounter', Joyce moved on to the use of third-person narratives with representative figures in different occupations who were in analogous situations. The span from 'Araby', one of the first stories, to the last story, 'The Dead' (completed in 1907), has been interpreted in autobiographical terms as the passage from the child Joyce of North Richmond Street and the Christian Brothers' School to the adult Gabriel Conroy, what Joyce would have been had he remained in Ireland. Between these stories are the typical personalities of the city. Through such a cross-section, Joyce sought to depict the actual spread of what he regarded as a debilitating paralysis which afflicted both himself and his countrymen:

> I have tried to present it to the indifferent public under its four aspects: childhood, adolescence, maturity and public life. The stories are arranged in this order. I have written it for the most part in a style of scrupulous meanness.[15]

But aside from the actual subject matter, Joyce had to defend his sultry prose to his publisher, who was raising objections set forth by the printer. That printer was actually refusing to publish certain

stories without some specified deletions of vulgar words and expressions. Joyce argued that these stories presented a series of predicaments emerging from the everyday situations of the streets. He had only exploited what would have been readily 'seen and heard'.

This exploitation involved the artistry which in the case of the stories proceeded from minimal experiences. Stanislaus went out of his way to emphasise in *My Brother's Keeper* that little actual personal experience contributed to these stories and that, in fact, most of the material came from him. Despite such a statement, bits and pieces of experiences from the Joyce family and their surroundings can be gathered as ingredients for *Dubliners*. Joyce had only to look within his own family and acquaintances to find a microcosm of the whole society. It is as if Joyce were searching for himself amidst the Dublin daily life, finding himself first in the child figures of the first section, finding his abusive father in father figures throughout the stories, and ultimately contemplating vicariously through Eveline and Gabriel Conroy the dead-end situations he would have been subjected to had he remained in Ireland. This material seems to preface the artist persona which will evolve in the major works. The processes in the stories are those of transfer and elaboration.

Joyce seems to have rescued disparate haunting images of his youth – an idle chalice, a closing bazaar, a busy port, a boarding house, the feel of clay, an annual Christmas party – and converted them into signs of a decaying society. It is documented, for example, that the old josser dressed in greenish-black in 'An Encounter' stems from Joyce's actual experience. Stanislaus states: 'my brother describes a day's miching which he and I planned and carried out while we were living in North Richmond Street, and our encounter with an elderly pederast.'[16] This story, along with 'Araby', reveals through epiphany-like effect sudden realisations impressed on a young boy with whom Joyce identified. According to Ellmann, Joyce may have heard about a decadent priest in his childhood which he then elaborated in 'The Sisters'. He also may have heard about a laundress, a relative on his mother's side, whom he then placed in 'Clay', stylised in a diminutive appearance. He may have remembered neighbours on North Richmond Street who were sources for the Eveline story, and might have been intrigued by her love for a sailor. What Joyce did in such stories is to proceed from apparently insignificant situations to produce an understatement for the recurring picture of a stagnated Ireland. When Stanislaus claims that he had given Joyce the materials for the story 'Grace', he

commented that Joyce 'used this thin material, transforming it in his own way'. The drunken figure at the beginning of the story was in fact his father, whom Joyce went on to camouflage somewhat as an acquaintance of his father. Similarly, Stanislaus notes that Joyce created the story 'A Painful Case' out of the 'unpromising material' that Stanislaus had recorded of an encounter at a concert-hall. Stanislaus even identified himself in that story as the banal principal character, Mr Duffy, who was writing some sort of diary.

Joyce transforms this minimal material, whether personally experienced or vicariously perceived. Stylisation removes these stories from the mimetic mode, and this is what Joyce himself was suggesting when he called the series 'epicleti'. This foreign word was drawn, in part, from the ritual of the Eastern Orthodox Church designating the conversion of the sacraments of bread and wine to the body and blood of Christ. Joyce used the analogy of conversion to chart the process from the real to the artistic:

> Don't you think . . . there is a certain resemblance between the mystery of the Mass and what I am trying to do? . . . converting the bread of everyday life into something that has a permanent artistic life of its own.

The significant words are 'conversion' and 'everyday'. For in amassing the dregs of the sordid grey Dublin life, Joyce stylises them as they relate to a collective environment. Joyce perceives the collective experience through a series of representative ordinary individuals, some of whom resemble family members, who emerge from the Dublin streets. Therefore, often identifying with such abject specimens, he moves from simple representation to a level of quasi-parable.

There are traces throughout these stories of Joyce's father and mother, although none are specifically paralleled as they are in Joyce's novels. In the stories, their characteristics seem to be amalgamated in the general types of degenerate father and beleaguered mother. The examples are many. Joyce presents a series of drunken, irresponsible father figures, many of whom are abusive in relation to children or victimised women. 'Eveline', for example, alludes to the 'father's violence'[17] and the mistreatment of the deceased mother. In 'The Boarding House', there is reference to Mr Mooney, who 'began to go to the devil. He drank, plundered the till, ran headlong into debt'. This description reminds the reader of Joyce's

own father who gradually lost his assets through sheer irresponsibility and alcoholism. In the story, Mrs Mooney assumes responsibility for her daughter, attempting to marry her off through immoral means. In 'Counterparts', Farrington, the father of five children, abruptly leaves his job when contested, pawns his watch and goes off to drink with his buddies at Davy Byrne's pub: 'He had done for himself in the office, pawned his watch, spent all his money.' When he arrives home and abuses his child, his wife is out at the chapel, anticipating his reckless state and resorting to prayer as a mechanism for protection. Finally, 'Grace' presents most poignantly the image of an inebriated and debilitated salesman, fallen at a bar. Again, according to Stanislaus, the fall in the bar actually happened to their father. The person in the story is nameless at the beginning, stressing his anonymity, and later is camouflaged as an acquaintance of his father, possibly being the father of Eveline. Through such transfer, Joyce seems to be amalgamating his father in a general type and circumstance: 'he was quite helpless. He lay curled up at the foot of the stairs down which he had fallen.' The Jesuit church in Gardiner Street, a church that can be seen today with a cross-like structure, provides a realistic setting for a typological character. Stanislaus claims that he provided realistic material for the story through his letters and diaries; John Joyce had actually attended a retreat for businessmen in the Gardiner Street church. But Joyce himself may very well have glanced at the assorted congregation of this church as a young boy, and found his father or a similar type attending a service. A section of *Stephen Hero* makes reference to such an incident in which Stephen, witnessing from afar his father and two friends attending a Good Friday service, feels hypocritically satisfied. In this work the anonymity is discarded.

It is obvious that this collection of irresponsible father figures, which may be take-offs from Joyce's own observation of his father and his like, prompts Joyce to depict his own father more specifically in the next work, *A Portrait*. In this light, these lesser fathers become a rehearsal for attacking his own more blatantly. And after his own father is depicted, as the character Simon Dedalus, in total decline in the episode of Cork in *A Portrait*, the optic changes in *Ulysses*, where Joyce depicts a quest for the father figure, dimly portraying a Simon Dedalus in the background.

As for the mother figures, they emerge in another process of transposition. One key is found in the allusion to the deceased mother of Eveline, whose memory haunts the nineteen-year-old

girl – enough to prevent her justifiably from fleeing her abusive father. In that story, there is a flashback to the dying mother – who is like a premonition of the moribund figure that is to emerge prominently in *Ulysses*. Eveline muses:

> She knew the air. Strange that it should come that very night to remind her of the promise to her mother, her promise to keep the home together as long as she could. She remembered the last night of her mother's illness.[18]

Eveline accepts the responsibility laid upon her by her mother, and refuses to flee. In another story, actually entitled 'A Mother', the mother in question, Mrs Kearney, fights for the rights of her daughter, whose contract for a singing engagement at a concert hall is suddenly annulled. It seems highly significant that the mother's plea is totally ignored by the male-dominated society of concert administrators. The mother remains devoted but ineffectual *vis-à-vis* the corrupt ruling order. These hardworking mothers and wives in the stories are for Joyce fictions of the abused motherland in atrophy.

The early stories, then, distance these figures as national types; the later works mythologise them as conscience. In *A Portrait*, the mother, more closely resembling Joyce's own, is pictured at the end, faithfully packing the bags of her 20-year-old son, who is about to leave his motherland. This benign figure is subsequently annihilated and even distorted into a degenerate milkmaid at the beginning of *Ulysses* and as a moribund figure thereafter in Stephen's dreams. Feminist interpretations, like that of Suzette Henke, read Joyce's early work as misogynist but then find a substitution figure in Molly Bloom who, as they see it, represents the new Ireland – vital and sensual. In the presentation of the mother figure, Joyce moved from the distanced portrait of comparable types in the stories to the more personalised versions in *A Portrait* and eventually to the depersonalised, mythic rendition of *Ulysses* – relegated to the medium of the dream and thereby becoming part of a collective unconscious.

If many of the stories seem to reflect parental figures, several of the characters suggest Joyce's view of himself had he remained in Ireland instead of rebelliously leaving for the Continent a second time in 1904. After all, many of these stories were composed at that time and a bit later in faraway Trieste. In particular, Little Chandler of 'A Little Cloud', Eveline in the story by that name, and Gabriel

Conroy in 'The Dead' reflect predicaments over which Joyce had triumphed. Little Chandler is intentionally made diminutive as a frustrated writer who is a dreamer, a reader of poetry, caught in a life of drudgery with dreams never realised. Aesthetically speaking, he incarnates in his diminutive presence the possibility of effacement and seems more like a caricature than a type. Joyce, too, might have seen part of himself in the young girl Eveline, who allows herself to lose the chance to flee Ireland with her lover sailor. This story undermines the possibility of flight in direct contrast to Joyce's reallife situation of fleeing Dublin with his lover in October 1904 after 'Eveline' was published. So if it is far-fetched to associate Joyce with Eveline, it is fully justifiable to connect Joyce with Gabriel Conroy of 'The Dead', as many critics have done.

'The Dead' has been considered the most transparent story, autobiographically speaking, and has been fully probed for parallels by such critics as Lionel Trilling, Harry Levin and Richard Ellmann. But what has not been discerned is the aesthetic moulding of such parallels. Let us first recall the story and then its referential components. The narrative describes a Christmas party to which Gabriel Conroy and his wife are invited. It is an annual dance given by two spinster sisters, the Morkans, who live in a dark, gaunt house at Usher's Island. The same guests reappear at this event each year, certain musical performances are given, a grand festive dinner is consumed, and a certain nostalgia for the past and old Irish values is always prevalent. Viewing the scene as an outsider is Gabriel, the devoted nephew of the Morkans who, as an intellectual of sorts set against Irish nationalism, looks toward Ireland's future. He gives an ambivalent speech, tolerates the niceties of the evening, and then retires to a hotel room with his wife. But in this second scene at a Dublin hotel, a crisis of consciousness occurs, in which he suddenly realises that his wife clings to the memory of a past dead lover named Michael Furey, who is suggestive of the Ireland of the past. Such a surprising revelation and disillusionment gives Gabriel an identity crisis, as he senses the ever-presence of the dead and the past.

As has been readily seen, 'The Dead' is actually a composite of facts stemming from Joyce's relationship with Nora. Actually, Joyce's letters of 1904–9 refer to the raw material of the story. Early in their relationship Joyce had been aware that Nora had had a lover in Galway who had died as a young boy. Joyce wrote to Stanislaus in 1904: 'She has had many love-affairs, one when quite young with a

boy who died.'[19] Later, Joyce doubted (but only for a short period) Nora's fidelity to him because of a false accusation by his university friend Vincent Cosgrave. While travelling apart from Nora in 1909, Joyce communicated this fear in a letter to her: 'At the time I used to meet you at the corner of Merrion Square and talk out with you and feel your hand touch me in the dark and hear your voice . . . every second night you kept an appointment with a friend of mine outside the Museum . . . you lifted your face and kissed him.'[20] It is clear that Joyce's infatuation with Nora, accentuated during his visit to Dublin, had prompted jealousy to emerge as a dominant emotion. At this very time, Joyce clearly communicated to Nora that she was indeed the woman in 'The Dead': 'Do you remember the three adjectives I have used in "The Dead" in speaking of your body. They are these: "musical and strange and perfumed" . . . my jealousy is still smouldering in my heart.'

Joyce confirmed that another ingredient had nourished the story. Following the above letters to Nora, Joyce had proceeded to Galway. There he was introduced to Nora's mother, Mrs Thomas Barnacle, who apparently sang to him the tantalising song *The Lass of Aughrim*. Joyce reported this to Nora in another letter: 'She sang for me *The Lass of Aughrim*'.[21] But days later he called it Nora's song since it was actually from her that he had first heard the ballad: 'I was singing an hour ago your song *The Lass of Aughrim*. The tears come into my eyes and my voice trembles with emotion when I sing that lovely air.' This cluster of references makes it clear that Nora was to be identified with Gretta Conroy of the story as the Galway girl. But in the story, Joyce makes the identifiable song function in a similar manner to the motif of the Vinteuil sonata in Proust's novel. It is used as a vehicle to provoke memory. In the climactic scene, Gretta admits to her husband: 'It was a young boy I used to know . . . named Michael Furey. He used to sing that song, *The Lass of Aughrim*. He was very delicate.'[22] This memory, initially identified with Gretta's or Nora's personal past, is transformed and universalised into the collective memory of Ireland's past as viewed by the writer figure who is looking into Ireland's future: 'His soul had approached that region where dwell the vast hosts of the dead.'

Joyce locates the story in the identifiable place of Usher's Island. Those who have visited Dublin know that Usher's Island is actually a quay on the south bank of the river Liffey with a full view of the Wellington monument. By the power of association, Joyce connects the snow on the Wellington monument with another real locale,

though far away, Galway: 'It was falling, too, upon every part of the lonely churchyard on the hill where Michael Furey lay buried.' It is interesting that Joyce visited Galway only after having written the story and that in 1912 he actually visited the graveyard of 'The Dead' and wrote to his brother: 'I cycled to Oughterard on Sunday and visited the graveyard of "The Dead". It is exactly as I had imagined it.' [23] As we shall see, Virginia Woolf goes through a similar process in *To the Lighthouse*; years after alluding to the Hebrides in the novel, she visits it, confirming her imaginings of it. In Joyce's story, the compounding of the near and the faraway place conflates the past and the present in the view of Ireland – the living and the dead. Furthermore, it has been said that actually having conceived that story in Rome, he was influenced by the ghosts of the Parthenon and the sense of the past which hovers over that ancient city. This atmosphere was also assimilated into the story about Ireland.

At the time he was writing 'The Dead' in 1907, Joyce was obviously contemplating the dilemma of flight which he was conceiving in the Stephen Dedalus persona. Writing this story near the beginning of his self-imposed exile, he gave vent to speculations on what he would have been had he personally forgone that flight and remained in his country. Like Joyce, Gabriel writes book reviews for the Dublin *Daily Express*, wears glasses, has chosen an Irish Galway girl as his life companion and is interested in the progressive ideas of Europe. Yet the fictionalisation of the life material turns the domestic story into an archetypal one. Contrasting the purely Irish Galway element of Michael Furey and Gretta to the Europeanised inclination of Joyce himself, Joyce creates a dialectic of death and life, of the old and the new. The Galway lover, though identifiable, is symbolic of Ireland's past. Gabriel, though linked with the author, is the consciousness of the future. Joyce adds the element of snow, symbolic of natural process, as the all-inclusive element which mediates between the past and the present.

After writing 'The Dead' Joyce returned to his life materials to remake his image in *Stephen Hero* and then again in *A Portrait*. In fact, Joyce returned to the narrative of his life, which he had not yet attempted to reconstruct in the stories. In the process of relating key experiences of his childhood, Joyce seems to have surveyed his life for facts which could be exploited in his art. In fact, his brother Stanislaus's account *My Brother's Keeper*, ending in 1904, along with his diary ending in 1905, substantiates many of the facts which are transposed in the fiction. What is considered to be the draft for *A*

Portrait, Stephen Hero, in the surviving fragment of the Harvard manuscript, parallels only the first two years of Joyce's university life (1898–1900) and reads like a crisis autobiography, chronicling the youth's rebellion against the Catholic religion and his domestic life. It is, in this sense, reminiscent of Victorian autobiography and in particular of Gosse's *Father and Son*. But unlike Gosse's work, *Stephen Hero* introduces certain artistic theories pertaining to the development of the artistic figure, Stephen. Along with the definition of epiphany, it describes the process of transposition that is crucial to the artist:

> The artist who could disentangle the subtle soul of the image from its mesh of defining circumstances most exactly and re-embody it in artistic circumstances chosen as the most exact for it in its new office, he was the supreme artist.[24]

It would seem that this process of poetic transformation of fact had not yet occurred in *Stephen Hero* and was awaiting the mythical substratum which would be added to *A Portrait*. For 'Stephen Hero' merely declares in flatly unpoetic ways that he would be an artist, lacking the actual epiphany at 'The Bull', which occurs in *A Portrait*.

Nonetheless, a series of associations are unleashed in this rather primitive work which are then further developed and configured in *A Portrait* and *Ulysses*. In the course of describing certain achievements of his university life, Joyce refers to domestic scenes which shape his perceptions. There is the presence of his devoted brother Stanislaus in the guise of Maurice who keeps a record of conversations with Stephen; such a character never reappears. Joyce focuses in *Stephen Hero* on the death of his brother George, which is not included in the other works yet understandably was a traumatic event for the family. For in *My Brother's Keeper*, Stanislaus goes into quite vivid detail, describing the agonising state suffered by his younger brother 'Georgie' who was afflicted with typhoid fever and died of peritonitis at the early age of 14 in 1902. Stanislaus describes the close bond between his mother and her then-favourite son: 'When during the crisis his pains became acute, he would put his arms around his mother's neck and remain so until they abated.'[25] He recalls also the very night of George's death, when James apparently had gone downstairs to the piano to sing a melancholy chant he had set to verse and 'very shortly afterwards the symptoms of perforation of the intestines appeared . . . He [George] died that

evening.' The reference to George's death is the subject of two of Joyce's collected epiphanies. But in *Stephen Hero*, even that epiphany is transformed into another which distances Joyce from the character by creating a fictional character, Isabel, as the sister of Stephen, to replace his real brother George. The death is also dated two years earlier than it actually occurred, since, in the chronology of *Stephen Hero*, it happens just before Stephen's second year of university. Contrary to the definition that Joyce had given, this epiphany is outside the range of the trivial or ordinary, as it conveys a dramatic, shocking event in graphic terms:

Do you know anything about the body . . . He heard his mother's voice addressing him excitedly like the voice of a messenger in a play:

What ought I do? There's some matter coming away from the hole in Isabel's . . . stomach . . . Did you ever hear of that happening? [. . .]

I don't know . . . What hole?

The hole . . . the hole we all have . . . here.[26]

Joyce expresses death in terms of the physicality of the body. Following this scene, *Stephen Hero* describes the 'mean' and 'lowly' funeral at Glasnevin cemetery. Stephen's contemplation of the corpse seems to anticipate Bloom's attitude in Paddy Dignam's funeral in *Ulysses*. Indeed, this death prefigures the obsession with death in the larger novel where the physicality is transferred to the description of the dying mother.

Stephen Hero also situates Joyce's crisis over religion, for it shows Stephen telling his mother in person that he will not make his Easter duty. This is a confrontation which is dwelled upon in the later works. But in *A Portrait* the Stephen figure merely reports such a conversation to his friend Cranly, and in *Ulysses* the refusal of Communion is linked to the image of the dying mother and the stagnant Irish sea. In *Stephen Hero* the discussion emerges realistically in the restrictive personal environment of the family. The dialogue over religion between the Irish mother and the wayward son takes place in the kitchen over a cup of tea. This particular conversation is suddenly heightened by the reference to the ailing 'sister' in the background so that the rejection of religion is obliquely connected to the portent of death. The connection of the two themes is merely suggested in this episode.

These are a few instances which illustrate the use of narrative in *Stephen Hero* instead of the poetic transposition of fact that occurs in the subsequent *A Portrait*. For the most part, the earlier work chronicles the actual achievements of the university years and is full of conversations that the precocious student has with his contemporaries and mentors. A large space is given to the writing, reception, and presentation of the essay 'Drama and Life', which Joyce actually gave to the literary society of his university in 1900. His fervour about Ibsen had created a controversy, but in *A Portrait* this achievement is not even mentioned. The manuscript of *Stephen Hero* ends abruptly with a reference to a scene in the North Bull area of Dublin, where Stephen expresses his disappointment with his university and an awareness of his future vocation as an artist. Yet the epiphany connected with this scene and the dramatisation of it is waiting to be elaborated in *A Portrait*.

Stephen Daedalus of *Stephen Hero* turns into Stephen Dedalus of *A Portrait*. Despite the alteration of the spelling from the Greek original, the second Stephen becomes much more linked to the Greek archetype and the theme of the myth. For in *A Portrait* the exploitation of the Daedalus reference enriches the recasting of Joyce's life by adding a mythic dimension to it. The focus on *A Portrait*, which was not evident in the draft, is upon the flight of the persona with which Joyce identifies. Joyce had attempted to move the subject matter of his life from the lyrical to the dramatic in the ten years that separate *Stephen Hero* from *A Portrait*. And although *A Portrait* contains much more of the immediate 'I' than *Stephen Hero* does, that 'I' is at once personal and depersonalised in the transformation of the alienated Irish boy into the generalised artist figure. The Daedalus–Icarus myth serves Joyce's purposes for suggesting a threefold situation of constriction, art and flight. After all, in the celebrated myth, Daedalus was the supreme artificer who had constructed the labyrinth on the island of Crete to house the monstrous minotaur. He had also created the wings with which his son Icarus sought to fly. Appropriately, then, Joyce adapts the myth to his modern purposes as Stephen focuses upon birds and flight: 'He watched their flight; bird after bird; a dark flash, a swerve, a flash again, a dark aside, a curve, a flutter of wings.'[27]

As is well known, an entire section of the fourth chapter focuses on Stephen's recognition of his identity through an association with the mythical figure. An extended epiphany is created in the scene at North Bull Island, a real site which Joyce must have vis-

ited many a time in his youth. As an island on Dublin Bay, it is connected to the mainland by the wooden bridge of the Bull. Walking beyond the bridge to the breakwater, one has views of the commanding Howth Head, rolling distant mountains and Dublin port. One leaves behind in the distance Dublin, which becomes barely visible, and one can suddenly be overtaken by nature. By contrast to the confines of the city, there all the senses are assaulted by the vaulted sky full of clouds, the fresh sea breeze, the brackish red seaweed which is baked into the spongy sand. The strand where Stephen sees the wading girl is readily visible today and one can actually reincarnate the scene by replacing the wading girl with any passer-by looking out towards Dublin Bay and beyond. It is especially striking that patches of clouds above the Bull can very well pertain to the poetic phrase which Stephen utters: 'A day of dappled seaborne clouds.'

From this realistic setting, there is a transposition from sight to insight. A pleasurable experience emerges from the use of language, as in the case of Proust's aesthetic response to the steeples of Martinville and the ensuing experimentation with language and creation. In both instances, the artistic calling is associated with the transfer to language. Stephen is uplifted in an ecstasy of flight:

> His heart trembled; his breath came faster and a wild spirit passed over his limbs as though he were soaring sunward. His heart trembled in an ecstasy of fear and his soul was in flight. His soul was soaring in an air beyond the world ...

The image of a wading girl in the distance is the intermediary through which the artistic awakening is experienced.

Such is the re-presentation of poetic inspiration, which writers have often associated with some muse, but in this case is identified with a concrete place to which Joyce himself had fled for solace from the confines of his restrictive environment. Within the work, however, it continues to be suggested that the material that the artist 'forges' is the 'sluggish matter of the earth',[28] since the artist's ultimate task is to 'recreate life out of life'. For, after all, Joyce was using the 'dregs' of his childhood and adolescent experiences as the raw material of his art. An aesthetic image which captures this process is found in the fifth section of *A Portrait* in which the university student Dedalus, on the verge of becoming an artist, recalls his boyhood at Clongowes in its negative perspective:

He drained his third cup of watery tea to the dregs and set to chewing the crusts of fried bread that were scattered near him, staring into the dark pool of the jar. The yellow drippings had been scooped out like a boghole and the pool under it brought back to his memory the dark turfcolored water of the bath in Clongowes.

This is an example of involuntary memory reminiscent of Proust. Recollected experiences are the raw materials of his art. The aesthetic images and scenes which are created consist of 'life purified in and reprojected from the imagination'. Joyce is describing a process of distillation, in which the essence of experience is extracted and reproduced.

This is the very process by which he charts the different stages of his life in *A Portrait*. Although he moves in a chronological manner from infancy to the age of 20, the year of his departure from Ireland, he presents in his narrative a series of scenes which have focal points of transition. His first memories, of course, pertain to Bray, that idyllic seaside town where Joyce spent his early childhood. The particular house, 1 Martello Terrace, still stands, separated from the sea by a huge sea wall; it is the first of eight terraced ballustraded houses. A visitor today can tour the actual dining-room which is the setting of the politically charged Christmas dinner scene of *A Portrait*. Another set of memories pertain to Clongowes Wood College, in County Kildare, the Jesuit Boarding School to which Joyce was sent at the age of six-and-a half, the youngest boy in the school. Upon reaching Clongowes one is astounded by the magnificence of the allée leading to the gigantic fourteenth-century limestone castle which has served as a school. The playing fields surrounding the castle are large in expanse; so too is the area inside. Joyce had felt alienated in this environment and could recall the abuses of childhood at the hands of the Jesuit fathers – the source of his rebellion against the Church. The next stage is the recall of the streets of Dublin, through which Joyce had roamed while attending Belvedere College and the crude awakening at the age of sixteen on the trip to Cork with his father. Finally, the years at University College, Dublin, come to light, where as a literary-oriented student, Joyce engages in dialogues and prepares his wings for flight.

Joyce has created a persona which very much embodies his own life; the parallels are obvious, particularly so because the places

are not camouflaged and relate precisely to Joyce's own life story. In the first chapter of *A Portrait*, Joyce juxtaposes the two simultaneous memories of his life at Clongowes and Bray. Clongowes appears immense in proportion to the young boy who is left there at six-and-a-half, much younger than most of the boys, whose average age was eleven. Joyce emphasises this disproportion. Alienated from his fellow students, Joyce paints a vision of himself minimised in 'the wide playgrounds swarming with boys'. Another vision of the boy is the one whose Christmas dinner is disturbed by the boisterous dispute over Parnell between his father and 'aunt' Dante, who is modelled on Joyce's governess Hearn Conroy. Yet another sharp recollection is the sensuous pain he feels after having been unjustly hit on the hands by a Jesuit priest. Unlike Rousseau who intellectualised a scene of injustice, Joyce reintroduces the emotional content of it. Yet such early crises are compounded by those of his adolescence, which involve his resolve not to go into the ministry and the shift to art as a substitute. Revelling in carnal sin among the prostitutes heightens the conflict between religious remorse and sensuous indulgence which the artist figure endures. Each of these scenes exudes an atmosphere which transports the writer into his past through an empathy with the persona. The immediacy with which each incident is related again has extracted the essence from the scenes and recast it in an objectified form. Here, unlike in other works, there is no effort to camouflage the identification of writer and persona. The date of Parnell's death puts the narrative in historical time and is a gauge for the chronological parallels between Joyce's life and Stephen's. In his documentation of Joyce's life, Stanislaus avows that James uttered a rebellious phrase in 1902, 'Ireland is the old sow that eats her farrow' – a phrase which is incorporated verbatim in *A Portrait*, as Stephen responds to Davin's plea for nationalism. While there is little effort to distance the persona from the author, the persona transcends the personal identification by being presented in a typological context as the narrative charts a biological gestation of a creative power.

The distillation of experience and sensibility during these stages can be illustrated in specific scenes. For example, the period in which Joyce attended Belvedere College, from 1893–8, brought the young adolescent onto the urban scene. Joyce wants to communicate his search for something vague beyond the confines of his restrictive environment. This yearning is translated into Stephen's

search for the fantasy girl called Mercedes. An intentional ambiguity is sensed in the non-delineation of this figure. Instead, Stephen is pictured wandering with a certain freedom through the streets of Dublin out to the area of the docks:

> Dublin was a new and complex sensation . . . He passed unchallenged among the docks and along the quays wondering at the multitude of corks that lay bobbing on the surface of the water in a thick yellow scum . . .[29]

Joyce transforms Dublin from a locale into a sensation, as Anaïs Nin later does with her places. As his persona focuses on the yellow scum, a sense of stagnation is communicated along with the awakening to the sense of the beyond. At a next stage, the focus is on the city of Cork, a place identified with the loss of innocence, as the young boy witnesses his father's demise and is totally disillusioned by him:

> Nothing stirred within his soul but a cold and cruel and loveless lust. His childhood was dead or lost and it his soul capable of simple joys.

At a later stage, the same persona wanders through the Dublin streets to satisfy his awakened lust:

> His blood was in revolt. He wandered up and down the dark slimy streets peering into the gloom of the lanes and doorways listening eagerly for any sound.

Joyce transfers to his persona the emergence of his lust as if he were peering at himself from a distance. Such are the stepping-stones for the breakthrough of the artist. Although such stages may well have related to his own personal experience, they are presented in an objective fashion, open for analysis.

It seems justifiable that Joyce should end his *Portrait* with a diary format which refers to certain life facts that have not yet been elaborated in dramatic scene. These are facts which create a turning point in his life away from crisis towards the establishment of an identity independent of any restrictive locale. Joyce lists the meeting with Nora, 'met her today pointblank in Grafton Street', and the separation from his mother and motherland, 'Mother is putting away my new secondhand clothes in order. She

prays now'.[30] Alluding to both his mother and Nora in the year 1904 involves a manipulation of facts since Joyce had effaced from chronology the death of his mother (which had occurred in 1903) and his earlier sojourns to Europe in 1902–3 when he had been a student in Paris. In other words, he fuses his 1902 departure from Ireland with a second, less climactic one of 1904 right after his mother's death. Shifting therefore to 1904 and the time of his departure with Nora from Dublin, Joyce sets the stage for *Ulysses*. By amalgamating such facts, Joyce dissociates them from a particular historic time and infuses them into a created time or Bloomsday.

Compounding is the technique that Joyce uses throughout *Ulysses*, as he assembles a series of significant life facts and creates a substratum regarding the myth of Odysseus. Joyce moves away from the chronological progression that he had used in the rendering of life facts in *A Portrait* to create a new chronology in the framework of a single day which amalgamates the events of a lifetime. In moving his life facts into the time frame of *Ulysses*, he creates a strange admixture of clock time with mythic time as if he were inventing a new dimension with which to view a life in epic proportions. Parallels and the simultaneity of events expand the day into historic proportions of its own.

A conglomerate of facts surround the year 1904, which in turn are infused in the fictional Bloomsday of 16 June. It is a curious coincidence that the very same year of 1904 was a rich source for the literary work of Joyce's exact contemporary, Virginia Woolf, as we shall see. Her madness had reached a peak during that summer, and some of those experiences would be later transferred to *Mrs Dalloway*, a work which must have been modelled after the *Ulysses* notion of a 'life-day'. As for Joyce, certain facts precipitated this momentous year. We recall that it was on 17 January 1903 that Joyce actually left Dublin for Paris, having already fled there briefly a month earlier. It was in Paris that he first attempted to study medicine at the prestigious *École de Médecine* but he quickly gave it up to write reviews for Dublin newspapers. Then on Good Friday, 10 April 1903, he received an urgent telegram from his estranged father: 'Mother dying come home father.'[31] That ominous message made him return immediately to Dublin, and on 13 August he witnessed the agonising death of his mother from incurable cancer. Numerous reports, those of Gorman and Ellmann, have confirmed Joyce's obstinate refusal to pray at his mother's bedside: a traumatic experience

which was incorporated in the opening section of *Ulysses*. Ellmann recounts the behaviour leading to this dramatic refusal:

> Her fear of death put her in mind of her son's impiety, and on the days following Easter she tried to persuade him to make his confession and take communion. Joyce, however, was inflexible . . . His mother wept, and vomited green bile into a basin, but he did not yield.[32]

Despite disputes over the authenticity of such a scene, Joyce's brother Stanislaus has reported that he and his brother actually refused to kneel at his mother's deathbed, even when they had been ordered to do so by his uncle. Perhaps the greatest obsession of Joyce's life was this 'betrayal' of his mother and her religion. It is no wonder, therefore, that three specific references to the haunting image of Joyce's mother's death appear in *Ulysses*, two in the Telemachus section and one, later, in the Circe section. Whereas in Virginia Woolf's *To the Lighthouse*, as we shall see, the mother figure is resurrected as she is universalised as a life principle through a symbol of the lighthouse, in *Ulysses* the mother figure is linked to death and deadened forever through her association with the putrid Irish sea. In both instances there is a transposition of the human factor into an aesthetic image created by the author which severs the personal connection and creates an impersonal significance. The turmoil created by Joyce's conflict with his mother is transposed into two sequences of Stephen Dedalus's musings at Martello Tower. In one of the most arresting passages of the novel, Joyce transforms the memory of the dying mother into the image of the Irish 'snotgreen' sea:

> Silently, in a dream she had come to him after her death, her wasted body within its loose brown graveclothes giving off an odor of wax and rosewood, her breath, that had bent upon him, mute, reproachful, a faint odor of wetted ashes. Across the threadbare cuffedge he saw the sea hailed as a great sweet mother by the wellfed voice beside him. The ring of bay and skyline held a dull green mass of liquid. A bowl of white china had stood beside her deathbed holding the green sluggish bile which she had torn up from her rotting liver by fits of loud groaning vomiting.[33]

It is a curious fact that below Martello Tower are rocks covered with algae which make the water look slightly greenish; Joyce associated this image with his view of a degenerate Ireland which is then further linked to the memory of his dying mother. It was the Existentialist Sartre who later 'de-Romanticised' the sea in *Nausea* in 1938, but before him Joyce had de-romanticised the Ireland of the past by associating its sea with putrefaction and illness. The detail of the white china basin at her deathbed brings the immediacy of that domestic scene into focus even as it is merged with a larger picture. As with his brother George, Joyce concentrates on the sheer physicality of such a death, intentionally removing it from any religious context. He also distances himself from the emotions associated with his mother's death by presenting her not as an individual personage but as a universal representation of the death of his motherland. In a subsequent section the memory of the mother's death is provoked once again, this time by the blasphemous Buck Mulligan, modelled on Joyce's poet friend Oliver St John Gogarty. It was this friend, a medical student as well as a poet, who constantly incriminated Joyce for having killed his mother by his open cynicism. Haunted once again by the reminder of that horrific image, Stephen blatantly rejects prayer in a dismissal of Ireland: 'No mother! Let me be and let me live!'[34] But Stephen is unable to cast off the memory, for in the Circe section where Stephen is wandering amidst the brothels of Dublin, the mother's image returns to haunt him. This stage is like the *Walpurgisnacht* of *Faust* where conscience returns. The cryptic question that Stephen asks of his mother, for the last time in the Circe section, 'Tell me the word, mother, if you know now. The word known to all men',[35] has been answered by some critics in their restoration of the so-called 'love passage' of the 'Scylla and Charybdis' episode.

Other facts converge nearer to the date of 16 June 1904, which provide the material for the three sections of *Ulysses* 'Telemachia': the Tower, the School and the Strand. By March 1904, having stayed in Ireland after the death of his mother, Joyce had become a teacher at the Dalkey school in the vicinity of Sandymount Strand, a position which lasted only until June. It is also known that Joyce spent four days in Martello Tower (9–14 September 1904) with Oliver Gogarty, who had rented the tower, and an Anglo-Irishman, Samuel Trench. Joyce's relationship with Gogarty was tensely competitive and strained. Stanislaus's diary note of 14 September 1904 documented the situation at the tower:

At present he [James] is staying on sufferance with Gogarty in the Tower at Sandycove. Gogarty wants to put Jim out, but he is afraid that if Jim made a name someday it would be remembered against him.[36]

As a matter of fact, Joyce virtually fled the Tower on that night of 14 September because of Trench's threatening nightmares and his shooting of a pistol. Joyce is then said to have walked the many miles back to Dublin and to have appeared at the National Library the next morning to recount the strange misadventure. Of course, many parallels of these facts can be found in *Ulysses*. It is not surprising that Stephen Dedalus should first be viewed in his role as schoolteacher at Mr Deasy's school near Martello Tower and that the long walk back to Dublin proper may have inspired Joyce to construe the walk in *Ulysses*. The motif of flight and of having been 'put out' of the Tower finds its way significantly into *Ulysses*. Also, the characters of Buck Mulligan and Haines have been identified with Gogarty and Trench.

So much for the sources which relate to Stephen. At the same time, there are obvious sources for Bloom and Molly, from the relationship which begins between Joyce and Nora just around the novel's date. It is well known that Joyce made literary history in creating his special 16 June as an eighteen-hour day of epic proportion. From a practical point of view, he may have been influenced by the fact that Ireland at that time of the year has very late daylight, giving one the impression of perennial day. But it is also recognised that Bloomsday, itself, was dedicated to Nora. It has been said that Joyce pursued the chambermaid of Finn's Hotel, having seen her for the first time walking down Nassau Street on 10 June 1904. A subsequent meeting was planned for the evening of 16 June; hence the true source of Bloomsday. That meeting and subsequent ones led to a lifelong relationship. Joyce was to leave with Nora for Europe on 8 October of that same year. This was to be his third flight from Dublin, and he was to return to Dublin thereafter only briefly in 1909 and 1912 before his self-imposed exile became definitive. As we know, the novel transfers the Nora–Joyce relationship to the fictional characters of Molly and Bloom, avoiding a straight one-on-one correlation with Stephen. Furthermore, the novel does not involve flight, as the previous ones do, but positions its two characters caught within Dublin. Such avoidance of direct parallels suggests that Joyce was seeking a fuller vision and

deeper vision of himself than that suggested by the Dedalus figure of *A Portrait*, and that he was exploring other facets of his personality.

It is significant that Joyce's rebellion against his country and religion had reached its peak in 1904. Certainly, it was to affect the creation of the Dedalus rebellion in *A Portrait*, but in 'reweaving' his image in *Ulysses*, Joyce situates the artist in the very quotidian against which he had previously revolted. The artistic elements emerge from the dregs of that society rather than from lofty elements overhead. It is a fact that on 29 August 1904 Joyce wrote a blasphemous letter to Nora during their brief and fervent courtship which communicated his attitude towards religion, his mother, the social order of Ireland, his fatherland and his personal father. Joyce wrote to Nora in outright rebellion:

> My mind rejects the whole present social order and Christianity – home, the recognised virtues, classes of life, and religious doctrines . . . My mother was slowly killed, I think, by my father's ill-treatment . . . When I looked on her face as she lay in her coffin – a face grey and wasted with cancer – I understood that I was looking on the face of a victim and I cursed the system which had made her a victim . . . Six years ago I left the Catholic Church, hating it most fervently.[37]

Here in 1904 was a total attack by Joyce on the religious and social values of his past provoked in part by the lasting image of his mother as a victim of the system which he had come to detest. In this fashion the death of his mother has universal implications for others. Likewise in his art, domestic situations are emblematic of a society at large.

It is no wonder that the year 1904 becomes the 'Bloomsday' year. It is a fictional construct coalescing various aspects of his personal life in synchronic time, or what Paul Ricoeur would call 'monumental time'. The sheer compounding of events and motifs is colossal, turning the day into a microcosm of human history, particularly with regard to the perception of the Irish nation. For Joyce himself, the passage from one woman to the next, from the old to the new, is a turning-point linking the personal history of the author with his conception of the passage of time from the old ailing Ireland to the new one – about to be born. The movement away from the ailing and battered mother to the Galway girl of eighteen

can be paralleled to the two different visions of Ireland: the snot-green sea at the beginning, the ripe Molly figure at the open-ended conclusion.

The evolution of Nora into the 'new' Molly figure has been dealt with by feminist critics and commentators such as Brenda Maddox, who rescues Nora from her image as chambermaid and instead re-evaluates her as a crucial factor in Joyce's life. However, we must also note her role in Joyce's art, for it is her very status of chambermaid that gave her literary potential in terms of Joyce's readiness to transform the quotidian into the artistic and mythical. For both Bloom and Molly are as quotidian as they can get, yet reach levels of the mythical and the universal as 'everyman' and 'everywoman'.

It also seems highly significant that the whole 'plot' of Molly's infidelity to her husband on that 'ordinary' day in June in *Ulysses* may have arisen from a passing comment that presumably was made to Joyce on 6, August 1909. At that time Joyce had travelled to Ireland with his son Giorgio, to introduce him to both families. On that trip Joyce is said to have met his old friend Vincent Cosgrave who boasted, as noted earlier, that he had had an affair with Nora during the summer of 1904 when Joyce had fallen in love with her. Cosgrave had been one of Joyce's friends at University College who became the disrespectful fictional character Lynch in *A Portrait*. But Cosgrave's assertion about Nora was 'a blasted lie',[38] according to Joyce's closest friend Byrne, the model for Cranly in *A Portrait*. Whether it was truth or fabrication is irrelevant, for the function of such a statement was to produce inordinate jealousy in Joyce, which he would transfer to characters in his fiction – first, as he already had with Gabriel Conroy, and then on to Leopold Bloom. In his own life, after having become suspicious of others, Joyce is said to have clung to Nora more than ever, writing erotic notes to her which were peppered with obscenities. If Joyce's jealousy of a past but negligible affair parallels the matter of 'The Dead', his very feeling of jealousy seems to have triggered the plot for *Ulysses*. The epic novel builds upon this near-fragmentary material to present a case of adultery inflicted upon a cuckolded spouse. From an ordinary conversation or confession of jest arises material for this monumental novel, and the sheer discrepancy between the source and the fictionalisation demonstrates the artistic method. Joyce enlarges his experience through negative fantasies, for there is no documentation that suggests infidelity on

Nora's part in their long relationship. Although the parallels between the real Nora and the fictional Molly are many – both having a son and a daughter, both being sexually liberated for their era, both having a taste for opera – the theme of infidelity seems to be an artistic elaboration. Joyce has taken the incidental and merged it with the image of a lasting archetype, and this very admixture is at the heart of the artistic conversion of the everyday material.

The building blocks for *Ulysses* are therefore many and variegated, but their convergence in *Ulysses* recasts them in a mythic mode. The vomited green bile, the blasphemy against the Catholic Church, the stay in Paris among the medical students, the writing for the Dublin newspapers, the visits to the National Library, the teaching position at the Dalkey school, the brief stay at Martello Tower, the chance meeting with Nora, the fit of jealousy five years later, all coalesce in the novel in the confines of a single June day. Joyce transmutes such facts into motifs as he both distils and elaborates their significance. He depersonalises these occurrences, moving from the particulars of his own 1904 life situation to the situation of his compatriots and to general experiences common to all men, which he had corroborated with the analogous Homeric ur-work.

Joyce, after all, had been attracted to the *Odyssey* as the most compelling classic precisely because he had read in it some very human themes. An ultimate building block for *Ulysses* is this literary experience which had infused his life; he had sought to translate its themes into the modern context. Joyce perceived Ulysses, one of the major survivors of the Trojan War, in the role of the wandering artist, returning to his homeland – to his son and wife who had been forsaken for 20 years. Unlike *The Aeneid*, whose heroes are superhuman, vying with the gods, *Ulysses* emphasises the human and domestic factor. Joyce comments on the unemphasised fact that Odysseus' heroics are those after the war itself: the perilous journey of his return and the facets of the domestic life he had left behind. He also notes that Ulysses is 'a great musician' who in the 'Scylla and Charybdis' scene has himself tied to the mast in order to enjoy the music without danger. The artistic element is introduced, mingling with suggestions of the heroics of the battlefield and the mundane activities of life. In the course of writing *Ulysses* in 1917, Joyce had explained to one of his language students in Zurich:

I find the subject of *Ulysses* the most human world literature . . .
the motif of wandering . . . the motif of the artist . . . And the
return, how profoundly human![39]

Joyce was to recast this 'return' in the third section of *Ulysses*,
entitled 'Nostos'.

Although parallels are fabricated on the thematic level, the actual
parallels between the characters of the two works are not consistent.
In fact, what exists are discrepancies between the two works precisely in terms of human character. Could Joyce be saying, as did
Virginia Woolf later, that human character had changed after the
great modern war? Ulysses is hardly a model for the ordinary
Bloom who seems cowardly and unenterprising in his confined
locale. The two-year-old son, Telemachus, left at home at the time of
the Trojan War, who is 22 at the time of Ulysses' return, could be a
fitting parallel for Stephen Dedalus, but that parallelism is blurred
by the memory of Bloom's infant son who died ten years before at
eleven days old. Ulysses' wife Penelope was given the epithet 'faithful' precisely for being true to her wayward husband for those 20
long years – in contrast to the adulterous Molly who is unfaithful
within the time span of a given day.

Furthermore, it is interesting that Joyce is actually shifting the
focus in his own opus from the Stephen Dedalus persona to his new
creation, Leopold Bloom. It will be seen how Virginia Woolf shifts
identification from one female character to another as her life and
perspective evolve. This technique of splitting the self is germane to
these autobiographical novelists. As for Joyce, his reading *The
Odyssey* as a domestic epic was highly significant in this stage of the
evolution of both his life and his art. At the time of starting *Ulysses*
in 1914, Joyce was already an established artist, having published
Dubliners and with *A Portrait* appearing in serial form. The figure of
Stephen leaving Ireland in pursuit of art in exile had been sketched.
What may have preoccupied Joyce in the subsequent years of his life
was his role as man, husband and father. In being attracted to the
role of Odysseus, Joyce created the character Bloom and weakened
his identification with Stephen – the youthful figure he was no
longer. A new perspective had awakened a new analogy. Although
the 22-year-old Stephen corresponds to Joyce's age in 1904, the Joyce
who was writing the novel from 1914–21 was in his thirties, nearer to
the 38-year-old Bloom. Stephen, after all, is a lesser character in the
background of Bloom's peregrinations on Bloomsday. Although he

is an artist in search of a father figure, that profile is less forceful than the one of the surrogate father figure Bloom, who is alienated culturally in the city in which he dwells.

The association of Bloom with Joyce is provocative precisely because the exterior parallel between Bloom and Joyce appear nil. We recall that Proust identified with a character like Swann only on some levels; the same is true of Virginia Woolf with Mrs Dalloway, as will be seen. But whereas these other writers were creating figures of the upper crust, Joyce went out of his way to explore the plebeian, as illustrated by the fact that Bloom is a lower-middle-class advertising agent, living at 7 Eccles Street, modelled on a butcher that Joyce knew in that area of Dublin. Bloom's traits – his Jewish origin, his globular physique, his lack of glasses – seem also totally unrelated to Joyce, the lean intellectual Irishman with poor eyesight. But in some manner, Joyce may have been peeking at a conventional life-style which he had avoided by his departure from Ireland. He was also experimenting with mythic themes beyond the paradigm of flight.

The intersection of the two persona, Dedalus and Bloom, on the Dublin streets seems to reflect different aspects of Joyce's own estranged identity. The splitting of Joyce's personality into two parts has been observed by the critics: Bloom the Jewish outsider in Catholic Dublin and Stephen the homeless intellectual-artist. Just as Bloom cannot relate to the Catholic funeral of Paddy Dignam, Stephen cannot relate to his rowdy contemporaries who jeer at him and then abandon him wandering drunk in a brothel in Nighttown. Bloom, the earthy mercantile 'everyman' is contrasted to Stephen, the exceptional dreamer. Despite the dissimilarities, Joyce's fusion of the two in a temporary relationship seems to convey a message: the sky-bound artist must be grounded to mingle with the ordinary, the sensual and the earthly. Ihab Hassan has stated succinctly that 'the *Portrait* depicts the Artist alone; *Ulysses* presents the Artist seeking Everyman'.[40]

Joyce compounds his own sense of alienation in presenting these two outsiders. Stephen and Bloom are actually perceived as walking on 'parallel courses', however different they may be. A comparison with Proust's trajectory is illuminating. Just as the narrator of the *Recherche* perceived the two ways as representing two sides of the brain, the one towards society, the other towards art, so the two walks in *Ulysses* parallel the artist with the man. Literally, after the brothel scene, the two walk on two sides of the street. As Bloom escorts Stephen home for shelter, Joyce posits a dialectic, opposing the 'scientific' side of Bloom to the 'artistic' one of Stephen. Their

friendship, however, suggests some sort of fusion of the human with the artistic, analogous to the fusion of the artistic and the social in Proust's perspective. This theme of parallelism runs throughout *Ulysses*. Early in the novel, it was Bloom who had contemplated the Ballast Office clock and had derived an interpretation of it, which was called 'parallax'. That scientific term refers to a displacement of an object from two points of view. Bloom had questioned this concept as he viewed the clock:

> Mr Bloom moved forward, raising his troubled eyes. Think no more about that. After one. Timeball on the ballastoffice is down. Dunsink time. Fascinating little book that is of sir Robert Ball's. Parallax.[41]

The notion of two sets of time, from Dublin to Dunsink, conjures up the idea of two perspectives, reflected by Bloom and Dedalus. In this particular instance, the Ballast Office clock triggers a series of associations which mediate between the perspectives of Bloom and Stephen. Since the Ballast Office had been previously connected to the concept of epiphany, it is appropriate that in this case it suggests the novel's themes.

The walk through Dublin itself, through recognisable places, is unlike the journeys to faraway places that we shall find in Woolf and Nin. For Joyce, the path of the artist is grounded in physical reality. Even the fact of 16 June being one of the longest days of the year, with sunlight disappearing in Ireland for only a few hours, may have been the living reality for the extended limits of the fictitious day in *Ulysses*. Joyceans annually trace the Bloomsday walk from the Post Office on O'Connell Street to Davy Byrne's Pub in Duke Street and on to the National Library in Kildare Street, with many stops on the way. It is an itinerary which, of course, undercuts Odysseus' perilous journey. Joyce traces the pathway of the artist, not the hero, but by dissociating the one from the other, having sought them in earlier works such as *Stephen Hero* and *A Portrait*, he reintegrates the artist in ordinary life.

Another thematic pattern of the work involves the dialectic of life and death. Joyce incorporates his personal experiences of death, that of his mother and brother, into an expression of the passing of an era. Stanislaus Joyce has commented that the 'Hades' scene, where Bloom attends the funeral of a near-anonymous personage, Paddy Dignam, was composed from impressions that James had of his mother's and

brother's funerals. The detached manner in which Bloom contemplates the death of an Irishman reflects the distancing that Joyce had achieved by 1914 from his personal tragedies and his readiness to treat death in an abstract manner. He is associating these particular deaths with the death of an aspect of Irish society as a whole. He is also injecting his own agnosticism into the character of Bloom, who views the death in materialistic terms, focusing on the physicality of the corpse and the futility of the ritual of burial. Counteracting these morbid references, however, is the birth image suggested elsewhere in the novel by the prolonged accouchement of Mina Purefoy. As anonymous as Paddy Dignam, Mina joins Paddy in being a universal archetype of ordinariness. But unlike Paddy, Mina represents thematically the passage to rebirth, reflecting perhaps Joyce's own view of a modern age. This association is inevitably connected to the figure of Molly Bloom in the closing 'Penelope' section. The flowery image of the fertile Molly replaces these previous moribund references, which include not only the funeral but the snotgreen sea, the green bile and the old milkmaid haunting the Martello Tower. The revived relationship between Bloom and Molly at the end, after the years that had severed their rapport, due in part to the unfortunate death of their infant son, suggests a new beginning. The single relationship, in its ordinary setting, is a microcosm of the larger society.

Joyce thus uses certain particulars of plot to suggest a larger vision which he may have harboured in seeking a perspective with which to view his native Ireland, having forsaken it. He tints the real and verifiable in his recollections by the power of association and expands upon the minimal. The epic mode of his major work offers him a detachment from the personal elements that had so much filled his earlier writings. Although he creates types from the Dublin streets, he transforms them into indices of a modern humanity searching for life connections. Recasting his own image several times over, he reaches a universal level of apprehension of the human species as he converts the incidental into the significant. He recycles the ingredients of his own personal life into a collective corpus, exploiting the very drabness of his environment to arrive at an art work which shapes it with thematic structure and architectural design. Ultimately seeking myth to objectify his life story, he proceeded from the Daedalus myth of flight to the Ulysses myth of the wanderer. And, much like the craftsman Daedalus, Joyce maps out a labyrinth from which he, at once the father and the son, emerges in creative flight and liberation from the very ingredients of his art.

6

Distancing and Displacement in Virginia Woolf

Virginia Woolf's life has been persistently probed in recent years as rich ground for psychological inquiry and feminist pathbreaking. Yet no attention has been paid to her intense preoccupation with the relationship between art and life which incorporates but exceeds any neurosis or feminism that can be detected. Throughout her essays and letters, she dealt with the very subject of aesthetic autobiography, sensing a tenuous balance between 'bios' and 'autos', and she gave a warning of this fascinating complexity in her introduction to the 1928 American edition of *Mrs Dalloway*:

> For nothing is more fascinating than to be shown the truth which lies behind those immense facades of fiction – if life is indeed true, and if fiction is indeed fictitious. And probably the connection between the two is highly complicated.[1]

The interest in Virginia Woolf's life stems from its tumultuous psychological quality set against the background of late-Victorian decorum. Psychobiographies have been written focusing on sexual abuses by her half-brothers Gerald and George Duckworth, on mental abuses by the apparently unsympathetic doctors of her time who repeatedly committed her to mental institutions, and on emotional abuses by her sister Vanessa Bell, by her close friend Vita Sackville-West, and even by her devoted husband Leonard Woolf. Certainly, her act of suicide in the river Ouse in 1941 will continue to be the subject of critical speculations regarding her life and work for a long time to come. And then, feminist critics will continue to hail her as one of the first true feminists of the twentieth century who ardently fought against the vestiges of the patriarchal system of the Edwardian era. *A Room of One's Own* has been regarded as her

manifesto, and her fiction has been interpreted in semiotic terms as challenging the phallocentric orientation of the society of her time.

But for Woolf, the period in which the probing of the connections between life and fiction become most noticeable is one of relative calm in her life and great literary productivity. It is the 1920s, what her biographer-nephew Quentin Bell has labelled the 'years of ascent' (1922–31), in which, 'writing what are now her most celebrated novels, she formed and developed her own style'.[2] Offering theories of modern fiction in her numerous essays and commenting inadvertently on her own fiction in her diaries and letters of the 1920s, she gives clues to her creative process which recasts her life in the philosophical dimension of existential predicament, transcending her personal traumas. This period of relative peace and health in her life is marked by the creativity of her chief novels, *Mrs Dalloway* and *To the Lighthouse*, with *Jacob's Room* and *Orlando* in the background.

Woolf expressed thoughts about autobiography in her personal writings of that era, perhaps not fully realising that her life material was already being absorbed and dilated in her fiction. In her entry of 8 February 1926, Woolf had assessed her diary (begun in 1915 and extending to 1941) as 'rough material'[3] for her masterpiece, which was to be her memoirs to be written at the age of 60. Woolf came very near to that schedule, since it was not until the age of 58 to 59 in 'A Sketch of the Past' that she actually engaged herself in the writing of real autobiography, cut short of course by her untimely death in 1941. It has been said that Woolf felt that an autobiography in her time, written by a woman, would never reach the candour of a Rousseau. She was obviously not as free as the later writer Anaïs Nin, who, we shall see, turned her diary into a confidant and storehouse for her fiction. Woolf's reservations about the diary form might explain in part her motivation to develop a more veiled autobiography, which could reveal the intimate obsessions of her own life through indirect artistic means.

On the other hand, Woolf was closely exposed to biography writing by the two dominant male figures in her life: her father and her husband. In her early years she must have observed Leslie Stephen's activity as a Victorian biographer. After all, he was the first editor of the *Dictionary of National Biography*. Moreover, he had understood autobiography in its classic historic sense, making a comment anonymously the year before Virginia was born that 'an autobiography, alone of all books, may be more valuable in proportion to the

amount of misrepresentation which it contains'.[4] But he had been interested in the psychology of being false to oneself, not in the creative process that may have distorted the life truth for higher aims. Leonard Woolf, on the other hand, the author of a five-volume autobiography which was to span the years 1880–1969, seems to have made an unconventional statement regarding the genre: 'it is rather depressing for an autobiographer starting on a fourth volume to find in this way that most of his facts are will-o'-the-wisps and it is almost impossible to tell the truth'.[5]

It is as if Virginia later responded to her father's orientation by questioning the standard approach to the writing of biography. For even in this accepted form of non-fictional writing, she sensed the importance of ingredients beyond fact and chronology. In her 1927 essay 'The New Biography' she sought to identify the necessary ingredients of the modern biography, which would combine the 'granite-like solidity' of truth with the 'rainbow-like'[6] connotation of personality – and more. Whereas past biographers had been interested in the systematic order of events which made life 'eventful', the new biography should focus on the 'truth' of the personality of the subject, which could only be conveyed through artistic writing. It is interesting that Virginia herself experimented in her life with two forms of biography: the one on the life of her artist-friend Roger Fry and the other, a fictional biography of her close friend, Vita Sackville-West, in *Orlando*. Neither of these works, however, reached the level of fictional transposition of her well-known novels.

It was the autobiographical, therefore, not the biographical which was to be her medium for creativity. Fascinated by the deeper apprehension of life through the fictional process, she proceeded to amplify her own life experiences and relationships in her novels. The tragic loss of four close family members – her mother in 1895, her half-sister Stella in 1897, her father Leslie Stephen in 1904 and her brother Thoby in 1906 – made her seek their recovery in her fiction. She later dramatically stated in retrospect in 'A Sketch of the Past' that when she finished writing *To the Lighthouse* 'I ceased to be obsessed by my mother'.[7] Whether this purgation in 1927 was definitive or temporary is a matter for debate. But the actual transfiguration of her many obsessions regarding death, sanity, sexuality, time and war into artistic artifacts and characters is a process which can be detected in her fiction.

Woolf came out with a set of theories on fiction which have an immediate bearing on her autobiographical transposition. Perhaps

her most haunting statement was the one looming from her 1924 essay 'Mr Bennett and Mrs Brown': 'On or about December, 1910, human character changed.'[8] She went on in this same essay to amplify what could be considered an arbitrary and even capricious declaration with the following comment: 'all human relations have shifted – those between masters and servants, husbands and wives, parents and children'. She was obviously noticing the change in the traditional hierarchies of her day. Her choice of 1910, and December for that matter, has often been connected with the artistic innovations of the time. In particular, some readers have linked Woolf's statement with the First Post-Impressionist exhibition of November 1910 which took place in London and startled the public with the abstract experimentations of Cézanne, Matisse, Picasso, Van Gogh and Gauguin. Woolf herself later took note of this public reaction in her account of the exhibition in her biography of Roger Fry.

But Woolf was really saying that her fiction was to bear the marks of a new era. 1910, also the year of the death of Edward VII, was for Woolf the beginning of a new time. She related such changes in the collective psyche to the literary context. Her statement regarding the basic change in human character with its link to changes in artistic form was suggesting that the modern novelist thereafter was to have the complicated task of depicting life in a more complex manner than that of mimesis and representation. Certainly, the aesthetics of Roger Fry and his followers were stressing this point. For Fry wrote in the preface to the catalogue of the Second Post-Impressionist Exhibition of 1912:

> Now, these artists do not seek to give what can, after all, be but a pale reflex of actual appearance, but to arouse the conviction of a new and definite reality. They do not seek to imitate form, but to create form; not to imitate life, but to find an equivalent for life.[9]

In his accent on formal representation of life materials, Fry and others were dismissing photographic representation and introducing the concept of analogy in art. It will be seen how Virginia Woolf was attempting to go in the same direction in the theory and practice of her literary art, using the method of analogy in her aesthetic autobiographies.

Woolf's essays of the 1920s, therefore, are an attack on traditional methods of representation. Woolf took an ardent stand against the conventional realism as practised in her country. In her view, Britain

was behind in the progress towards modernism which was occurring in the field of arts on the Continent. She attempted, therefore, in her manifold essays to create a platform for her fiction. She questioned the very definition of 'reality' which had been so narrowly understood by writers such as Mr Arnold Bennett. In that essay of hers, 'Mr Bennett and Mrs Brown', she created the parable of a Mrs Brown, who seemingly ordinary, was to emerge as the life source itself: 'she is an old lady of unlimited capacity and infinite variety: capable of appearing in any place, wearing any dress, saying anything and doing heaven knows what . . . for she is, of course, the spirit we live by, life itself'.[10] According to Woolf, this universal Mrs Brown had actually been expressed in the persons of Ulysses or Prufrock. Woolf, here, was analysing the power of the quotidian – what had been explored by T. S. Eliot and James Joyce before her, and what she too had been incorporating in her fiction.

Woolf praised those modern novelists such as her exact contemporary, the young James Joyce, who was attempting to come 'closer to life'.[11] In an essay 'Modern Fiction' (1924) she pointed out, in this regard, Joyce's attention to the particular and detail. Writers should be concerned with 'an ordinary mind on an ordinary day', she explained – obviously under the influence of Joyce. She was putting this premise into practice in writing her *Mrs Dalloway* – a novel in which she fused that everyday with the universal: moments of 'non-being' with moments of 'being', as she called them. Although she had earlier in 1922 actually criticised Joyce for the paltriness of his subject-matter, the notion of the quotidian as a resource for artistic transmutation had obviously struck her as his saving grace.

Woolf was also attracted to the artistic exploitation of the commonplace gleaned from life material by the earlier writer Proust. As early as 1917 she had heard of a 'new' French genius through Roger Fry who had announced this discovery to a second-generation Bloomsbury – the 1917 club. Proust had been added to the collection of writers such as T. S. Eliot, Katherine Mansfield, James Joyce, Ezra Pound, who were being discussed by the avant-garde members of the club. Thereafter, Woolf absorbed Proust, as her numerous references to him in her letters and essays testify. Also, in 1928 she and Leonard published at the Hogarth Press her brother-in-law's short book on Proust. Clive Bell, who was singing the praises of Proust, had also noticed at this time Proust's use of the familiar and everyday to reveal the mysteries of life. Bell wrote:

He observed banalities after the manner of his beloved Impressionists, staring at familiar objects till they gave up their secrets, till he had penetrated the dust and dirt and discovered underneath that thrilling reality which is the thing itself.[12]

Likewise, in her essay of 1929, 'Phases of Fiction', Woolf made it known that she was aware of this tendency in a recent writer whom she had read and assimilated:

The commonest actions, such as going up in an elevator or eating cake, instead of being discharged automatically, rake up in their progress a whole series of thoughts, sensations, ideas, memories which were apparently sleeping on the walls of the mind.[13]

Woolf used her discussion of Proust to warn her readers that the purpose of art was *not* to provide psychological insight into the author, for 'truth' had to measured by the standards of art rather than life:

Indeed, the enormous growth of the psychological novel in our time has been prompted largely by the mistaken belief, which the reader has imposed on the novelist, that truth is always good; even when it is the truth of the psychoanalyst and not of the imagination.

To speculate on the life and adventures of the novelist behind the work returns the novel to a personal level, which was not the domain of the modern novelist, as Woolf saw it. An aesthetic orientation toward the use of life material was apparent here, similar to that of Proust who had countered Sainte-Beuve. But Woolf, in particular, was fighting against the 'accuracy of representation' which, in her view, was material for psychologists, not artists.

Psychoanalysis, practised by Freud and others, was viewed by Woolf as an enemy which locked her up in institutions, keeping her away from the few people who she felt loved, respected and understood her. Unlike Anaïs Nin, who was to exploit the uses of psychotherapy for artistic purposes, Woolf fled from it. This flight may have been due in part to her very private nature, her 'room of her own', which she never wanted to expose fully and open up to public view. The incentive of her art would therefore be to hide or camouflage her selves in others, through the process of transfer and

projection. Such an orientation, of course, can and has been analysed psychoanalytically in her case, but what is interesting in this
context of autobiographical art is the artistic process which contains
the personal yet objectifies and universalises it.

Quentin Bell reports that Freud, seeing her for the only time,
when on his deathbed, offered her a narcissus.[14] Ironically, narcissism was the last thing she would have wanted to be associated
with. Leonard Woolf, in alluding to this instance of meeting Freud
on Saturday, 28 January 1939 (eight months before his death) said
that 'almost ceremoniously he [Freud] presented Virginia with a
flower'.[15] In any case, this contact with Freud must have been dis-
tasteful to Virginia, who claimed to have paid no attention to the
psychoanalyst even though the Hogarth Press, from 1924 on, had
published English translations of his early writings and she herself
had set the type of two volumes of Freud's *Collected Papers. The Ego
and the Id* had been published by the Press in 1927, the same year as
To the Lighthouse. But in *To the Lighthouse* she claimed, as if her art
were in competition, to have psychoanalysed herself: 'I suppose that
I did for myself what psycho-analysts do for their patients. I
expressed some very long felt and deeply felt emotion.'[16]

Yet the expression of that emotion would be, for Woolf, achieved
through a process of depersonalisation in art. It is easy to see that
she detested the personal as being trivial. When she admitted to
weaving family members into her fiction, therefore, she explicitly
stated that she extracted from them, or herself for that matter, the
'typical', the 'universal' and the 'representative'. Her use of autobiographical data thus involved the transfer from the individual to the
archetypal, from the temporary to the enduring.

Therefore, along with her attack on traditional methods of representation in her essays of the 1920s, there is throughout Woolf's letters and diaries a constant denigration of the ego and personal
emotion. As early as 1920, before writing any of her major works,
Woolf considered the possibilities of writing in an autobiographical
mode but cautioned herself against what she called the 'danger' of
the 'damned egotistical self'.[17] In order to hide the personal element,
which she knew would saturate her fiction in an obsessive way, she
sought formal structure. She again commented in her diary in 1924:

> I think writing must be formal. The art must be respected. This
> struck me reading some of my notes here, for, if one lets the mind
> run loose, it becomes egotisical, personal, which I detest.[18]

One wonders, in this instance, if she is not under the direct influence of Roger Fry – applying his commentary on artistic creation as formal equivalence of life to the realm of her autobiographical writing. It is especially interesting that she wrote the above lines in her diary as she was 'driving [her] way through the mad chapters of *Mrs Dalloway*', the novel in which she 'hid' her madness in an *alter ego* figure, Septimus Warren Smith. The formal structures which she alludes to are the aesthetic structures of 'the double' and simultaneity in which the personal elements are embedded. Elsewhere, in speaking of *To the Lighthouse* in a letter to Vita Sackville-West,[19] she asks if her allusion to her parents is sentimental in that novel, for it is precisely the romantic and sentimental which she wished to avoid in her writing. It will be seen how she seems to have transcended such nostalgic sentimentality through a certain abstraction and distancing in the narrative which universalises these root figures in a cosmic context and translates and aggrandises her obsession with death into terms of universal incipient darkness.

The most specific clues to Woolf's fictional method come from her memoirs, entitled 'A Sketch of the Past', written at the end of her writing career and life as a sort retrospective assessment of the relations of her life to her fiction. This document assimilated the keys to her fiction that had been conveyed earlier in her letters, diaries and essays. But it went beyond those earlier comments by highlighting memory as a selective process which shaped life facts into artifacts. For Woolf, memory functions according to the concept of the privileged moment which extracts the essential from the everyday; that treasure then becomes imprinted on the mind for eternity. The elements of the artistic can be seized by the artist from the constant blending of 'being' and 'non-being'. From the everyday arises the significant, the meaningful; accordingly the philosophical novelist blends the existential with the essential:

> From this I reach what I might call a philosophy; at any rate it is a constant idea of mine; that behind the cotton wool is hidden a pattern, that we, I mean all human beings are connected with this, that the whole is a work of art; that we are parts of the work of art.[20]

Her memory, then, is an artistic process which retrieves the past in seeking the pattern behind the 'cotton wool' of the everyday and seizing those moments of being for eternity. The narrative of her

novels, therefore, re-enacts this combination of the quotidian with the essential through what she calls 'scene making'. She points out that such scenes are not just 'novelistic' but, rather, part of her process of perception and recollection: 'I find that scene making is my natural way of marking the past. Always a scene has arranged itself: representative; enduring.'

This notion of selective memory which arranges scenes according to their enduring patterns catches life synchronically and may be representational in terms of the temporality expressed by Paul Ricoeur's viewpoint. From the temporal she sought the permanent; and from the everyday self she proceeded to the universal one. Her portrayal of her own self would therefore involve a process of objectification. Extracting herself from her childhood scene, she therefore commented:

> If I were painting myself I should have to find some – rod, shall I say – something that would stand for the conception. It proves that one's life is not confined to one's body and what one says and does; one is living all the time in relation to certain background rods or conceptions.

The story of Virginia Woolf's early life clearly emerges from 'A Sketch of the Past', which recaptures her idyllic childhood in St Ives, Cornwall, and it was this extended scene that she was to transpose in *To the Lighthouse*. It was in St Ives that the Stephen family spent many a happy summer until the time of Julia Stephen's death on 5 May 1895 which abruptly ended Virginia's childhood: 'For after that day there was nothing left of it . . . everything had come to an end.'[21] Leslie Stephen immediately sold Talland House, the lovely white house which was perched on a hill overlooking St Ives Bay and the Godrevy lighthouse – all of which can be seen today.

Like Proust, Woolf sought to recover the idyllic past of her childhood. But she achieves this retrieval in a two channel outlet of both fiction and memoir. In the memoir written after the fiction, she tries to communicate the actual sensations of her childhood in the St Ives ambience. Her earliest reminiscences recapture the sights and sounds from the perspective of the nursery:

> It is of lying half asleep, half awake, in bed in the nursery of St Ives. It is of hearing the waves breaking, one, two, one, two, and

sending a splash of water over the beach; . . . It is of hearing the blind draw its little acorn across the floor as the wind blew the blind out. It is of lying and hearing this splash and seeing this light.

The sound of the waves and the little acorn on the blind are accompanied by remembered colours of yellow, silver and green, luminescent hues. A second memory follows, marked by fragrance and touch:

> It still makes me feel warm; as if everything were ripe; humming; sunny; smelling so many smells at once . . . The gardens gave off a murmur of bees; the apples were red and gold; there were also pink flowers; and grey and silver leaves . . . It was rapture rather than ecstasy.

In a Proustian fashion, perhaps specifically under the earlier writer's direct influence, Woolf comments that she herself was merely the vehicle for the sensation, which is what is remembered and preserved: 'I am hardly aware of myself, but only of the sensation. I am only the container of the feeling of ecstasy, of the feeling of rapture.' Even in this strictly autobiographical piece the evasion of the self is noticeable. As Woolf went on to recall the looking-glass in the hall at Talland House, she commented that at the age of six she would tiptoe to see her face in it but was ashamed of doing so. In fact, she vaguely remembers a horrifying dream of a terrible monsterlike animal peering over her shoulder in the mirror – obviously an image which can be psychoanalysed in terms of childhood guilt. It can also suggest a fear of self – what Anaïs Nin, in fact, expresses as a minotaur which must be faced and conquered.

Central to the descriptions of the idyllic summers at St Ives are the images of the lighthouse and Julia Stephen. In describing Talland House, perched as it is on the hill, on several acres of garden and lawn, Woolf describes the perfectly open view of the Bay and the Godrevy lighthouse:

> The bay was a large lap, many-curved, sand-edged, silver green with sandhills, flowing to the Lighthouse rocks at one end, which made two black stops, one of them with the black and white Lighthouse tower on it.[22]

The actual description of Julia Duckworth Stephen looms from this reminiscence as the most compelling memory:

> Certainly there she was, in the very centre of the great Cathedral space which was childhood; there she was from the very first. My first memory is of her lap . . . She was the whole thing; Talland House was full of her.

Woolf then comments on the 'astonishing beauty' of her mother, which is immediately understood as the archetypal or life principle: 'She was keeping what I call in my shorthand the panoply of life . . . – in being.' One senses how this supreme mother figure was the creator of the happy world of Virginia's childhood – all of which vanished on the fateful day of Julia Stephen's untimely death.

It has been readily seen and acknowledged that *To the Lighthouse* was composed as an elegy to Julia Stephen, the mother of six, who died when Virginia was thirteen. One of the most compelling autobiographical statements ever written was Woolf's comments on her mother's death and its connection with that novel:

> Until I was in the forties, I could settle the date by seeing when I wrote *To the Lighthouse* . . . the presence of my mother obsessed me . . . But I wrote the book very quickly; and when it was written, I ceased to be obsessed by my mother. I no longer hear her voice; I do not see her.[23]

Thus, up to the age of 45, she tells of being haunted by the memory of her mother, the centre of her life and the limit of her childhood. In her novel, she transforms her mother into a constant factor in the midst of variables, as the personal element is upgraded to the artistic register.

Virginia's letters and diaries of the mid-1920s shed light on her attitude towards the writing of this novel and the personal element therein. In the genesis of the novel, the centre had actually shifted from her father to her mother. On 14 May 1925, Woolf noted in her diary:

> This is going to be fairly short; to have father's character done complete in it; & mother's; & St Ives; & childhood; & all the usual thing I try to put in – life, death &c. But the centre is father's character sitting in a boat, reciting . . . [24]

Subsequently, in a letter of 13 May 1927 to Vita Sackville-West, there is already apparent a tension regarding the primacy of the role of father or mother: 'as my mother died when I was 13 probably it is a child's view of her . . . she has haunted me; but then so did that old wretch my father.'[25] It is interesting that simultaneously Virginia received a letter from her sister Vanessa, who had just read the book for the first time; Vanessa commented on the primacy, authenticity and centrality of her mother in the novel:

> Anyhow it seemed to me that in the first part of the book you have given a portrait of mother which is more like her to me than anything I could have ever conceived of as possible. It is almost painful to have her so raised from the dead. You have made one feel the extraordinary beauty of her character, which must be the most difficult thing in the world to do.[26]

In response to this letter, Virginia wrote that she was flattered that her recollection, that her childhood view of her mother, could be considered so authentic:

> I'm in a terrible state of pleasure that you should think Mrs Ramsay so like mother. At the same time, it is a psychological mystery why she should be; how a child could know about her; except that she has always haunted me, partly, I suppose her beauty; and then dying at that moment.[27]

By the time of the publication of the book, therefore, it seemed clear and confirmed that Mrs Ramsay was at its centre, 'raised from the dead' and seen from a child's perspective. The father figure in the novel had become a peripheral character. Elsewhere, Woolf had stated that she refused to examine any letters of her mother, suggesting that she wanted to retain that pristine memory of her for her fiction.

The facts relating to the fiction are quite clear and transparent and have led to standard autobiographical readings. The Mrs Ramsay figure, aged 50 at the beginning of the novel parallels Julia Stephen who died at 49. Mrs Ramsay, the mother of eight children, most of whom the reader only knows vaguely, is a distinct parallel of Julia, who had seven of her own (in two marriages) and added Laura, the mentally disturbed child of Leslie Stephen's previous marriage. Virginia had called her half-sister her 'idiot sister'. Mr Ramsay is an

obvious match to Leslie Stephen, considerably older than his wife, and engaged in intellectual matters. Virginia later described her father as being 'Spartan, ascetic, puritanical'; the stern manner is transferred to Mr Ramsay who, constantly seeking sympathy and encouragement from his protective wife, categorically refuses to go to the lighthouse with his son James who consequently develops a hatred for his father. Finally, Lily Briscoe, who is 33 years old at the beginning of the novel, is 43 by its end and approaches the age of the Virginia Woolf herself, who completed *To the Lighthouse* at 45. The two Ramsay children who die in the 'Time Passes' section, Prue and Andrew, correspond to Stella Hills and Thoby Stephen. Virginia had witnessed the drama of the lives of these two siblings. Stella's romance and marriage to Jack Hills had been followed sadly by her death from peritonitis while newly pregnant in 1897; in *To the Lighthouse*, 'Prue Ramsay died that summer in some illness connected with childbirth.'[28] Another shock had been Thoby's sudden death from typhoid at the age of 25 in 1904; he had contracted the disease on a trip with his siblings to Greece. In *To the Lighthouse*, Woolf created the image of a young man dying in war: 'A shell exploded. Twenty or thirty young men were blown up in France, among them Andrew Ramsay.'

One of the first alterations of such facts for the fiction is to attribute Thoby's death to the Great War. Both in *Jacob's Room* and in *To the Lighthouse* Woolf intensifies the significance of Thoby's death by relating it to the devastation of the Great War. Although a marginal character in *To the Lighthouse*, he is the central character of the earlier novel, *Jacob's Room*. This experimental novel condenses 20 years of Thoby's life into what appears like one year marked by the passage of time through seasonal change. It chronicles the stages of the young man's life from his childhood at St Ives, to his stay at Trinity College, Cambridge, to his travels to Greece. Unlike the later novel which was to camouflage St Ives in the Hebrides, *Jacob's Room* situates it precisely in the authentic place and may have been inspired by an actual memory of Thoby associated with St Ives Bay which Virginia Woolf much later documents in her memoirs: ' I recover . . . one actual picture of Thoby: steering us in round the point without letting the sail flap.'[29] Framing Thoby's equivalent in the novel by the setting of the real locale could be seen as an effort to preserve Thoby there.

That image of Thoby in the boat, however, was followed by the series of deaths which afflicted her family. In her memoirs, in fact,

Woolf is reluctant to continue her narrative about her family and her past because she would have liked to keep the image of Thoby sailing carefree in his boat instead of following it with his and others' painful, premature deaths. *Jacob's Room* therefore communicates with respect to Thoby an atmosphere of pervasive and relentless death; the novel starts with allusion to the death of Jacob's father, Seabrook, and ends with reference to his own death. The year 1906 looms in the novel as a date associated with Jacob's stay at Cambridge; yet it is focused upon because it is the date of Thoby's death and the narrative is an attempt at an elegy for him. Although the elegy of *To the Lighthouse* is, to be sure, a more skilfully constructed artifact, here the mood of fragmentation of life incident conveys a mournful quality. An isolated litote, that of the shoes left behind in Jacob's room, and the mother pathetically wondering what to do with them, transmits the effect of pathos and loss. Actual artistic devices are minimal, however, in a novel which emanates atmosphere and chronology rather than symbol and universality and can be read unilaterally according to biographical reference.

In contrast, *To the Lighthouse*, proceeding as it does from the biographical material, transcends this base through the higher power of analogy. The nagging theme of the novel, to get to the lighthouse, may well have proceeded from an incident of frustration which was actually recorded in 1892. Quentin Bell has quoted the *Hyde Park Gate News* for September 1892 as stating:

> On Saturday morning Master Hilary Hunt and Master Basil Smith came up to Talland House and asked Master Thoby and Miss Virginia Stephen to accompany them to the lighthouse as Freeman the boatman said that there was a perfect tide and wind for going there. Master Adrian Stephen was much disappointed at not being allowed to go.[30]

This incident could very well have been the *donnée* for the novel, as Bell suggests – what Woolf expands into symbolic proportions and connects to Julia Stephen's presence. It is interesting that Woolf later reports in 'A Sketch of the Past' that of the eight children Julia Stephen cared for, Adrian was her favourite: 'him she cherished separately; she called him "My Joy" '.[31] In the novel, of course, his equivalent, James Ramsay, is the youngest child, the six-year-old, who is prevented from going to the lighthouse in the first section of the novel.

Such is the bare incident that may have propelled the beginning of the novel, particularly since Virginia Woolf must have chosen out of the many incidents of her life the one she could artistically enhance and most closely connect with her mother. In some respects, in its seeming triviality, it resembles a screen memory in Freudian terms. Its negative nature reminds one also of 'the drama of the kiss' in Proust and the pandying incident in Joyce. Such traumatic occurrences connected with childhood have central influence and are also material for fictional transmutation and elaboration. Yet the artistry starts with the sheer selection of such material.

On the other hand, far greater material with much wider implications infiltrates the central section, 'Time Passes', which has been called Woolf's *tour de force*. Woolf transposed a dark period of her life into the fiction, which she later identified in ' A Sketch of the Past': 'I shrink from the years 1897–1904 – the seven unhappy years.'[32] These were the years immediately following Julia Stephen's death, when Leslie had sold Talland House and trips to St Ives had ceased. It was also the period between Stella's and Leslie's deaths. Certain variations occur in the transposition to the novel. First, in the novel there cannot be any selling of the house after the death of Julia Stephen's equivalent, Mrs Ramsay, for the family returns ten years later to pick up the pieces of their lives. Secondly, the seven years are expanded to ten in the final version of the novel, and actually include the death of Mrs Ramsay. These years also include constant allusion to the First World War, thereby altering the dates and expanding the loss and devastation from that of a single family to a population at large. This central section of the novel with its dramatised scenes of deterioration and loss could not have existed without the element of aesthetic choice regarding the house as opposed to mimesis. The haunting presence of the Great War compounds the deaths, transferring the personal to the universal and even the cosmic. It is to be remembered that virtually all the novels of this era referred to the war in some manner. Woolf uses metaphoric language to convey the threat to the life principle – in particular the image of an abandoned house and the personification of darkness:

So with the lamps all put out, the moon sunk, and a thin rain drumming on the roof a downpouring of immense darkness began. Nothing, it seemed, could survive the flood, the profusion

of darkness which, creeping in at keyholes and crevices, stole round window blinds, came into bedrooms, swallowed up here a jug and a basin, there a bowl of red and yellow dahlias.[33]

This highly visual language is effective in portraying wholesale destruction – not on the battlefield, however, but in the individual household which could be perceived as a microcosm of the collective experience. Woolf has gone well beyond the single reference to the war in *Jacob's Room*, conveyed as it is through Jacob's death. The holographs of *To the Lighthouse* show that the first versions give direct reference to the Great War, whereas the later revisions replace the specifics of the war with more lasting allusions.

The transposition in this novel of locale from St Ives, Cornwall, to another real but faraway setting, the Hebrides, distances Virginia Stephen's own 'cathedral space' of childhood in both time and place. It is interesting that Virginia had never visited the Hebrides until well after the writing of *To the Lighthouse*, as Joyce had not visited Galway until after writing his story 'The Dead'. In both instances, the writers selected places which served as euphemisms for the remote and the faraway. It was only in 1938, over ten years after writing the novel, that Virginia and Leonard went on a holiday trip to Scotland, specifically to the island of Skye in the Hebrides, the very island she construed as the setting of the novel. Yet Virginia's description of Skye, in a letter to Vanessa of 25 June 1938, corresponds to the impression of it suggested by the novel:

> Well, here we are in Skye . . . completely remote . . . One should be a painter. As a writer, I feel the beauty, which is almost entirely colour, very subtle, very changeable.[34]

The sense of remoteness which figures prominently in the novel was later experienced by Virginia on this trip; however, it had already been anticipated by her imagination in the novel. In fact, just prior to the actual trip in 1938, Virginia had written a letter to Vita Sackville-West saying: 'We think of driving up to The Hebrides, the furthest seas – where the cuckoo calls. What's the quotation I'm thinking of?'[35] Nigel Nicolson has identified it as being from Wordsworth's poem 'The Solitary Reaper':

> A voice so thrillin' ne'er was heard
> In spring time from the cuckoo bird

>   Breaking the silence of the seas
>   Amongst the farthest Hebrides.

One fictional reference had led to another, since also in this simple poem the Hebrides had been associated with distance and 'the faraway'.

Ironically, Woolf's literal-minded readers objected to her use and description of the Hebrides on the grounds that it was unauthentic. Virginia wrote in a letter of 22 May 1927 that Lord Olivier had objected to her inaccurate description of the natural setting, of its flora and fauna:

> Lord Olivier writes that my horticulture and natural history is in every instance wrong: there are no rooks, elms, or dahlias in the Hebrides; my sparrows are wrong: so are my carnations.[36]

How, then, in 'Time Passes' could darkness 'swallow up' a 'bowl of red and yellow dahlias'? Virginia herself explicitly stated in the same letter that she was not out to defend any accuracy in such matters. In a letter to Violet Dickinson of 5 June 1927, Virginia showed her awareness of her poetic license and her intention to blur any exact equivalence: 'People in The Hebrides are very angry. Is it Cornwall? I'm not as sure as you are.'[37]

Woolf had manipulated place for the purpose of art. The substitution of the Hebrides for Cornwall was an artistic process which depersonalised what could be regarded as a transparent story, allowing it to acquire an ambiguity which no one could clarify but to which all could relate. On the personal level, since the separation from her childhood and her mother was the focus of the novel, she sought to give that impression of distance. Since the family never returned to Cornwall after Julia Stephen's death, that death had distanced the place in real life. On a universal level, Woolf went beyond Proust's notion of recapturing a personal past in memory to render elements of that past eternal and objective through art.

The symbolisation of the lighthouse becomes the shift towards objectivity. Moving the actual Godrevy lighthouse of St Ives to the Hebrides is the first step in endowing it with larger repercussions than those associated with its physical site. As James commented toward the end of the novel, there were two lighthouses, the tangible one that was reached and seen at close quarters and the imagined or 'other' one that had always been seen from afar and

had become an objective. Like her character, Woolf had proceeded from the 'real' one to the created one, the artifact of the imagination.

Any visitor to St Ives today can ascertain that the Godrevy light-house is within viewing distance of Talland House and a dominant presence from the perspective of the house. It must have been a haunting image for Virginia in her earliest years; she would wake up and see it standing there sharp and clear; at night she would sleep following its beams. She would also have contemplated the gulf of the bay that separates the lighthouse from the projecting peninsula. It is true even now that little boats are warned against going into that little inlet because of sudden currents that could smash them against the jagged rocks which surround the base of the lighthouse. Realistically speaking, it may indeed become a journey to reach this lighthouse right off the coast because of the unpredict-able dangers surrounding it. Such impediments regarding some-thing so near adds an oxymoronic quality to the lighthouse: a combination of closeness and distance, which Virginia exploited in her novel to suggest her emotional relationship to her past. The Hebrides, then, increased that sense of remoteness; situating the lighthouse there makes it even harder to reach. Furthermore, the actual peninsula in Cornwall which projects toward the lighthouse is wild and uninhabited, with scattered brush. This landscape is turned into a 'moonlike' terrain in the novel and may have been suggestive to Woolf of the primitive nature of parts of the Hebrides:

> The hoary Lighthouse, distant, austere, in the midst; and on the right as far as the eye could see, fading and falling, in soft low pleats, green sand dunes with wild flowing grasses on them, which always seemed to be running away into some moon country, uninhabited of men.[38]

Despite the life analogies in her fiction, Virginia Woolf refused to foresee any one distinct 'meaning' in the lighthouse image. She states this point explicitly to Roger Fry in a letter of 27 May 1927, saying that her use of symbolism in the novel was vague and generalised and that the novel would serve as the repository for the readers' emotions:

> I meant nothing by The Lighthouse. One has to have a central line drawn down the middle of the book to hold the design together. I saw that all sorts of feelings would accrue to this, but I refused to

think them out, and trusted that people would make it the deposit for their own emotions – which they have done, one thinking it means one thing, another another. I can't manage Symbolism except in this vague, generalised way. Whether its right or wrong I don't know, but directly I'm told what a thing means, it becomes hateful to me.[39]

She was responding to Roger Fry's statement that 'arriving at the Lighthouse has a symbolic meaning which escapes me'.[40] Actually, she was unconsciously under the influence of the Symbolist poets on the Continent, providing as they had done in their art a rich ambiguity of interpretation. In avoiding direct allegory she would prevent an overt biographical reading of her work which would return it to the personal level.

Woolf unwittingly fulfilled the Symbolist approach through the larger implications of her novel. She had translated the personal loss of a mother who was the centre of her existence to a philosophical dilemma of modern man or woman in an existential position confronting the void. This modernist predicament becomes the 'pattern' behind the death of her mother. Woolf introduces artistic objects (the lighthouse), a persona (Mrs Ramsay) and situations (Lily's painting and the journey to the lighthouse) to construct a mythology regarding the loss and substitutions. It is tempting to identify the artist figure with Woolf herself and the painting with the writing because of the analogies that Woolf had always made between writing and painting, with her close affinity with her artist-sister Vanessa. Yet at the same time the impersonality of the artist figure and her measured distance from Mrs Ramsay enables Woolf to position herself with respect to the memory of her mother and that consuming loss.

If the novel itself was prompted by the need to eradicate once and for all the haunting death of a beloved mother, it ultimately succeeds in altering the perspective from death to life, from subject to object, through the prevailing lighthouse image at the end. Woolf depersonalises her mother through a double transfer: creating the Mrs Ramsay figure who identifies herself with the beams of the lighthouse which then replaces her as the guiding light. Through this movement from the subject to the object, Woolf triumphs both over the personal loss and over the sense of morality which was a personal obsession and the undercurrent of this novel. She also turns the personal into an abstraction, since the lighthouse

ultimately suggests a goal and guide for all of humanity 'lost at sea' and searching for an anchor.

The very process of association which links the memory of the mother to the lighthouse scene is explained much later by Woolf in a section of 'A Sketch of the Past'. As will be seen in Anaïs Nin's *The Novel of the Future*, Woolf analyses in retrospect significant aspects of her fictional technique regarding autobiographical transposition. She illustrates what she calls symbol making and scene making. First, in referring to the death of her half-sister Stella, Woolf recalls the tragic and agonised figure of Stella's husband, Jack Hills. Woolf recounts that at the time of Stella's death there was a certain tree, resembling a skeleton, standing prominently outside the garden house. Woolf perceived that particular tree in terms of the effect of Stella's death on Jack Hill as 'the emblem, the symbol of the skeleton agony to which her death had reduced him'.[41] This transfer from the bereaved figure to the object objectified the emotion and kept it for eternity. In an analogous manner, Woolf must have gone about creating the symbol of the lighthouse in her art. But the lighthouse, instead of simply designating a loss, was further elaborated into a vehicle of substitution and turned into an abstraction.

In this process of 'symbol making' an aesthetic object is produced in the transfer of the actual Godrevy lighthouse of Woolf's childhood days to the fabricated one in the Hebrides. Since the scene or symbol is grounded in reality, Woolf notes that they 'are not altogether a literary device' but a natural means of capturing the past and making it 'representative; enduring'. She considers her susceptibility to the recollection of representative scenes to be the source of her creativity. Such 'scene making' was the process used to capture her mother from the past and suggest a larger significance. Woolf was to explain this fully in 'A Sketch of the Past':

> in all the writing I have done, I have almost always had to make a scene, either when I am writing about a person; I must find a representative scene in their lives.

Analogy, as formulated in her aesthetics, is the means by which Woolf links the life facts to the artifacts in her novel. It is readily seen from the start that the lighthouse is connected to the Mrs Ramsay figure: 'and pausing there she looked out to meet that stroke of the Lighthouse, the long steady stroke, the last of the three, which was her stroke'[42] The Mrs Ramsay figure, in turn, reflects the

Mrs Stephen one. The remoteness of the Hebrides distances both Woolf's mother and her memory of her, yet the fact that the Hebrides is a real place rather than a fabricated one emphasises the 'real' dimension in coping with the problem of loss. The lighthouse becomes the artistic material anchor which harbours the memory of the mother – as Proust's material objects mediate his process of memory. Analogous to the association of Mrs Stephen with the Godrevy lighthouse is the identification of Mrs Ramsay with the fabricated Hebrides lighthouse. As both mothers, real and fictional, are eradicated, the lighthouse remains the lasting symbol of them and their significance.

Another analogy is constructed with respect to pictorial art through Lily Briscoe's painting, which is finally completed. The picture itself has been an enigma to many readers of the novel especially with respect to the line drawn down the middle and the relation between the masses: the wall, the hedge and the tree. Avrom Fleishman, in his book on Woolf, equates the line with the lighthouse itself – as the connecting link between the near and the faraway, between the garden and the bay, between the vision and the journey. The obvious reading is that Lily offers the artist's view of the mother and the positioning of her in relation to the world of nature and the indifferent universe. Like Virginia with her pen, Lily aims to 'break the vacancy'[43] with her brush, 'the one dependable thing in a world of strife, ruin, chaos'. Early in the novel, Lily counters William Bankes, the scientist who questions the abstractions of her painting, as he is accustomed to precise, representational art:

> The truth was that all his prejudices were on the other side, he explained. The largest picture in his drawing room, which painters had praised, and valued at a higher price than he had given for it was of the cherry trees in blossom on the banks of the Kennet . . . But now – he turned, with his glasses raised to the scientific examination of her canvas. The question being one of the relation of masses, of lights and shadows, which, to be honest, he had never considered before . . .

Here, the prosaic literalist view is distinguished from the artistic, poetic one of the modernist painter and writer. Woolf, like Proust before her, is projecting her own aesthetic orientation into that of a painter-character. For Lily Briscoe can indeed be compared to

Proust's Elstir, whose marine landscape recreated the observed scene as it eliminated strict boundaries between land and sea. Although Proust's Elstir has been associated with Impressionist aesthetics whereas Lily has been connected to Neo-Impressionism, there is a striking similarity in the focus on the artists' movement away from strict representation – as almost a metaphor for the writers' aesthetics of autobiography.

It seems apparent that Virginia Woolf was incorporating Roger Fry's aesthetics into Lily Briscoe's painting, which in turn was to shed light on her own autobiographical art. Once again, as in the case of Proust, the aesthetics of the pictorial artist within the novel reflects that of the artist's creator. In the first section of the novel, the reduction of the portrait of mother and child framed by the window to an equivalent form or purple shadow may indeed shock the literalist William Bankes: 'Mother and child then – objects of universal veneration . . . might be reduced, he pondered, to a purple shadow without irreverence.' But beyond the obvious interpretation, this reduction reflects precisely the use of formal analogy that Fry had explained in *Vision and Design*: 'not to imitate life but to find an equivalent for life'. Lily Briscoe has in fact found 'an equivalent for life' in her recreation of mother and child through shapes and colour. Woolf had also found an equivalent for her search for her mother through the narrative of the journey to the lighthouse. The aesthetics of the painting is therefore analogous to the writer's treatment of her life.

Moreover, a technique of condensation is used in the final reduction of Mrs Ramsay or the triangle to the line drawn down the middle of the painting by Lily Brisoce, who thereby has her vision or epiphany at the end of the novel. This particular stroke had been much anticipated throughout the novel, as Lily toyed laboriously with the idea of moving the tree to the middle. The tree, an artifact in the painting, becomes the analogy for the life centre, displacing the void created by the physical death, and superimposed, as it were, onto the inert lighthouse. By a series of associations, therefore, Mrs Ramsay is connected to the line, and the three components, the human, the natural and the object, are included in the painting. Again, it is interesting that Roger Fry had theoretically dealt with the positioning of masses and had specifically analysed the quality of line: 'the condensation of the greatest possible suggestion of real form into the simplest, most easily apprehended line'.[44] Hence, Mrs Ramsay is condensed into a line and simultaneously substituted by

the lighthouse, which in turn can be equated to a tree, the equivalent for her as a life force. These analogies to the second degree highlight similar processes used by the author in her fiction, as she presents two approaches to the problems of loss. One can be called the life approach – the journey to the lighthouse and the acceptance of direction; the other would be the artistic approach – the painting and the novel itself. The condensation to the single journey and the sole painting sets the memory in formal terms. The technique of analogy succeeds in objectifying and transcending the very personal material of the novel.

We have seen how Virginia Woolf's own approach in writing the novel is analogous to Lily Briscoe's act of painting. To have made Lily a writer would have been too representational, and Woolf obviously avoided the risk, run by Proust, of being directly associated with a writer figure. Instead, there is the ambiguity of the source for the artist Lily, who could suggest Vanessa Bell or Roger Fry as well as Woolf. Instead of direct identification, there is an analogous association of Lily with the author.

Both the author and the artist character insist on the transformational rather than the representational qualities of their art in keeping with Roger Fry's statement that the purpose of literature is 'the creation of structures which have for us the feeling of reality, and that these structures are self contained, self sufficing, and not to be valued by their references to what lies outside'.[45] Hence, in the process of transformation, the referential factor becomes negligible as the artistic analogy has transcended it. The autobiographical ingredients are less than the sum total of the aesthetic product, which is true of all four writers considered in this mode.

Like the alteration of place, there is manipulation of the time dimensions in this novel to suggest the relativity of time to counter the finality of death. It has already been noted that Woolf shifts the dark period of her own life forward a decade to the war years which engulf her personal tragedies. Within this period, expansion and condensation of time occur, which amount to another aesthetic device destroying mimesis. The novel juxtaposes the 'before' and 'after' of a haunting presence. In first recovering a September afternoon and evening in the first section, 'The Window', the novel lets time lag and concentrates on the activities of life. The commanding presence of a Mrs Ramsay is felt through protracted mundane occurrences: the walk to the town with Mr Tansley; the knitting of the sock for the lighthouse keeper's son; the reading of a fairy tale to

the youngest son James; a visitor losing a brooch and getting engaged; and the *boeuf en daube* dinner at the end of the day. In contrast, the middle section, 'Time Passes', counters the sense of duration with that of mortality and vicissitude. One evening multiplies into ten years of darkness as the war years are spanned and numerous deaths are charted.

Most striking are the brief parenthetical statements concerning the death of Mrs Ramsay, Prue and Andrew – which would not have been made for the real-life equivalents. In the condensation of these three deaths into impersonal declarative statements of facts, Woolf juxtaposes the insignificance of individual human lives with the multiple deaths suggested by a Great War and with the inevitable vulnerability of the humankind. First, she frames a scene to communicate succinctly the pathos of the death of Mrs Ramsay:

[Mr Ramsay, stumbling along a passage one dark morning, stretched his arms out, but Mrs Ramsay having died rather suddenly the night before, his arms, though stretched out, remained empty.][46]

This particular death, which is treated in a controlled, unsentimental way, is distanced from the original autobiographical emotion. It is dislocated further by being subsumed within the multiple deaths suggested by the war:

So with the house empty and the doors locked and the mattresses rolled round, those stray airs, advance guards of great armies, blustered in . . .

Woolf continues to compound deaths not in a scene but in a subsequent bracket which is a capsule of the death of her half-sister. Finally, in yet a third bracket, Woolf frames a statement regarding her brother's death, here attributed to the Great War as it had been in *Jacob's Room*. These three incidents, perfunctorily stated in objective telegraphic style, are made to diffuse the sentimentality that might normally accompany them in real life terms and absorb these tragedies into the larger scheme of mortality, suggested here by the Great War. The use of parenthetical brackets is an ironic understatement of the devastation – both personal and collective – which haunted Woolf and her contemporaries.

Against this cruel reality are the housekeeper's slow movements in picking up the pieces left dispersed in the abandoned house. Unlike Virginia, who was prevented from revisiting Talland House and the past it harboured, the characters in the novel eventually return to the sense of the past and move forward with substitutions. The 'morning after' the ten years of absence resumes the sense of prolonged time communicated at the beginning of the novel. The focus of this third section, the art of Lily Briscoe, is a counterpart to the reality of living and is suggestive of Woolf's own perspective with respect to her past. For in the novel it takes Lily as much time to draw a definitive line down the middle of the painting as it does to live the lives of the Ramsays. Art serves as a solace, creating a *durée* against the ephemeral nature of human existence. The vision of Lily captures Mrs Ramsay in an enduring moment. A slow morning counteracts the preceding ten years' passage, and a vision is achieved which suggests means of attaining a secular sense of mortality. That is to say, the 'irreverence' that Bankes had referred to in the painting is interpreted at the end. In the place of the mother and child and their 'religious' connotation is substituted an abstract painting of shapes, colours and lines which appear definitively when the actual journey to the lighthouse is accomplished. What is being suggested is that memory is immortalised in the painting and transferred to the material lighthouse as its anchor by the power of association. The transfer of the subjective feelings to the objective lighthouse, as the three members of the Ramsay family reach the goal of their excursion, is a process which parallels the transfer from life into art which Woolf herself achieves in the composition of her novel.

Whereas in *To the Lighthouse* Woolf had concentrated on preserving the memory of her mother's presence, in *Mrs Dalloway*, the earlier novel, she had sought a funnel to explore her own personality, particularly with respect to her personal metaphysical angst. In a sense, this novel may have been a more complicated work since it was a question of analysing her own split personality which she defensively desired to hide and camouflage. As we have seen, Woolf's distance from Freud must have involved an inherent fear of revealing selfhood, which can actually be deduced from her fiction. But in proceeding from the personal to the existential self in this novel, Woolf projects her obsessions with madness, suicide and death onto her renditions of identity.

The actual figure of Mrs Dalloway was drawn, according to Quentin Bell, from a certain acquaintance, Kitty Lushington, who

had been a guest and protégée of Julia Stephen at St Ives and had been engaged to Leo Maxse in 1890. When Kitty succumbed to a mysterious death, falling down stairs in 1922, Virginia interpreted it as a suicide. However, to claim this reference as a source would be, as Daniel Ferrer has noted, 'a reductive conception of fiction and reality',[47] particularly since Woolf herself had actually attempted suicide in 1904. One might say, rather, that the news of this particular death along with Woolf's own obsessions became the impetus for the suicide element in *Mrs Dalloway*.

The novel compounded the various deaths that Woolf had bereaved along with her own hidden flirtation with suicide and obscured them in a double. In her diary entry of 14 October 1922, Woolf follows the notation of Kitty Lushington's bewildering death with an analysis of *Mrs Dalloway*, her book in progress at that time:

> Mrs Dalloway has branched into a book; & I adumbrate here a study of insanity & suicide: the world seen by the sane & the insane side by side – something like that; Septimus Smith? – is that a good name? – & to be more close to the fact than Jacob, but I think Jacob was a necessary step, for me, in working free[48]

Earlier in the year she had connected her writing of *Jacob's Room* with the consciousness of death: 'I meant to write about death, only life came breaking in as usual.'[49] If previously she had dealt with the death of her brother Thoby, in the case of *Mrs Dalloway* she interweaves the society lady's death with the potential of her own.

It is a fact that Woolf's original plan was to have Clarissa kill herself, as indicated in the introduction to the 1928 American edition of the novel; but she then decided to create the *alter ego* figure of Septimus Warren Smith to bear that burden. Having already tried suicide twice in her life, Virginia had the materials for this character. In 1904, shortly after her father's death, Virginia had thrown herself out of the window while being cared for by her close friend Violet Dickinson in Burnham Wood. Interestingly, this is the method she gives to Septimus Warren Smith, who actually succeeds in killing himself. In another instance, in 1913, just after her marriage to Leonard Woolf, she was found unconscious after taking a hundred grams of veronal. Having complained of 'hearing voices' at numerous instances of insanity throughout her life (even to the very end in the letter she left to Vanessa in March 1941 at the time of her suicide), Virginia had at first hand the materials for the insane character. She

had, after all, been confined in a Twickenham nursing home on four occasions: 1910, 1912, 1913 and 1915. During that time she had developed a mistrust of her physicians, Doctors Savage and Craig; they have been perceived by recent critics as having upper-middle-class, late-Victorian attitudes unsympathetic to Woolf's artistic temperament. In *All that Summer She was Mad*, a title taken from Quentin Bell's characterisation of the summer of 1904, Stephen Trombley sees Virginia Woolf as a victim of what Michel Foucault would call 'the discourse of power'. Trombley suggests that Woolf's animosity toward the doctors who were treating her was due to their lack of understanding of her real condition as a woman artist. Anaïs Nin was later to express the same concerns.

In discussing the four doctors who actually treated Woolf, Trombley singles out Dr T. B. Hyslop as specifically antagonistic to Woolf's artistic milieu. Citing Hyslop's article, 'Post-Illusionism and Art in the Insane' (1911) as declaring 'the collective insanity'[50] of the Bloomsbury painters, Trombley summarises Hyslop's reactionary views:'the criteria we may extract from Hyslop's comments make two things clear: plastic art, to remain within the bounds of sanity must be representative'. Hyslop had written:

> The distorted representations of objects, or partial displacements of external facts, are known technically as 'illusions' . . . Postmaniacal illusionism is almost invariably distorted, and the faulty representations bear little significance except as manifestations of disease.[51]

Such authoritarian views indicate that Woolf's aesthetics would have been viewed as aberrant by the very doctors who 'treated' her insanity.

The antagonism was obviously mutual. Trombley also comments on the overt carry-over to the novel: 'In *Mrs Dalloway* Virginia presents a sustained attack on psychiatry as she experienced it. The two doctors – Holmes and Sir William Bradshaw – are modelled on the four doctors [Sir George Henry Savage, Sir Maurice Craig, Sir Henry Head, and Dr T. B. Hyslop].'[52] It is indeed true that as early as 26 November 1904 Virginia confessed to Violet Dickinson in a letter: 'My life is a constant fight against Doctor's follies, it seems to me.'[53] Such negative feelings are, of course, transferred to Septimus Smith, who flees his psychiatrist Sir William Bradshaw when he tries to commit him to an institution. The therapeutic measures designed

for the 30-year-old Septimus echo those offered to Virginia in her early thirties – what she herself would have abhorred. The novel undermines Bradshaw's prognosis:

> To his patients he gave three-quarters of an hour . . . Health we must have and health is proportion . . . order rest in bed; rest in solitude; silence rest; rest without friends, without books, without messages; six months' rest; until a man who went in weighing seven stone six comes out weighing twelve.[54]

Even the reference to necessary weight gain suggests Virginia's weight-loss during her bouts of madness.

From such specific hints it is obvious that despite the fact that an actual model can be found for Mrs Dalloway, there is a certain transfer of Woolf herself into this figure. But again, what occurs in the formation of this character is simultaneously an identification and a distancing. Septimus Smith, the nondescript shell-shocked war veteran, is a second derivative and conglomerate of the sources anterior to Mrs Dalloway, the intermediary. He is also a representative character, whose very individuality paradoxically reflects the collective identity. Ultimately, therefore, the novel reaches an abstract level, personifying the twentieth-century Self and its existential undercurrents in the aftermath of the Great War.

The allusions to the Great War through the character of the shell-shocked war veteran intensifies the preoccupation with death and mortality throughout the novel. Septimus, desensitised to the point of not accepting the death of his friend Evans during the war, is a symbolic figure of humanity as a whole in the postwar era: 'London had swallowed up millions of young men called Smith.'[55] Woolf herself had proclaimed her hatred for this war as 'the preposterous male fiction', and here, as in *To the Lighthouse*, she has it seep through the crevices of the narrative to be the spiritual basis of the unease of her characters. At the same time it is sensed as having tormented her own individual soul.

Starting from the personal, Woolf projects two sides of her personality into two characters, the society hostess and the war veteran, thereby splitting that self into two objective segments. A similar splitting, we recall, occurred with Joyce *vis-à-vis* his characters Stephen Dedalus and Leopold Bloom. But Woolf highlights the notion of segmentation even further by also splitting the Mrs Dalloway figure from the public presence to the private self known

as 'Clarissa', who in turn mirrors the Septimus figure in its solitude
and separation. As the inner, hidden self is projected onto Septimus,
the parallels become all too clear. The alienation, the bouts of insanity accompanied by the hearing of voices, the jumping from the window, the suspicions of the Establishment and in particular of
society's physicians are components of the Virginia Woolf that was
anguished and alienated. On the other hand, the Mrs Dalloway figure who is the wife of the Member of Parliament represents the conventional self which at times surmounts the inner one. The evening
dress that Mrs Dalloway repairs in the course of the day reflects a
successful achievement of the integration of personality and completeness. As the hours progress towards evening, she heroically
stitches that potentially divided self back together in a silken fabric
of selfhood.

Chronologically speaking, *Mrs Dalloway* was published two years
before *To the Lighthouse*, and it is interesting to observe the evolution
of the female characters from the one novel to the next. As already
noted, there are subtle but marked tensions in the Mrs Dalloway
character – between her domestic duties as wife, mother and hostess, and her separateness and individualism, which surge forth
intermittently, seeking expression in the course of the fateful day.
The desire for the narrow bed, the feeling of distance that she often
has with her husband, the sudden and intense empathy she has for
the unknown Septimus Smith, all relate to that proclivity for individualism and significance which her social self must dutifully sup-
press. Early in the novel and early in the June day, Woolf catches the
private side of her character through highly suggestive figurative
language:

> Like a nun withdrawing or a child exploring a tower, she went
> upstairs, paused at the window, came to the bathroom. There was
> the green linoleum and a tap dripping. There was an emptiness
> about the heart of life; an attic room. Women must put off their
> rich apparel. At midday they must disrobe . . . Narrower and
> narrower would her bed be.[56]

The narrow bed and the attic room are objectifications of Mrs
Dalloway's inner self, 'which could not dispel a virginity preserved
through childbirth which clung to her like a sheet'. These interior
spaces seem to anticipate areas of the self which Anaïs Nin was to
identify in a much more elaborate way in her *Cities of the Interior*, as

we shall see. As for Mrs Dalloway, her feeling of prolonged virginity sustains her separateness despite her marriage. Woolf translates Mrs Dalloway's reticence into an allusive description which suggests a degree of self-analysis:

> Lovely in girlhood, suddenly there came a moment . . . – when, through some contraction of this cold spirit, she had failed him . . . She could see what she lacked. It was not beauty; it was not mind. It was something central which permeated; something warm which broke up surfaces and rippled the cold contact of man and woman, or of women together.

Through a variety of means which involve the creation of conflicting persona and symbol making, therefore, Woolf succeeds in objectifying the tensions between the two selves. The party metaphor in this novel has been acknowledged by many critics as reflecting the celebration of the life factor, and it is clear that Woolf was working with this image in the outline for *Mrs Dalloway*, what she first contemplated calling 'At Home, or, The Party'. In the story 'Mrs Dalloway in Bond Street', which preceded the novel, the Mrs Dalloway figure appears frivolous compared with the compelling concerns of the later novelistic character. This latter version of Mrs Dalloway achieves integration of the divided selves in the unity and celebration of the party of life. The female figure is ultimately cast as a stereotype, using her traditionally unifying ways to bring together herself and the disparate people who are present at her party. In this process of giving and relating outwards, Mrs Dalloway wards off the death factor of separateness and time – which were obviously troubling Virginia Woolf herself: 'What business had the Bradshaws to talk of death at her party? A young man had killed himself.'

Along with the two 'anonymous' personae, Septimus Smith, the victim of war, and the old lady neighbour, the victim of time, are such symbols as Big Ben and the Serpentine in Kensington Gardens. The geographically identifiable places in London are suggestive of the obsessive death factor which is the undercurrent of the novel. Mrs Dalloway, in fact, is made to interpret the two personae. She understands all too well the act of suicide by an unknown war veteran and human compatriot: 'Death was an attempt to communicate; people feeling the impossibility of reaching the centre which, mystically, evaded them.'[57] Similarly, she observes with compassion the elderly neighbour, quietly going to bed and tolerating the

passage of time which has had its inevitable effect on her. Connections are also made with the geographic places. On her walk, Mrs. Dalloway associates the throwing of a penny into the Serpentine with the throwing away of a life by suicide. Later, as she gazes out of her window at a particular moment of Big Ben's toll, she observes the old lady's fatal conditioning to the tyranny of time and links the person to the object:

> Big Ben struck the half hour. How extraordinary it was, strange, yes, touching, to see the old lady (they had been neighbours ever so many years) move away from the window, as if she were attached to that sound, that string. Gigantic as it was, it had something to do with her. Down, down, into the midst of ordinary things the finger fell, making the moment solemn.

This mosaic of interconnected persons and places lends a symbolism to the narrative which is reminiscent of Proust's conflation of the real and the fictional.

Even more specifically, like Joyce and his Ballast clock in Dublin, Woolf has expounded upon a very visible and quotidian structure of London life. The giant clock is conveyed in its material presence. Its foreboding aura, with its objective pronouncement of the passage of time, subsumes Woolf's obsessions with death. In the novel, it is readily identified with the irrevocability of ageing; both old lady and bell, at once, objectively embody and engulf instincts of singleness and death. The novel, with its designated tollings of Big Ben and other London bells, communicates the pervasive consciousness of death and the passage of time. Simultaneously, however, Woolf has her key character, Mrs Dalloway, counter this tolling with her commitment to life. In setting life against death through the contemporaneous existence of Mrs Dalloway and Septimus Smith, Woolf has life loom as the triumphant factor.

When it came to creating representative female characters, Woolf obviously envisaged a plurality of role models due to her historic period and the changing stereotypes of her time. Unlike Anaïs Nin, who later proliferated her many selves into basically one type of modern woman, Woolf considered a variety of types. In her own particular environment, she was exposed to three types of women: her domestic mother, the artist figure which she and her sister Vanessa represented, and the outlandish androgynous exemplar of her friend and lover, Vita Sackville-West. Her novels of the 1920s

manage to depict each of these three types, as she seeks to situate herself among the various evolving roles that women were assuming.

The Mrs Dalloway figure, despite its tensions, combined tendencies to independence and domesticity. But when Woolf reached *To the Lighthouse*, she must have realised that such a reconciliation was no longer plausible. For in this next novel, she went on to create two very different women: Mrs Ramsay and Lily Briscoe, as we have seen. The pure mother, altruistic and giving, is set against the selfish, introverted artist. Mrs Ramsay is much more integrated than Mrs Dalloway, with no apparent tensions in her personality, because she is all-giving. As a kind of earth mother of eight children, in contrast to the less fertile Mrs Dalloway with her single, disloyal child, Mrs Ramsay with her maternal aspect is heightened into total domesticity. As the centre of the lives around her, she brings them all together until her untimely death. But in Mrs Ramsay's devastating death, Woolf seems to be putting an end to this Victorian woman, as a former type of woman, who may be no longer viable in postwar society. The very allusions to the war, in the course of which she dies, create a historical barrier between her and the modern world. On the other hand, the Lily Briscoe character emerges from the war to complete the painting and to leave her mark as an emergent modern woman.

It is striking that, just prior to writing 'A Room of One's Own', Woolf was evolving her feminism by allowing the artist woman to prevail, despite what was perceived to be her singleness, separateness, selfishness and general alienation. In *To the Lighthouse* the very failure of the marriage of Paul Rayley and Minta Doyle in the years after Mrs Ramsay's death also puts that singleness into a more common context of general humanity. In the creation, therefore, of these two very distinct women in *To the Lighthouse*, Woolf has removed the tensions of the previous Mrs Dalloway and moved on to the first expressions of 'the new woman' with whom she could no doubt associate.

The tendency on Woolf's part to blur identifications of herself even as they are suggested, as was the case with both Mrs Dalloway and Lily Briscoe, suggests her ultimate desire to prevent autobiographical readings in her prevailing demand for privacy. Perhaps, also, not fully satisfied with a mirror image of herself as a model for 'the new woman', she went on to further experiment, even in jest with the androgynous figure in *Orlando*. Here, there is no ambiguity

in the source of the title character: Virginia's beloved aristocratic friend and lover, Vita Sackville-West. In a letter of 9 October 1927, Woolf had made her designs whimsical but quite clear:

> But listen; suppose Orlando turns out to be Vita; and its all about you and the lusts of your flesh and the lure of your mind . . . Shall you mind? Say yes, or No.[58]

Vita's response in a letter two days later was positive, giving Woolf leeway in the development of the character: 'My God, Virginia, if ever I was thrilled and terrified it is at the prospect of being projected into the shape of Orlando.' Shortly thereafter, Vita fully accepted that identity by signing her letters 'Orlando'.

It would seem that Woolf was seeking 'the other' in the model for Orlando, an approach to her self which she had not yet attempted. The passionate Vita, who fascinated Virginia for at least ten years (the height of their relationship ranged from 1925–35), was what Virginia was not, despite the fact that both were writers. For Vita was descended from an ancient noble lineage and had the huge manor estate of Knole which had been in the family since Elizabethan times. Incongruously, she had a Spanish gypsy grandmother, who had added the spice of illegitimacy to the family line. Furthermore, Vita had an unconventional lifestyle; as the mother of two sons and wife to Harold Nicolson, she remained a free spirit who admitted to open homosexual practices. Bilingual in French and peripatetic, an ardent lover of nature and expert gardener, she exuded adventure and earthiness. Virginia had marvelled at her radiance and ripeness and capacity to 'control silver, servants, chow dogs; her motherhood . . . her being in short (what I have never been) a real woman. Then there is some voluptuousness about her . . . .'[59] Such was rich material for the novelist, and Virginia thought about equally scintillating devices she could use in the recreation of this personality: 'And instantly the usual exciting devices enter my mind: a biography beginning in the year 1500 & continuing to the present day, called *Orlando*: Vita; only with a change about from one sex to another.'[60]

Using Vita as her model and dedicating the mock biography to her, Woolf had an opportunity to intentionally upset and 'revolutionise' (as she put it in her letter to Vita) the standard notion of biography by dealing with a 20-year life span over a 400-year history. In giving hints of the formidable history of the Sackvilles through the one char-

acter, she creates a historical composite, spanning the years from about 1570 to 1928, moving from Elizabethan youth to the modern woman writer, aged 36 – the very age of Vita at the time of the book's publication. Manipulating the time dimension once again, she moves 'the self' over time, creating an irreconcilable multidimensional personality. As she moves Orlando into the twentieth century, she attributes to her the complexities of the twentieth-century self.

But Woolf does not allow Orlando to find what she called 'a Captain Self' as Mrs Dalloway had. In focusing on Orlando's androgyny, along with the sex change, Woolf seems to have incorporated in this character some of the notions of Proust regarding selfhood. One recalls that, in the discussion of Swann's loves, Proust had written about one self dying, yielding to another. In *Orlando* Woolf sums up the genealogy of the self as she traced it in the biography of her fictional character:

> For she [Orlando] had a great variety of selves to call upon, far more than we have been able to find time for, since a biography is considered complete if it merely accounts for six or seven selves, whereas a person may well have as many as a thousand.[61]

Leaving Orlando in the early twentieth century seeking 'a Captain Self', Woolf paints her incomplete, open-ended and problematic. Woolf selects a crisis year for Vita: 1928, the very year of the death of her father Lionel and the resulting loss of Knole to her uncle Charles, the fourth Lord Sackville and the next in line. The last views of Orlando are therefore of a woman driving a motor car in London, a writer with a certain amount of success from her nature poem 'The Oak Tree', and a woman visiting the old manor home, which appears now more as a museum with ghosts of the past lining the imposing corridors. Once again, Woolf touches upon a sense of history, the passage of time, the tension between the past and the present in the very existence of a young woman entering the future with uncertainty.

What began as a mock biography of a living loved one became a serious questioning of the status of the twentieth-century intelligent, liberated woman. Instead of creating a fictional character as she had done with her other works, Woolf obviously saw a type right before her, who harboured many of the dilemmas that the modern woman might confront and whose audacity surpassed a fabricated persona. The transparency with which Orlando reflected

Vita, substantiated by the dedication and photographs, merged the fictional and the real. Also, experimenting with the fusion of the male and the female in Orlando, Woolf challenged the stereotypical antitheses of the sexes that were assumptions in *To the Lighthouse.*

If *Mrs Dalloway* and *To the Lighthouse* could be considered acts of therapy for a writer trying to rid herself of certain obsessions, *Orlando* was no longer therapeutic but prescriptive. The friendship with Vita had given Virginia much comfort during the years of ascent, as Vita, though ten years younger, was like a surrogate mother to her. Virginia stated that Vita 'lavishes on me the maternal protection which, for some reason, is what I have always most wished from everyone'.[62] Since Woolf knew nothing consciously of psychological transfers, she could never admit to herself the fusion with 'the other', as Anaïs Nin later did in the creation of multi-faceted selves. As has been seen, Woolf separated selves into distinct characters whose boundaries were set. Hence, the persona of Orlando remains distinct from her own and not a projection of an aspect of her psyche.

The attic room of Mrs Dalloway was to become the private room of the woman artist of the twentieth century, who was struggling to emerge and be recognised. Woolf seems to have been moving away from her individual self even more in her next piece of writing, 'A Room of One's Own', as she sought to generalise her position and appeal to the women of the future. Through an intense period of writing autobiographical fiction and innovating new devices in this medium, she had temporarily at least governed her obsessions and exploited them in art. Her principal approach was one of multi-level transfer from real characters or situations to fictional ones which then proceeded, often by analogy, to a level of abstraction. Ultimately, Woolf brought an aesthetic dimension to her fiction, distilling character and object to a certain 'significance', as she moulded life experience into the symbolisation of art.

Woolf's aesthetics did involve a number of specialised techniques. As if she were sculpting a reality of her own making for her fiction, her artistic method started with her choice of life material followed by the craft of substitution. As we have seen, she was constantly manipulating time and locale in her fiction, at once distancing and drawing near, according to different perspectives. Selecting certain incidents from the past, she proceeded to de-emotionalise them, avoiding a self-expression of them. As she dramatised ordinary events, she diminished her own personal

connection with them. Whatever life facts she chose as her materials, she intentionally blurred them with elements of ambiguity and suggestiveness which altered their veracity but inevitably led to the truths of fiction more accessible to a greater variety of readers. Perhaps her largest challenge was to examine her own selfhood both by splitting and combining selves in her female figures. Keeping her distance from those figures, she nevertheless endowed them with traces of her obsessions, which she explored beyond the confines of her own individual behaviour. The artistic world she created in her fiction was a fabricated region which drew in the chosen life material and provided constructs to absorb and reshape them. Ultimately, Woolf seems to have borrowed from the great literary movement of Symbolism still permeating literary circles with its two basic features: substitution and ambiguity. This gave her creative perception of her life a larger and richer parameter of reader response, aside from the sheer curiosity factor associated with standard autobiography, and led her from Cornwall to the Hebrides and then beyond.

7

The Mythification of Selfhood in Anaïs Nin

Anaïs Nin's notion of the interconnectedness of life and art went further than that of her predecessors. This cosmopolitan writer of mixed European background sought a delicate balance between her daily habit of diary writing and her fiction. Peripatetic as she was, and living through the Second World War, she was impermeable to her epoch and environment. Moving as she did between Paris and New York with a few side trips to more exotic places such as Fez and Acapulco, she had no particular city with which to fully identify. She therefore transported the notion of place to a created locale, 'the cities of the interior', which served to lodge the multilayers of her psyche. Although much of her fiction is transparent and reflects in part her own person or others, the creative component reintegrates the living material into a mythic and universalised mode. Her was an aesthetics of transmutation, which saw art as alchemic, and she qualified that movement from fact to fiction by fixating on the prefix 'trans'. Through the words of the collage artist Jean Varda, Nin describes this process:

> What I wanted to teach you is contained in one page of the dictionary. It is all the words beginning with *trans*: transfigure, transport, transcend, translucent, transgression, transform, transmit, transmute, transpire, all the trans-Siberian voyages.[1]

Like Varda's, her belief is that the flux of life can be rendered into something permanent only when it is transposed into myth.

Nin's artistic creed was that through art the intensely personal becomes the universal, and for this reason she sought every opportunity to live life intensely through dream and experience. She declared adamantly in her diary, the receptacle or 'laboratory' for her immediate experience, that she would not 'stop living to write'.[2] Rather than reject the personal, as previous writers did, she

heightened it for her art: 'The personal life, deeply lived, takes you beyond the personal', she stated.[3] Hence, the life-long diary (1914–74), begun at the age of eleven, would register those moments of flux of experience, and her fiction would universalise them, rendering them quasi-permanent in mythic worlds created by the artist.

These mythical worlds stem from the lost Atlantis, which she identifies as her life source in *House of Incest*, and proceed through a labyrinth of interior places comprising the mythic realm of *Cities of the Interior*, the title of her serial novelettes. Unlike Joyce, who stylised his native city, or Proust, who renamed his villages, intentionally misrepresenting them, Nin internalises her cities, endowing them with configurations similar to dreams. For Nin, the place inhabits the person instead of the person the place. Therefore, an imaginary place like Golconda is inspired by the atmosphere of an actual one in Mexico 'where the life force is vital and expansive'[4] and the labyrinthine inscape was in fact suggested by the intricate nature of Fez whose layers 'are like the layers and secrecies of the inner life'.[5] Ultimately, the last city in *Seduction of the Minotaur* resembles another maze, the labyrinth of the Grecian myth, transposed to the inner region of the psyche.

If place is transported in Nin's fiction, persons are transfigured, as in the case of her own personality. In anticipation of critics who might reduce her fiction to autobiographical readings, as she felt Painter had done with the work of Proust, Nin admitted that her fiction proceeded from the real, and in some cases the autobiographical, but then insisted on the notion of 'transplant' into the fictionalised, magical realm of her art:

> Which does not mean that all my fiction is autobiographical, nor does it mean as some believe, that I am all the women in the novel (it would be pleasant in one life to be so many women!). It simply means that the psychological reality of each character had been taken first from a living heart. Whether or not the transplant was successful, I leave to the critics.[6]

Hence, if there are certain correspondences that can be found between the three principal women of the fiction – all artist figures in some way – and Nin herself, there are also dimensions in these characters which surpass the real. Elemental in nature, each corresponds to an element – Sabina to fire, Djuna to air, and Lillian to earth – and like the goddesses of the past they are prey to the

passions established through metaphors in their modern-day predicaments. But perhaps Nin herself saved the fourth element, that of
water, primarily for an 'ur' self. The resonant lines of the narrator of
House of Incest, 'my first vision of earth was water veiled', can be
specifically linked to Nin because of the fact that she allowed her
voice to be used to utter them in her husband Ian Hugo's film *Bells
of Atlantis*. Throughout the fiction, the proliferation of the self into
selves is rendered vivid through the succession and interplay of
these mythical personalities.

Nin's process of fictionalisation had two motives: the actual protection of personalities, on the one hand, and the symbolisation and
creation of myth on the other. Mythification involved recomposition
and recreation of any life facts that might have been culled into symbolic and universal dimensions. For Nin knew well the limitations
of mimesis: 'Faithfulness to life I sometimes found limiting. In life I
could not see the complete development of a character's destiny. In
fiction I could use my imagination'. Fiction expands, deepens and
develops, and the resulting art produces what Nin calls patterns,
and even lies, which paradoxically yield another level of truth.
Fiction, therefore, would add dimensions to the material registered
in the diaries. Characters in the fiction would be composites larger
than any originals.

So while Woolf had declared that the relationship between life
and art was very intricate and had sought exterior formal structure
and abstraction in her treatment of life materials, Nin went on to
deny and blur any separation between her life and her craft:

> There is no separation between my life and my craft, my work.
> The form of art is the form of art of my life, and my life is the form
> of the art. I refuse artificial patterns.[7]

Admitting a certain indebtedness to Proust, as already noted, she
made the following statement: 'My self is like the self of Proust. It is
an instrument to connect life and myth.'[8] In Nin's view, the self was
the intermediary to transform alchemically life into the mythical
patterns of fiction, universalising the personal into what Jung would
have called, as already noted, the 'suprapersonal'. In the analogy of
the ragpicker, a persona in one of the leading stories from *Under a
Glass Bell*, Nin, like Joyce before her, collected the dregs of her life as
components for her art. But beyond Joyce, Nin magically
transmuted these fragments into a rarefied sort of fiction, recreating

the scraps of experience into a higher fictionalised reality. She described this miscellany of life in *The Novel of the Future*:

> The final lesson a writer learns is that everything can nourish the writer. The dictionary, a new work, a voyage, an encounter, a talk in the street, a book, a phrase heard. He is a computer set to receive and utilize all things. An exhibit of painting, a concert, a voice, a letter, a play, a landscape, a skyscape, a telephone conversation, a nap, a dream, a sleepless night, a storm, an animal's greeting, an aquarium, a photograph, a newspaper story.[9]

Such miscellaneous material drawn from her experiences is reintegrated into the artistic composite. Sharon Spencer's early study of Nin, *Collage of Dreams*, viewed Nin's life work precisely as an 'immense collage of experience, art, exploration, and dream'.[10] It is like the alchemy of transmuting base metal into the precious gold that is art.

The most succinct model of this very process of transformation from the real to the artistic can be drawn from the story 'Ragtime', first published in 1938 and then included in the collection *Under a Glass Bell*. Nin herself later commented on the juxtaposition of the experience in the diary and the story. She observed: 'In the diary I documented a visit to the ragpickers. In the story I showed how it became more than that.' The 'more than that' is the mythic, larger dimension that the experience acquires in the context of fiction, with its compelling message that one can't throw out one's past. The process turns the real and the documentary into a metaphor and derives a pattern from the interpretation of that derivative form of expression.

The source of the story is documented in volume 2 of the *Diaries*, where Anaïs and her Peruvian friend Gonzalo visit a ragpickers' village on the outskirts of Paris in August of 1936. This particular experience is recounted in a straightforward, descriptive way with little if any intervention of emotional reaction. Nin describes what we would call the homeless – ragpickers who live in primitive shacks made of tin, cardboard and newspapers. These poor souls are surrounded by a series of disparate, 'mismated' objects, scraps and pieces, thrown-away items, odds and ends taken from garbage cans – nothing whole or new. Surrounding the ragpickers is a tribe of gypsies who live in similar conditions, one of them in particular living in a shack covered with sea-shells, another a cripple without

hands or legs. Contemplating this scene, Nin comments, 'I could write here', and Gonzalo replies, 'I could draw here.'[11] The transposition of this scene into the story demonstrates to what extent the human document is the material for the art. In the story, composed shortly after the actual visit, Nin creates a ragpicker character and a persona, the narrator 'I', suggesting herself. Instead of the particular places of Paris, the setting is simply a city – any city; this abstraction suggests the universal nature of this experience and conveys the notion of cities of the interior which Nin was to develop in her novelettes. However, a change does occur which turns the observation into an introspective account; the male ragpicker seems to be an adversary of the female subject, threatening her own integrity. Having observed the fragments around her, including the fragmentation of maimed bodies, quasi-human, she begins to question her own completeness. In a hallucinatory way, she finds amidst the debris her own torn blue dress that she had worn when she was seventeen and in the frenzy of adolescent love. She is suddenly awakened to a past world that is resurrected through the vision of objects: 'The ragpicker gave me a wisdom tooth, and my long hair which I had cut off.'[12] As with Proust and Joyce, objects trigger an epiphany-like awareness that the past is latently ever-present. The female persona is forcefully made aware of her fragmentation, which is objectified in the final gesture of the ragpicker putting her, along with the other objects, into a bag.

The lyric which ends the story with the theme 'the new not new' is a chant reminiscent of Ariel's sea-change poem in Shakespeare's play *The Tempest*. The image of the sea-shells and the catalytic power of night reinforce the notion of transformation. As in the context of the Shakespeare poem, the theme is that nothing is lost; everything is transformed – suggesting Nin's own artistic credo. The narrative 'I' is that of the artist who is able to transform in an alchemic change the base elements of existence into artifacts. The 'I' is doubled and objectified further by the ragpicker character. The objects suggest the raw material with which the artist works, and in this instance they evoke the past and are significant ingredients for the autobiographical novelist's art.

Through this process of objectification, transposition and internalisation, in a story so short yet rich in suggestiveness, Nin offers the technique of her own art for scrutiny. But unlike Joyce, who stylised the lowly and the ordinary, Nin symbolises them and transposes them into the mythic world of the artist. The story reads like a

parable. Like the other autobiographical writers, Nin treats the role of the artist with distancing yet thereby comments upon her own aesthetics.

Nin's earliest printed novelette, *House of Incest* (1936), which preceded 'Ragtime' by two years, presents a more elaborate agenda for her fiction in a work replete with phantasmagoric images. The dominant house image itself, with its many windows and ivy covering, resembles the actual house at Louveciennes where Anaïs and her husband Ian Hugo (whose real name was Hugh Guiler) had stayed intermittently from 1929 to 1936. Nin described this house fully in the first volume of her diary. In this suburb of Paris, which can be approached by what Nin likened to a Proustian train, Nin spent some years preparing for her art. Domestic as she might have been with her husband 'Hugo', the Scottish bank employee whom she had married in 1923 at the early age of 20, she had already realised that her self was to interact in many relationships. This period of 'the house' was the time when she developed intimate rapports with the Millers, who added sensuality and excitement to her life and when she opened herself up to the psychoanalytic realm of René Allendy and Otto Rank.

Nin described the house of Louveciennes in her diary as a 200-year-old house with eleven windows, one of which was only a pair of shutters with no room behind them, being placed there just for the purposes of symmetry. A visit today confirms the diary description of a house in decrepit condition, with rusty fixtures and iron gates, mostly hidden from view by a thick, heavy stone wall, overwhelmed with ivy and brush. There is something secretive and ominous about this abandoned and neglected edifice in what is otherwise a standard and ordinary French town reached from the Gare Saint-Lazare. In her time, Nin obviously exploited the mysterious anomaly of the window without a room, transforming it into a secret room in the fiction of both *House of Incest* and, later, in *Children of the Albatross*. Like Proust with the house of Illiers, she reverses the reality a bit, for in *House of Incest* the narrative 'I' seeks the 'room without a window'[13] – the 'fortress' of an incestuous love – instead of the window without the room. The transformation of the physical house into an internal container or psyche is the beginning of the process of interiorisation that Nin was to develop in her 'cities of the interior'.

Characterising the house as incestuous, Nin uses incest in metaphoric terms. The subject-matter of the novelette, that of lesbianism

and brother–sister incest, is a foil for the narcissism which she finds in herself and from which she eventually seeks to be liberated. This house image is later to be replaced by the labyrinth in Nin's fiction, which perhaps more graphically expresses the complexity of the interior, as will be seen. But the claustrophobic feeling of the house conveys the confinement created by the various form of self-love which the characters Sabina and then Jeanne practice in their unusual relationships. If Sabina indulges in a lesbian affair with the narrator, suggesting the attraction to 'sameness', Jeanne never even consummates her relationship with her brother who resides in the hidden room of her consciousness. The ultimate desire is for escape and liberation: 'If only we could all escape from this house of incest', says the modern saviour who seeks to free the women. But the house, as it stands, is a sterile state which is marked by 'the failure of transmutation'.

Nin herself provides even at this early stage a solution to her own dilemma of self-love. And though this solution may appear temporary, since parallel situations occur among women figures in the later novelettes, it is the definitive one. Here the narrative persona states in a revealing way: 'I walked into my own book, seeking peace.' The book might have been capitalised to designate her opus. Yet in the course of this engagement with art, she admits: 'As I move within my book I am cut by pointed glass and broken bottles in which there is still the odor of sperm and perfume.'[14] This odour of sperm and perfume is a euphemism for life, for the life facts which Nin cannot totally leave behind in her work. They are like the rags of the rag-pickers, fragments of love, which, though transmuted into art, remain to haunt her in her life. For the truth behind the windows is the truth that even art cannot fully hide from the artist. It is also the truth that the writer divulges to the reader in a confessional mode clothed in stark metaphor: 'The morning I got up to begin this book I coughed. Something was coming out of my throat . . . I have just spat out my heart.'

Despite such reminders, however, art was for Nin the only process which could liberate her from the maze of selfhood, and that liberation was only possible at the heights of her artistic sensibility after the passage through the dangerous depths of the psyche. In all the works that were to follow, this same tension recurs, and Nin in fact simulated in her fiction situations comparable to those in her life which were difficult for her to endure unless art periodically saved her.

Hence, in contrast to the image of the house there is the image of the boat. It is interesting that Nin herself likened Louveciennes to the village where Madame Bovary had lived, for that was another way of saying that it was bourgeois and boring. It is a fact that after 1936 Nin and her husband moved back to Paris and sought an unconventional form of lodging in a houseboat on the river Seine in Paris. Obviously, for her, this abode was liberating as it suggested free movement. At the very time, then, of the writing of *House of Incest* she was making this transition in lifestyle – to better conform to her personality. The boat image, therefore, became an alternative to the house image and is elaborated upon in her fiction to suggest liberation and life flow. This was already apparent in *House of Incest* where Nin vacillated between the static house and the floating ship. As a variation to this dichotomy, she had also created the image of a wrecked ship, impeded in its journey. Nin recorded in her diary that, in fact, her most recurrent dream was that of 'a boat stuck in the ground, unable to sail for lack of water'.[15] Hence, Nin proceeded from an authentic dream to a fictional one in her first novelette: 'I awoke at dawn, thrown up on a rock, the skeleton of a ship choked in its own sails.'[16] Awakening out of a dream in which water prevails amidst suggestions of free sailing and swimming through wall-less rooms, the narrator confronts the constrictions of reality – the house and the incestuous state of her relationships. Along with the boat image, Nin was to create images of bird, music and dance to suggest the creativity and liberation which art provided. In this early work, therefore, she suggests the symbiotic relationship between her life and art.

Nin's own formal aesthetics of the novel was formulated well after her own novel writing. In *The Novel of the Future*, her treatise on the future of fiction after 1968, Nin went out of her way to attack the social realism that she felt prevailed in modern fiction (especially in American fiction), despite the pathblazing attempts of Joyce, Proust and Woolf (writers she specifically names) to decompose structures inherited from the conventional novel of the previous century. She called for a 'new synthesis' or 'ultimate integration', going a step further from the fissions initiated by these early twentieth-century novelists. In an effort to define the poetic novel of the future, Nin drew analogies between the novelist and the psychoanalyst in search of new dimensions of selves buried under the many layers of reality. The novelist would make discoveries from the collective richness of the subterranean world, which could be likened to a lost Atlantis.

If the multiple selves explored in her fiction are facets and layers of her own fluid and vibrant psyche, they also reflect aspects of women in general. This strategy of multiplication transformed the single self into the many, and the various personae in her fiction were presented as variations on a theme. Dismissing what she wittily called 'passport identification' of characters, Nin, like Proust in *Contre Sainte-Beuve* before her, dispelled '*le moi quotidien*', or everyday self, to explore the aesthetic self in various facets and appearances. It was Marcel Duchamp's painting of the *Nude Descending the Staircase* which crystallised her own theory of the succession of selves she felt she was. Unlike Woolf, Nin felt no split personality because of the series of selves she donned during her lifetime and clothed in the various personae that surface in her novels. Although a disciple of Dr Otto Rank, she basically refused to accept the notion of an integrated self which Rank had proposed and instead kept dealing with the fragmentation and proliferation of selves 'on frontiers of an identity'.

Shedding and reclothing selves was to Nin as common as donning and removing clothes, for her aesthetic personality was in constant masquerade on a stage which was life. In fact, Nin projects this aspect into the Stella and Sabina figures with their fleeting natures and their actress personalities. Unlike Woolf, Nin was not afraid of ultimate dissolution since her ragpicker instinct always enabled her to make new collages of composite selves which were moments of stasis within an eternal flow of an ever-evolving personality. The notion of any fixed state was the closest Nin would ever come to a living 'death'. In continuous flux through the landscapes of her continuous novels, she gave free passageway to the selves' motion. The major lesson she had learned from her diary was that there was no finite and circumscribed self since it was in a constant state of becoming in that genre. She sought to transpose this fluid relativism to her fiction with characters continuously developing through interpersonal relations and open-ended narrative with no conclusion to circumscribe any character.

Perhaps the most significant 'life fact' that affected Nin's writings was the desertion of her and her family by her father, the Spanish composer and pianist, Joaquin Nin. This traumatic incident occurred in 1913, when Nin was merely ten years of age. The memory of that irresponsible but charismatic Don Juan figure haunted her all her life and was the motivation of her first diary written at the age of eleven – on the boat trip to the United States from

Barcelona. Psychologically, the abandonment of a young girl by a father can leave lasting traumas. Nin herself admitted in retrospect: 'I felt hysterical sorrow when he abandoned us. And all through my schooldays in New York I craved for him.'[17] But she managed to deal with this situation in a 'healthy' way by incorporating it in her writing. *Linotte*, begun at the age of eleven, was written as a continuous letter to her father in his first absence, 'an imaginary letter', as she called it. At 30 she commented again: 'so he could follow us into a strange land, know about us'.[18] She had intended to send it to him: 'The diary began as a diary of a journey, to record everything for my father.'

Such was the beginning of what was to become a life-long habit of diary writing, but in the chronological context of this first volume there is an understated 'crisis' entry which has a strong bearing on her work. Unlike standard autobiographers who, as we have seen, would have highlighted such a moment, Nin simply records a conversation with her mother, Rosa Culmell Nin, in 1919. At the age of sixteen, the young girl is suddenly made aware by her bitter mother that the possibility of her father's return was a 'romantic illusion'. Nin notes this turning point in her attitude toward a father she had idealised throughout her youth:

> 'But Maman,' I said, trying to defend my poor illusions, 'at my age, you would have believed the same thing. Fortunately, until now I have been a little girl, but now, alas, I have changed! I will use your 40 years of experience as my own!'[19]

If on this verge of womanhood Nin suffers one disillusionment, she nonetheless maintains an idealised illusion of her Don Juan father, which is not qualified until 20 years later, when she actually meets him in Paris for the first time since the original childhood separation. Volume 1 of the *Diaries* recounts this momentous meeting in May of 1933, when she is 30 years old. Anticipating it, Nin already comments:

> I find my father again when I am a woman. When he comes to me, he who marked my childhood so deeply, I am a full-blown woman.[20]

Rationalising perhaps, she prefaces this long-awaited meeting with an *a priori* negative statement:

> My father comes when I no longer need a father . . . My father comes when I have gone beyond him; he is given to me when I no longer need him, when I am free of him.

This seemingly definitive statement is modified, however, by a subsequent admission:

> Yet the child in me could not die as it should have died, because according to legends it must find its father again.

Nin then proceeds to describe that climactic meeting with her debonair, Spanish-speaking father who generates an aura of egotism and charm. At the age of 30, she then realises that this attractive creature is her 'double': 'He incarnated all the dangers of my illusory life, my inventing of situations, my deceptions, my faults.'[21] Yet she concludes that although the child in her will be forever attracted to him, her own deeper feelings are to be distinguished from his 'superficial and worldly aims'. So, despite the fact that she looks like him and is akin to him in her rebellious, explorative and unconventional nature, she consciously rejects him: 'When he left, I felt as if I had seen the Anaïs I never wanted to be.'

This interchange between father and daughter and the juxtaposition of their personalities shed light on Nin's own personality and the perspective she has as she becomes a woman artist. On the one hand, she is affirming the multiplicity of selves she herself harbours; one of which remains the child in search of the father, another of which incarnates in her very being the father himself. On the other hand, she is striving for ultimate liberation in rejecting her father and subsequent male figures and moving on to the independence and sovereignty of her art. The split with the father coincides with the inception of her art.

Paradoxically, then, within the context of her art, her father is expanded upon, less as a force than as a haunting persona, forever living and enlarged upon. Through the very comparison of the father in the diary and the father figure in the fiction, we witness the process of transmutation in her art. In the second volume of the *Diary*, Nin states:

> As I read the diary I was aware of all I have left unsaid which can only be said with creative work, by lingering, expanding, developing.[22]

She then goes on to apply this notion of transformation to the case of her father, which proceeds from the one-dimensional record of him in her diary to the artistic transmutation of him in her creative writing:

> I do feel that the portraits in the diary are only done at the moment a person is important to me. The person rises and sinks, appears and vanishes only in relation to the range of my vision, in relation to what I see of him . . . What is this bigger thing I captured in my book on my father that was not in my diary? A day so full. Is it that the record prevents the supreme flights? Every day of record counts against this bigger thing . . . Is the flowering possible only with forgetting, with time, with the rotting and the dust and the falsities?

The 'bigger thing' is Nin's fictive re-presentation of her father in her art. The book in question was, of course, *Winter of Artifice*. But unlike Virginia Woolf, who claimed to have written a book that had purged her of her obsession with her dead mother, Nin realised that she was not able to alleviate the pain of the final separation from her father which occurred in February of 1939. Volume 2 of the *Diary* describes this scene in Paris where Nin sees her father for the last time and witnesses his collapse from a stroke while he performs at a concert. Realising that this might be the final separation (although her father did not actually die until ten years later in Cuba), Nin commented on her inability to 'bury' forever this love in her art:

> I thought I had reached detachment and that I would not feel the separation. Now I know I will never see him again. It hurt me deeply even when I say I no longer love him . . . Does love ever die, I ask, and will die asking. For years I buried it, I buried it in a novel which will appear while he is sailing away, I buried it when I decided to let him go to Cuba . . . Yet when he left, the night before he sailed, I wept over him, and awakened in the morning thinking of him.[23]

The complexity of Nin's relationship with her father and its artistic transposition are visible in this novel and others.[24] The very title crystallises the emotional climate which the rapport creates. The life facts are quite transparent: the abandonment by the father; the voyage of Djuna and her family on the ship to New York, during

which the young girl starts to write her diary. Djuna is in fact simultaneously aged 11 and 31, since the major event of the novelette is the reunion of father and daughter 20 years later – a period during which she has yearned for him. Ultimately, however, the series of scenes charts a process by which Djuna becomes totally disenchanted with her father, to the point of declaring that the need of a father had died.

Through a process of condensation, the relationship is conveyed in a sharp image:

> They looked at each other across miles of separation. His fear of emotion enwrapped him in glass. The glass shut out the warmth of life, its human odors . . . The glass walls were a prison intended to eliminate the dangerous, and in this artificial elimination life itself was deformed.[25]

The father incarcerated in a glass compartment suggests an artificial hothouse enclosing a decadent flower. The glass suggests both the communication and the barriers between father and daughter, and ultimately the sterility of the relationship which is devoid of basic human warmth – hence, the wintry theme. It is therefore no surprise that at the end of the novel the female figure Djuna discards this artificial father, the Don Juan personality who cared only for his appearances and pleasures as a pianist. But perhaps even more intriguing is the superimposition of another traumatic life fact onto the desertion theme to compound the sense of devastation. As she realises the extent of this emotional death, Djuna attempts to cover her past in oblivion, and reference is made to ether: 'She was coming out of the ether of the past.' She then links her current metaphorical ether to a literal past one, when she emerged from childbirth to the reality of a dead infant: 'a little girl with long eyelashes and slender hands. She was dead.' At this point, Nin is incorporating her own actual painful experience of delivering a six month stillborn child in 1934,[26] just a year after her meeting with her father. By cleverly mingling the metaphorical ether with the literal one, she is making a metaphor out of a real, concrete fact. Although the stillborn birth was fully documented in volume 1 of the expurgated *Diary* and sensationalised later in the 1938 'Birth' story of *Under a Glass Bell*, its insertion in the novelette is for the purpose of conflation: 'The little girl in her was dead too. The woman was saved. And with the little girl died the need of a

father.'[27] This compounding of the theme of dead love through the two life incidents fully supports the stark title of the novel, which was no doubt suggested by a spontaneous and succinct statement in the gory description of the birth scene in the *Diary*: 'Ice and Silence'.[28]

However forceful, this *Winter of Artifice* is only the beginning of that continuous portrait of a father which persists throughout the evolving fiction. The Freudian Allendy, with whom Nin had psychoanalysis back in 1932, had analysed for her the lasting effects that such a desertion would have on her love-life. Nin exposed Allendy's view in the first diary's unexpurgated pages, now known as *Henry and June* : 'Instead of trustingly giving yourself entirely to one love, you seek many loves.'[29] Hence, in the two novelettes which were eventually included in the Swallow edition of *Winter of Artifice*, 'Stella' and 'The Voice', Nin picks up the obsession with the lost father and follows its further into the labyrinth of her work. It is as if her father has 1000 lives and is to be reincarnated in various personae. In 'Stella', for example, the title character (who is often considered a predecessor of Sabina) finds that her love for her father is affecting her other loves and is destroying her other relationships. Two abortive liaisons (with Bruno and with Philip) suggest that Stella cannot free herself from the burden of her past. As an actress, she confronts a dilemma: she wishes to be loved for her true self instead of for her false one, but in the process of falsification, she has lost her 'real' self. Nin carefully designates her characters as actors in order to highlight the problematics of identity. Stella's private love affairs are failures because of the experience with her father. But there are no images in 'Stella' as there are in *Cities of the Interior* to translate Stella's predicament. 'Stella', reading more like Volume 2 of the *Diary*, chronicles the vagaries of emotions of a restless woman trying to divest herself of a past compulsion in order to proceed with her life.

Finally, however, 'The Voice', the third novelette of the eventual volume, uses imagery and persona to reinterpret this predicament. Nin projects the father figure into the psychoanalyst who insists the Stella cannot get rid of her past, a past which includes the memory of her father. The dream sequence which ends this novelette incorporates, as *House of Incest* already showed, what was to be one of the most compelling images of Nin's fiction: the landlocked boat struggling to meet its native element of flowing water:

This boat I was pushing with all my strength because it could not
float, it was passing through land. It was chokingly struggling to
pass along the streets, it could not find its way to the ocean.[30]

It is significant that Nin's *Diary* of the 1930s records two experiences
of the boat: the first one, already noted, was the houseboat in which
she lived on the river Seine; the second was that of an abandoned
old sailboat which she saw in the yard at Maupassant's house at
Etretat. These images, at this point in her fiction, become the matrix
for the conflict between the constraining webs of life and the liberation that was her art. Such artistic metaphors emerge in confronting
the trauma of the lost father and the link to the past which the artist
cannot yet sever.

It is as if these works are the preamble for the more intricate
exploration of this traumatic obsession in *Cities of the Interior*. The
five novelettes which comprise this collection feature, as already
mentioned, three problematic women characters, Djuna, Lillian and
Sabina, who yearn for completion. As has been seen, Nin ultimately,
in *The Novel of the Future*, disclaimed the identification of herself personally with these women characters. But earlier in her third diary,
she did admit that these were not others but herself. And the general resemblance between the fictional women and the character of
Anaïs has prompted critics to interpret them as her satellite personalities. Such critics have identified the fiery Sabina as Nin's id, the
flawed earthy Lillian as her ego, and the ethereal Djuna as her
superego. If such classifications seem reductive, perhaps the firmer
basis for identification is the fact that the three personae are indeed
artist figures: specifically Lillian as the jazz pianist, Djuna as the
dancer, and Sabina as the actress. Yet Nin's focus on women artists
surpasses the feminist standpoint of Woolf in the context of *A Room
of One's Own*. Nin was answering the standard psychiatrists' opin-
ion that art proceeds from neurosis by creating female artistic personalities with a creative dynamism which was not subject to a
pathological or chauvinistic interpretation.

The first of the five novelettes, *Ladders to Fire*, introduces the persona Lillian, the red-haired wife and mother of two children who,
despite her conventional life and ten-year marriage, launches on a
series of adventures to attempt to fulfil her 'hunger' for experience.
That particular drive is for the sampling of passionate love. Plunging
into extramarital relationships, first a short one with Gerard, then an
extended one with the painter Jay, she fails to satiate that hunger and

instead disperses herself on the road toward fragmentation. Again the brief reference to a miscarriage at six months, the father being Jay, is used as a sign for the problematic character of that relationship. Lillian, speaking to the child in her womb, calls her 'a child without a father'.[31] It is no surprise, therefore, in the sequel to the Lillian story, *Seduction of the Minotaur*, that the reason given for her chronic failure in matters of love is her loss of her father at an early age. Lillian is thus an extension of the previous Djuna, and the psychological causes for her blatant failures will be exposed most forcefully in the frightful image of the minotaur in the last novelette of *Cities of the Interior*.

Especially characteristic of *Ladders to Fire* is the use of symbolic metonymies to convey the psychological makeup of the characters. Physical images abound. As far as the title of this earlier novelette is concerned, it is to be noted that 'only Sabina's ladder led to fire', and that the ladder is thrown up suddenly for Lillian in the middle of the metaphorical city of the interior. That is to say, Lillian's one moment of heightened experience in her search for passion is found in her relationship, not with a man, but with a woman. The only liberating factor for Lillian is the Sabina figure who is designated later as the firebird, becoming prominent in *A Spy in the House of Love*. But already, in moving from one figure to the next and juxtaposing them in the process, Nin is splitting the 'I' into multiple personae. Through these figures Nin renders the different aspects of the self concrete, so that it is like one self confronting another: 'Sabina desiring Lillian's newness, and Lillian desiring Sabina's deeply marked body.' Lillian has a shock of recognition when she explores Sabina, seeing her like the 'Other' and therefore thinking: 'I recognize you. I have often imagined a woman like you.' Nin thereby describes the meeting of selves through the concrete ana-logy of a passionate encounter which reaches a point very near lesbianism: 'Tendrils of hair raising their heads to the wind in the finger tips, kisses curling within their conch-shell necks.' Yet at this peak of passion, conveyed through physical metonymic expression, the author makes it clear that they were not seeking to possess each other but to become the other and that these parts of being 'could not be exchanged through an embrace'.

To find a real life source for Sabina is another matter. It can be well argued from an analysis of *A Spy in the House of Love* that she is the 'real' Anaïs. From a more literal standpoint, however, the seductive nature of Sabina has led some critics to associate her with June Miller, and Jay the painter, who is supported and encouraged by Lillian,

with Henry Miller. It becomes increasingly evident, as the unexpurgated diaries emerge, that from 1931 this couple opened up avenues of
sensual experience and experimentation to Nin. Henry had compared
his wife June to Proust's Albertine. Was Nin exploring in her own life
and fiction the makings of such a provocative individual? One
wonders, indeed, if Nin did not consciously exploit her relationship
with this couple in order to gather new, ripe material for her fiction. In
a retrospective commentary on *Ladders to Fire*, Nin confessed: 'I was
interested at the time in clarifying what prevented people from living,
from loving, from immersion in experience.'[32] She also emphasised
specifically in reference to Henry Miller that 'a composite may
become something more than one artist, writer, painter, more than
one person – a unit'. In a sense, Nin might have found that zest for
life, crude and earthy, in the behaviour and activities of this lusty
couple. On the other hand, whatever sources she may have used are
internalised into mythic aspects of the psyche. The fictional Sabina–
Lillian relationship is in keeping with Nin's notion of the 'give and
take' which occurs in human rapports, the self being in constant flux
because of its assimilation of the series of 'Others'.

The search for the self or selves, as re-presented by the Lillian figure, reaches an intensity in *Seduction of the Minotaur*, the last novelette of the volume. There, Nin transplants the classic myth of the
minotaur into the modern domain of the psyche, tracing its mean-
derings. Notably, the labyrinth had become a favourite image of
modern writers to suggest the precarious pursuit of the self. Nin
herself fully exploits the image, beyond Joyce's earlier evocation of
the Daedalus myth, to suggest the intricacies, the sense of possible
entrapment, the dangers, but also the hints of Daedalean liberation.
Lillian is seen in a more deliberate attempt to liberate herself, but
this time she is confronted by a psychoanalyst figure who dismisses
her escapist tendencies. Well before the writing of this novel, at a
time in her life when Nin herself first sought out psychoanalysts,
she had concocted the minotaur image as a challenge to self-searching: 'the modern hero was the one who would master his own
neurosis . . . who would enter the labyrinth and fight the monster.
This monster who sleeps at the bottom of his brain.'[33]

The setting of Golconda in this novel, a fictional city created from
Acapulco, is the 'drug' that is equivalent to the Sabina force of the
earlier novel. The very beginning of Volume 5 of the *Diary* chronicles a journey to Acapulco, Mexico, in the winter of 1947–8, which
contains many of the ingredients of the novel: the move to the trop-

ics, the sultry atmosphere, the meeting with a Dr Hernandez and engineer Hatcher, the comparison of the city to a labyrinth. Like Morocco's Fez, Mexico's Acapulco intrigued her as another exotic place which made her 'blood rhythms pulsate.'[34] She also was attracted to the fact that Mexico seems present-oriented: 'the past is dissolving in the intensity of Acapulco'. But characteristically, the novel goes further to elaborate and fictionalise, moving from the real Acapulco to the fictional Golconda to the suggestions of a modern-day Crete. It spanned at least 20 years of self-searching, as noted in the ingredients from Volumes 2 and 5 of the *Diaries*.

Golconda is a true city of the interior, because the character not only visits the city but imbibes its very essence in her being. And it is in describing Golconda that Nin really gives a definition to the metaphoric title of her *roman fleuve*:

> Each one of us possesses in himself a separate and distinct city, a unique city as we possess different aspects of the same person. She could not bear to love a city which thousands believed they knew intimately. Golconda was hers.[35]

Golconda is therefore Lillian's private city, an area of her psyche, and in what seems like an archaeological exploration, she reaches a hidden self, suggested by the minotaur, which frightens her but also alerts her to another stage of awareness. Rather than distance a locale, as Woolf did with the St Ives, or camouflage one fictionally, as Proust did with Illiers, Nin re-invents one, internalising it to lodge an emerging facet of the self.

Elaborating further on the metaphor of the landlocked boat seen in her earlier fiction, Nin has it reach the magical Golconda:

> she would give this ship, once and for all, its proper sea bed . . . She had landed in the city of Golconda, where the sun painted everything in gold . . . With her first swallow of air she inhaled a drug of forgetfulness well known to adventurers.

If Golconda is likened to an opiate that enables Lillian to forget her restrictive past, that forgetfulness, though liberating, is temporary. For aside from the immediate memory of her husband Larry in the bourgeois setting of White Plains, New York, is a deeper memory of her father and the curious mixture of pleasure and pain which his presence had created in the distant past.

The introduction of the doctor figure, Dr Hernandez, although a real person whom Nin befriended on her trip to Mexico in 1947, is used for the interpretation of Lillian's flight. Hernandez seems to be the representation of Dr Otto Rank, with whom Nin began psycho-analysis in 1933. Despite the fact that Nin went on to practise lay analysis with Rank in New York, there were major disagreements between them, Nin exploiting what she learned from psychiatry for artistic purposes instead of therapeutic ones. Hernandez mirrors Rank's categorical view that the past cannot be eradicated:

> Golconda is for forgetting. But it is not a permanent forgetting. We may seem to forget a person, a place, a state of being, a past life, but meanwhile what we are doing is selecting a new cast for the reproduction of the same drama, seeking the closest reproduction to the friend, the lover, or the husband we are striving to forget.

This citation is also reminiscent of Proust's notion in his *roman fleuve* of the recall of recurrent patterns in the lifetime of his characters. Here, Lillian denies the doctor's advice, even as Nin often questioned the opinions of Rank. Yet in the midst of her journey, travelling into a deeper recess beyond Golconda, San Luis, Lillian meets a man, Hatcher, who suddenly reminds her involuntarily of the past:

> Hatcher had hair on his fingers, like her father . . . She had been unable to live for three months a new life, in a new city, without being caught by an umbilical cord and brought back to the figure of her father.

In a Proustian way, a detail, the visual stimulus of Hatcher's fingers, brings back the image of her father and his dominant impact on her life. Despite her physical displacement from any recognisable locale and associations, she realises that indeed she is not free. Instead, the undercurrent of childhood remains, below Golconda and forever prevailing. This sudden realisation unleashes a string of images of her parents and her childhood, as she remains attached, as if by a permanent umbilical chord of memory, to the past. Forgetting is for her at constant war with remembering, as suggested by Nin's own recurrent dream of two solar barques, one flowing and one static. The escapist journey to Golconda is another version of such tensions.

Nin imbues this novelette with the context of professional psychology as if she were formally analysing herself. But the complexity of such analysis becomes artistically transfixed in the figure of the minotaur. Lillian encounters the minotaur on her journey home in the porthole of the airplane – a frightening revelation of her secret self, which she had unwittingly excavated in her passage through the labyrinth of Golconda. The monster was 'the hidden masked part of herself unknown to her, who had ruled her acts'[36] – what seems to be her father. Lillian has understood her reason for not loving any man totally: the formula for the love she is seeking is derived from the mixture of pleasure and pain that marked her relationship with her father and has not been discovered in any lover. Nin has aggrandised this obsession with her own father through this monstrous vision, which actually turns into a reflection of a masked woman, suggesting the aspect of 'the double' that her father represented for her. In the context of *Seduction*, the character submerges this vision as she returns to New York to her husband Larry, but her fate is uncertain. Obviously, Nin was unable to complete the portrait of her persona at the very end of her *roman fleuve* precisely because she saw no character as ever fully defined in the circular structure of her fiction which progresses and regresses in continuum.

In the novelettes between *Ladders* and *Seduction*, with less emphasis on Lillian, the search for the self continues in yet other fashions. *Children of the Albatross* (1947) seems to be in part a reprieve from the labyrinthine pathways which Nin's characters tread. The title suggests the illumination, the phosphorescence of youth, an aspect of selfhood which is alluring. Nin had apparently read about the albatross in a scientific journal which had explained why this particular bird has a metaphysical aura about it. Perhaps she had also wondered about the superstitious quality associated with it in Coleridge's 'The Ancient Mariner'. Nin had learned that the reason sailors had been traditionally reluctant to kill this large, awkward bird was that its entrails remain phosphorescent after death. Nin transfers this particular kind of glow and buoyancy to her characters, who in their youth are unburdened by moral or psychological constraints.

As Nin moves from the setting of a 'sealed room' to the cafés of Paris, she creates a series of successive scenes of adolescent characters carrying with them the traces of childhood, innocent in their exploration of interrelationships. The cafés, a variation on the theme of the cities, are the principal locales for such

activity. This is the most populated novelette, including as it does the three major female characters and several of the male lovers, such as Michael, Donald, Paul and Lawrence. Here Nin seems to be emphasising the move from the individual to the collective psyche. One wonders whether this section on adolescents wasn't in some way inspired by Proust's volume on *'les jeunes filles en fleurs'*. But if Proust had created an atmosphere of corruption veiled in ambiguity, Nin opened up a translucent realm of innocence. More specifically, she may well have been drawing from her acquaintance in the early 1940s in New York City with a variegated group of sensitive, artistic young men, several of whom were homosexuals. Nin mentions in the third volume of the *Diary* two individuals in particular, Robert Duncan and Paul (a pseudonym), who might well have contributed to the male figures in this work. However, the relocation of such a group in Paris distances any distinct source, although it may have captured a particular quality of relationship that she had not before observed in such collectivity, since she herself had concentrated on rather direct relationships of lasting significance which had more personal impact on her.

In *Children of the Albatross*, the shift from the 'sealed room' to the Parisian cafés can, of course, be seen as a symbolic parallel to Nin's own relocation in 1936 to Paris. As in the earlier case of *House of Incest*, Nin exploits the anomaly of the house of Louveciennes, but instead of changing it to a room without a window, here she is more faithful to the reality of an actual missing room:

But one shutter was closed and corresponded to no room. During some transformation of the house it had been walled up.[37]

She describes it as a dark or sealed room and assigns it this time, not to the little known Jeanne figure, but to the more fully explored Djuna, the character most obsessed by her past. But at the same time Nin heightens the symbolisation of the house by proliferating the rooms as correlatives of the many selves within Djuna, only one of which is the shuttered window:

Action taking place in one room, now in another, was the replica of experience taking place in one part of the being, now in another . . . The room of the heart in Chinese lacquer red, the room of the mind in pale green or the brown of philosophy, the room of the

body in shell rose, the attic of memory with closets full of the musk of the past.

Here are vivid images for the different parts of the psyche. Nin has created a metaphor from a real locale, the composite of the house, for the psyche which she then dissects into rooms and compounds those metonymies by finding an analogy with cells; the many-roomed house suggesting the many-celled body. Even the pun on 'cell' suggests this alliance. By calling it a 'house of myth', she stresses the transformation from the real to the universal.

At the end of the first section of *Children of the Albatross*, Nin has Djuna recoil from the walled-up room of her house because in it is 'lodged violence'. The emphasis is on the fact that there is only one such room which seems to lodge a frightening aspect of selfhood, comparable perhaps to what Lillian later experiences with the minotaur (who could have been lodged in a cell of the labyrinth which was its prison in the ancient myth). At one point injected in the narrative there is the disturbing image of Djuna suddenly feeling frozen by a memory in the guise of a modern-day Ariadne pulling at a thread within a maze: 'too much snow on the spool she was unwinding from the tightly wound memories'. But in the case of the ethereal Djuna, here aged 27, suffering still from the repercussions of the troubling relationship with her father in the past, there is an avoidance of the deeper probe at this instance. Nin quickly dispels the image of the maze, minimising the obstructive power of the past. Instead, she has Djuna retreat into a 'little room of gentleness and trust', which is the basis of her relationship with the younger adolescent Paul. She revives her own naive seventeen-year-old girl-self through this relationship with the younger man, who temporarily brings innocence back to love and protects her from her troubled self. Djuna experiences this phosphorescence in Paul, one of the adolescent males who 'had the skin of a child that had never been touched by anything of this earth'. Accordingly, at the time of the writing of this novelette, Nin modifies the notion of the house of incest by airing it and replacing it with the 'house of myth', stressing the variety rather than the singleness of selfhood.

This principal character Djuna, who has journeyed from the 'winter of artifice' to the cafés of Paris, is dissected further in the novelette that follows *Children of the Albatross*, *The Four-Chambered Heart* (1950). In this work, Nin fully develops a metaphor from a

scientific image, which seems to suggest in the most concrete way the multifaceted nature of her complex persona. Nin had found in science a reservoir of images that could be used by the artist; she commented later in *The Novel of the Future*: 'science is full of concrete images which could serve to represent an abstract psychological truth'.[38] Hence, Nin has her character Djuna choose a simple dictionary entry about the heart to be a physical rationale for her multiplicity of loyalties. Interestingly, this was a behavioural trait that Nin tried to justify all her life. Through the power of analogy, Nin objectifies her emotional makeup:

> The heart . . . is an organ . . . consisting of four chambers . . . A wall separates the chambers on the left from those on the right and no direct communication is possible between them.[39]

Reminiscent of Proust, Nin perceives love in physiological terms, analysing it through a physical analogy. She exploits the obvious image of the heart, focusing on the classic receptacle of the grand emotion. The context here is Rango's passionate love for Djuna which is unintentionally compromised by his devotion to his ailing wife, Zora. Djuna, in turn, has to convince her fiery lover that her previous love for Paul is hidden in another chamber of the heart and is irrelevant to her current emotion.

Graphically, then, the airy figure Djuna tries to reconcile her several loves – ranging from the gentleness of Paul to the violence of Rango – by shoving them into distinct chambers of her heart: 'the image of Paul into another chamber of her heart, an isolated chamber without communicating passage into the one inhabited by Rango'. As she realises that no one love fully satisfies her needs, and that in particular the fiery Rango is incapable of giving her a certain solace in life, she rationalises the necessity of keeping all the chambers of the heart occupied. Justifying her infidelities, therefore, she reasons that in order to love Rango she must not necessarily destroy the chamber occupied by Paul. To do otherwise would, in keeping with the analogy of the heart, cause insufficiency – a term which Nin might well have used had she pursued further her scientific investigation of the heart.

If, as Nin herself admitted, the character of Rango does represent Gonzalo, the Peruvian revolutionary who has already been associated with the ragpicker in the story, Nin does not hide this association, because she is convinced that she has recreated

him in her fiction. Her diary entry of 1948 reads very clearly: 'I am working at the fiction of Gonzalo become Rango [*The Four-Chambered Heart*].'[40] Obviously, this was a time when she had become disillusioned in the character of her former lover, admitting that 'the present Gonzalo is dead for me'. Yet she sought in her fiction to preserve her earlier appreciation of the excitement he brought to her life through his passionate Latin nature, his guitar playing, his fascinating tales of Peru. As in the case of her father, she has used the alchemy of art to transform the daily individual into a recreated specimen, whose illusion and totality can only be maintained in the art form. The person acquires a new and lasting life in the fiction – hence her startling statement after the diary entry on Gonzalo: 'The alchemy of fiction is, for me, an act of embalming.' 'Embalming' is a striking word to describe the chemistry of her art; just as embalming preserves a dead body, so does art preserve the memory of the real 'soul' of a person. 'Scientific' terminology, once again, nourishes this particular novelette and is a source for its metaphoric expression.

If, in Nin's view, science enriches the novelist's symbolism, so too does art. It is in this novelette and another that Marcel Duchamp's famous painting *Nude Descending a Staircase* serves to render vivid the notion of the multifaceted self. This type of selfhood, here represented by the Djuna figure, will reach its most dramatic incarnation in Sabina, who will also be associated with this painting in *A Spy in the House of Love*. As is well known, what is particularly striking about this museum painting is the definition of a fragmented woman through contours, which multiplies the one into the many in a downward gradation. Such is a fitting image for Nin's multi-selved women, who in their mythic identities remain figures or forms rather than rounded, fleshy characters. Sensual as they are, they are not corporeal; and this unusual anomaly renders them universal. For Nin, the painting described 'the movement of the many layers of the self'[41] similar to archaeological strata. She thus appropriates this pictorial vision to the depiction of Djuna's character in *The Four-Chambered Heart*: 'Not one but many Djunas descended the staircase of the barge.' The different dimensions of this character, ranging for example from the influence of her parents, friends, childhood, profession, nature, art, readings and loves contribute to the continuing evolution of the multilayered self. By this point in her fiction, Nin has translated this notion of multiplicity into a series of analogous metaphors. She has proceeded from the many-roomed

house, to the labyrinthine cities, to the four-chambered heart, to steps of the staircase, compounding the metaphors to suggest the vast layering of the interior.

Nin's theory of multiple selves reaches a point of climactic representation in the shift from Djuna to Sabina, who is the emblematic persona of *A Spy in the House of Love*. For Sabina, designated as Stravinsky's 'firebird' in this work, is the most potent incarnation of the fluidity of selfhood and perhaps the closest to Nin herself. Although examined earlier as a catalyst to Lillian in *Ladders to Fire*, in this later work she comes into her own and her singular behaviour is fully exposed. There is a certain transparency with respect to Sabina, which leaves her open to an autobiographical reading. For example, her wearing of a cape is reminiscent of the author herself, who often appeared in masquerade-like costumes. Those who knew Nin remember that she wore two different capes, a black one and a red one. Furthermore, her clothing had no particular period style but was simply theatrical. Her eyes, covered with black maquillage, gave the impression of an actress's face; so it is no wonder that Sabina is an actress character. Furthermore, those who knew her loyal and protective life-long husband Hugo (Hugh Guiler) cannot help but identify him with the faithful and trusting character Alan who only appears in this one book.

But perhaps the question of sincerity is the most pertinent to this evasive character and an issue which Nin felt compelled to treat with respect to herself. The 30-year-old Sabina, married to a loyal and devoted 35-year-old husband, Alan, leads an active extramarital love life, which includes one-night escapades with fleeting men. These men, ranging from an opera singer Philip to an African jazz musician Mambo to a young aviator John, fulfil different needs, as does her fatherly husband to whom she inevitably returns. Yet a different self emerges with each relationship, and the proliferation of selves prevents the possibility of any unitary one or any total love, for that matter. Through the city streets Nin follows the peregrinations of this passionate woman of the night and crystallises her makeup through the analogy of a spy:

> It was when she saw the lives of spies that she realized fully the tension with which she lived every moment, equal to theirs. The fear of committing themselves, of sleeping too soundly, of talking in their sleep, of carelessness of accent or behavior, the need for continuous pretending . . . [42]

As a 'spy in the house of many loves', Sabina is unidentified and and constantly engaged in acts of pretence and duplicity. This behaviour coincides with her training as an actress, but she envies those more professional actresses who are able to step out of their roles and return to a permanent self. Instead, like Stella before her, she finds herself in a position of perennial acting in her daily life. As she contemplates her many lovers, she envisages the dismemberment of her self and the impossibility of a single identity:

and she was afraid because there was no Sabina, not ONE, but a multitude of Sabinas lying down and yielding and being dismembered, constellating in all directions and breaking.

Nin has Sabina become the mythic composite of the many selves, but that composite is paradoxically not whole. Here again, Duchamp's painting is used to objectify the multiplicity of selves, as the actress sees in it a mirror of herself:

she understood Duchamp's painting of a 'Nude Descending a Staircase'. Eight or ten outlines of the same woman, like many multiple exposures of a woman's personality, neatly divided into layers, walking down the stairs in unison.

Given this multiplicity of character, the Sabina figure is subject to duplicity, forever 'choking' the truth. Although she may be sincere in each of her many relationships, that is the sincerity of the moment. Her fragmented makeup prevents her from reaching total sincerity, which could be construed as the prerequisite of total love. Nin herself had confessed to this dilemma in her diary: 'How difficult it is to be "sincere" when each moment I must choose between five or six souls. Sincere according to which one, reconciled to which one?'[43]

Hence, this problem is shared both by the persona and the author. As already noted, in real life in the early 1930s Nin sought out psychiatry to try to cope with her dilemma of her divided selves. It was Dr Rank who had tried to convince her that underneath was a unitary self which she must make efforts to find. Having been dissatisfied with Dr René Allendy, the more conventional Freudian psychiatrist, who simply classified her as a neurotic, she turned to Dr Rank, whose work *Art and Artist* of 1932 revealed that he was interested in artistic creativity and might analyse her in those terms.

Also, she was attracted to his writings on the Double, which no doubt would have a bearing on her relationship with her father. It is interesting that when in November 1933 Nin was on her way to meet Rank for the first time in Paris, she records in her diary her confessions to him of her need to rid herself of her lies: 'I am tired of lies and deformities.' Two years later, however, after practising lay analysis with Rank in New York, she broke with him because she felt that he had still been unable to understand the artist in her as a cause of her problems. After all, he had encouraged her cruelly to leave her true most faithful confidant, her diary, which in his view was her 'last defense against analysis'.

In *A Spy in the House of Love*, written years later, when in fact Nin had become totally disillusioned with what she regarded as male psychiatry, she transformed the psychiatrist, perhaps out of revenge, into a mechanical device. It is a lie detector, to which Sabina eventually confesses that in her life she had sacrificed truth for adventure. This male respondent can only warn her that in fact she has never found true love, and that only such a condition can extricate her from her entrapment with her selves. His diagnosis is that her psychological history is one of 'non-love'. Of course, where there is no transparency between the persona and the author, the fact is that the author has the saving grace of her art and the resort to her diaries, while the character has only her casual dabbling in acting and a sudden recourse to classical music to soothe her from the dire indictment of the psychoanalysis.

It is curious that Nin did not in fact end *Cities of the Interior* with *A Spy in the House of Love*, given the transparency of its principal character and the central dilemma which it exposes and which in fact pertains to all her variations of women. It remains the most focused and streamlined of all the works, as it singles out a paradigmatic character with an inscape that suggests a modern-day urban setting. But perhaps Sabina was too close to Nin herself, and Nin choose to distance herself a bit more at the end of her volume by returning to Lillian and the abstraction of the labyrinth of the Grecian myth. The minotaur, the most frightful image of selfhood, remains the haunting one at the end of the *roman fleuve*, suggesting perhaps the dangers of probing too deeply and the palliatives of the simple act of living.

It is interesting to trace the four different levels of expression through which Nin travelled. From the scintillating life facts she helped create, she moved to the unexpurgated expression of the

original diaries, to the edited ones for public consumption and then on to the supreme transformation of these life trappings into the permanence of her art. In many instances, she juxtaposed her diary with her fiction, speaking of the transformative act she was constantly engaged in. Already in the context of her early diary *Linotte* she chided herself as being by nature secretive and falsifying but thanked her diary, her confidant at that point, for forcing her to be truthful about things she had done: 'I find them written straight out, spread out here with all the love of the truth which is *not* in my character but which *you* have forced me to cultivate.'[44] She had envisaged her diary in the metaphor of a strainer which purified, improved and filtered out her thoughts. It was the first remove from the original level of life; later, her fiction could have been viewed as a transformer which heightened and transmuted even the filtered elements to gilded artifacts of the imagination. So that if even Anaïs had admitted that she was not by nature sincere, her fiction eventually was to transport her to a higher level of truth which reached a pitch of universality and myth.

If Anaïs was a woman who worshipped the spontaneity of the moment and savoured a certain intensity in her life, she was able to compensate for the sense of life's transience and fragmentation by the permanence she transfixed in her art. The particular techniques that she used to shape the experiences salvaged from her life are vital and enduring in the context of modern art. They include, as has been seen, a heightened use of metaphor drawn from concrete images, the proliferation of metaphor into metonymy, the use of analogy, and the variegated symbolisation of obsession. Whereas the earlier writers of aesthetic autobiography tended to use a strategy of bifurcation in the projection of selfhood, splitting themselves in two, Nin compounded the approach through a strategy of multiplication, splitting the 'I' into multiple personae in her works. Moreover, of the writers considered in this book, she was the most aware of the powers of the transformative process welding life fact into artifact. And the result of such artistry, nourished as it was by the savouring of life experience, is the mythification of the modern psyche for the generations to come.

Envoi

My choice of texts to illustrate what I have called 'aesthetic autobio-graphy' may appear idiosyncratic to some readers, but these writings are the very ones which inspired me to probe this aspect of autobiography. Inadvertently, I have used the four authors to set up a model that defines literariness in an age when there is difficulty in distinguishing between reportage and journalistic narrative on the one hand and literariness on the other. The juxtaposition of autobiographical communication and the indirect use of autobiography to construct a work of fiction helps to highlight that elusive element we call literature.

I am aware of the current unearthing of 'reportorial' autobiographies as 'archaeological' findings, giving insight to a collective group in a society. Such autobiographies are indeed sociological documents and, insofar as they are regarded as such, prove useful and enlightening. Their study currently involves an ideology of genre. Notably, the scrutiny of such autobiographies disqualifies a consideration of art, since art itself would individuate the very writers who are being viewed as representative of collectivities.

In contrast, what the four writers of autobiography featured in this book had most in common was their sustained commentary on art within and without the texts. These very writers were concerned with the aesthetic process even as they wrote. The genesis of art, the passage from fact to fiction, could be followed in these cases precisely because we have access to the process of creation through the available resources of notebooks, journals, letters and drafts. Extrinsic and intrinsic approaches can therefore be applied.

Naturally, other writers can be brought into this aesthetic pool, as the invention of fictive constructs to distort, enrich and transcribe life facts onto a universal plane is a process which perennially exists. For it is important to realise that this type of writing is not a fad nor a stylistic signature of a particular literary movement or epoch. The fact that it has been identified in the early twentieth century in the context of this book is because that was a propitious historical moment when self-expression was being analysed after the loose subjectivism of the previous century – and autobiography was the most obvious target for such scrutiny. Therefore, the methodology

used in this book to identify the fictionalisation can readily be applied to other texts and help in the crucial identification of the literary dimension.

This method goes beyond biographical and genetic criticism, for it takes those findings as means not ends in observing further their artistic transplantation. The same is true with the question of referentiality – a hot topic in literary criticism today – for references 'real' or otherwise are also means to the greater artistic goals. It is recognised that many psychoanalytical studies have been successfully conducted to observe the transfer of aberrant behaviour to the fictional realm. But as Freud himself admitted, such is not the study of art, for the concern is with subject-matter rather than with formal structure and metaphor. Many critics and commentators, including Freud himself, have alluded to this other area of study as a field to be probed, but specific methods have not been readily indicated or pursued.

The particular methodology I have used is necessarily a branch of aesthetic theory, illustrated in the many examples I have given and perhaps most vividly described by Proust's analogy of the artistic vision as a 'mirage caught on a canvas' – *'mirage arrêté sur une toile'*. When one analyses the way pieces of life information are gathered into a work of art, one marvels even more at that great unity of art which is always more than the sum of its parts. The designation I have given of 'aesthetic autobiography' categorises a form of autobiography which has been neglected and loosely alluded to, but might now be a classification which can be peopled with yet other revealing examples. And beyond its relevance to autobiography theory, I hope that this book will be a springboard for further investigation of the creative pathways into art.

Notes

1: Historical Paradigms

1. Cellini, *The Life of Benvenuto Cellini Written by Himself*, vol. I, p. 71.
2. Augustine, *Confessions*, p. 267.
3. Ibid., p. 40. The quotation in the next paragraph is on p. 46.
4. Ibid., p. 47. The quotation in the next paragraph is on p. 178.
5. See Egan, *Patterns of Experience in Autobiography*.
6. Symonds, 'Introduction' to Cellini, *The Life of Benvenuto Cellini*, vol. I, p. 5. It has been noted that Cellini's *Life*, written 1558–66, did not appear in a printed edition until 1728 and therefore did not become widely known in other countries until the nineteenth century.
7. Taine, *Histoire de la littérature anglaise*, vol. 1, p. xlvi. Translations from the French are my own except where otherwise indicated.
8. Franklin, *The Autobiography of Benjamin Franklin*, p. 44.
9. Rousseau, *The Confessions*, p. 170. Rousseau wrote his autobiography in a shorter period of time (1765–70) than Franklin's eighteen years. As a younger autobiographer with less interruption in his narration, Rousseau could give more spontaneity and immediacy to his account, and impose less selectivity on events, as he claims.
10. Ibid., p. 17. The quotations in the next paragraph are on pp. 169, 257.
11. Ibid., p. 21. The quotations in the next paragraph are on pp. 29, 30, 88.
12. Ibid., p. 327. The quotation in the next paragraph is on p. 262.
13. Gosse, *Father and Son*, p. 5. The next quotation is on the same page.
14. Ibid., p. 27. The next quotation in this paragraph is on p. 202.
15. Ibid., p. 5.
16. Gide, *Si le grain ne meurt*, p. 245. The subsequent quotations in this paragraph are on p. 22, 10.
17. Ibid., p. 10.
18. Neuman, *Gertrude Stein*, p. 60. The next quotation is on p. 76.
19. Leiris, *Manhood*, p. 158. The next quotation in this paragraph is on pp. 160–1.
20. Brée, 'Michel Leiris: Mazemaker', p. 206.
21. Leiris, *Scratches*, p. 232. The next quotation in this paragraph is on p. 233.
22. Lejeune, *Le Pacte autobiographique*, p. 209.
23. Sartre, *The Words*, p. 253. The quotation in the next paragraph is on p. 251.
24. Ibid., p. 252.
25. Soyinka, *Aké*, pp. 75–6.

2: Theories of Autobiography

1. Gusdorf, 'Conditions and Limits of Autobiography', p. 39. The subsequent quotations from Gusdorf are on pp. 28, 29.
2. Pascal, *Design and Truth in Autobiography*, p. 180.
3. Lejeune, *Le Pacte autobiographique*, p. 14. The quotations in the next paragraph are on pp. 241, 29.
4. Bruss, *Autobiographical Acts*, p. 14. The quotations in the next paragraph are on p. 127.
5. Spengemann, *The Forms of Autobiography*, p. xiii.
6. Coe, *When the Grass Was Taller*, p. 8.
7. Barthes, 'The Death of the Author', p. 142. The next quotation in this paragraph is on p. 147.
8. Foucault, 'What is an Author?', p. 988.
9. Thibaudeau, 'Le Roman comme autobiographie', p. 214.
10. Mehlman, *A Structural Study of Autobiography*, p. 14.
11. Renza, 'The Veto of the Imagination', p. 274.
12. Sprinkler, 'Fictions of the Self: the End of Autobiography', p. 325. The next quotation in this paragraph is on p. 326.
13. Barthes, 'The Death of the Author', p. 144. The next quotation in this paragraph is on the same page.
14. Genette, *Figures III*, p. 45.
15. De Man, *Allegories of Reading*, p. 15.
16. Hassan, *The Postmodern Turn*, p. 147.
17. Beaujour, *Miroirs d'Encre*, p. 348. The quotation in the next paragraph is on p. 258.
18. Olney, *Metaphors of Self*, p. 3.
19. Olney, 'Some Versions of Memory/Some Versions of Bios', p. 237. The subsequent quotations in this paragraph and the next are on pp. 22, 247.
20. Fleishman, *Figures of Autobiography*, p. 26.
21. Eakin, *Fictions in Autobiography*, p. 226.
22. Eakin, 'Narrative and Chronology as Structures of Reference', p. 34.
23. Ricoeur, *The Rule of Metaphor*, p. 229.
24. Ricoeur, 'Life: a Story in Search of a Narrator', in *A Ricoeur Reader*, p. 432.
25. Ricoeur, *Time and Narrative*, vol. 2, p. 158.
26. See Sekora, 'Is the Slave Narrative a Species of Autobiography?', pp. 99–111.
27. Watson, 'Shadowed Presence', p. 180. The next quotation is on the same page.
28. Frye, *Anatomy of Criticism*, p. 307. The next quotation in this paragraph is on p. 308.
29. Ricoeur, *A Ricoeur Reader*, p. 432.

3: A Theory of Aesthetic Autobiography

1. Taine, *Histoire de la littérature anglaise*, vol. I, Introduction, p. lxvi.
2. 'Nouveaux lundis', 22 juillet 1862, in *Oeuvres choisies de Sainte-Beuve*, p. 343.
3. T. S. Eliot, 'Tradition and the Individual Talent', in *Selected Prose*, p. 41.
4. Jung, 'On the Relation of Analytical Psychology to Poetry', in *Collected Works of C. G. Jung*, vol. XV, p. 71.
5. Proust, *Contre Sainte-Beuve*, p. 222.
6. Letter of 15 May 1871 to Paul Démeny, in Rimbaud, *Oeuvres complétes*, p. 251.
7. Joyce, *A Portrait of the Artist as a Young Man*, p. 215.
8. Diary entry of 26 January 1920, in *The Diary of Virginia Woolf*, vol. II, p. 14.
9. Nin, *The Novel of the Future*, p. 157.
10. See diary entry of 27 June 1925, in *The Diary of Virginia Woolf*, vol. III, p. 34.
11. Woolf, 'The Art of Fiction', in *Collected Essays*, vol. II, p. 53.
12. Woolf, *Roger Fry*, p. 164.
13. See Richard Ellmann, *James Joyce*, pp. 508–9.
14. See diary entry of 8 April 1925, in *The Diary of Virginia Woolf*, vol. III, p. 7.
15. Entry of August 1937 in *The Diary of Anaïs Nin*, vol. II, p. 232.
16. Nin, *The Novel of the Future*, p. 194.
17. See Brewer, 'What is Autobiographical Memory?' in Rubin (ed.), *Autobiographical Memory*.
18. Brown and Kulik, 'Flashbulb Memories', p. 73.
19. Woolf, 'A Sketch of the Past', in *Moments of Being*, p. 122.
20. Nin, *Winter of Artifice*, p. 143.
21. Diary entry of summer 1952, in *The Diary of Anaïs Nin*, vol. V, p. 93.
22. Diary entry of 8 April 1925, in *The Diary of Virginia Woolf*, vol. III, p. 7.
23. Woolf, 'Modern Fiction', in *The Common Reader*, p. 150. The next quotation is on the same page.
24. Proust, *A l'ombre des jeunes filles en fleurs*, in *A la recherche du temps perdu*, vol. II, p. 191.
25. Freud, 'The Moses of Michelangelo', in *The Standard Edition of the Complete Psychological Works of Sigmund Freud*, vol. XIII, p. 211.
26. Jung, 'On the Relation of Analytical Psychology to Poetry', in *Collected Works of C. G. Jung*, vol. XV, p. 69.

4: The Art of Misrepresentation in Marcel Proust

1. Proust, *Contre Sainte-Beuve*, pp. 221–2.
2. Proust, letter to Robert Dreyfus, 19 May 1908, in *Selected Letters*, vol. II, p. 374. When quotation is taken from Philip Kolb's translations of Proust's letters, the original French version is not given. When the translations are my own, the French text is included.
3. Proust, 'A Propos du "Style de Flaubert" ', in *Contre Sainte-Beuve*, p. 599.

4. Gide, journal entry of 14 May 1921, in *Journal: 1889–1939*, p. 692.
5. Mallarmé, *Oeuvres complètes*. Pléiade, p. 366.
6. Proust, 'Dédicace à Jacques de Lacretelle, 20 April 1918', in *Contre Sainte-Beuve*, p. 565.
7. Proust, letter of 27 September 1905 to Mme de Noailles, in *Selected Letters*, vol. II, p. 207.
8. Proust, letter of soon after 28 September 1905 to Robert de Montesquiou, in ibid., p. 208.
9. Hayman, *Proust*, pp. 258–89.
10. Proust, *A la recherche*, vol. 2, p. 641.
11. Proust, letter of 27 September 1905 to Mme de Noailles, in *Selected Letters*, vol. II, p. 207.
12. Proust, *A la recherche*, vol. IV, p. 486. All translations from *A la recherche du temps perdu* are my own.
13. Pierre-Quint, *Marcel Proust*, p. 20. Later in his book, Pierre-Quint makes one exception to his statement by saying that the Baron de Charlus was irrefutably recognised as the portrait of Robert de Montesquiou; see pp. 48–9.
14. Ferré, *La Géographie de Marcel Proust*, p. 118.
15. Bonnet, *Marcel Proust de 1907 à 1914*, p. 18.
16. Coulon, *Promenades en Normandie*, p. 17.
17. Proust, 'En memoire des églises assassinées', in *Pastiches et mélanges*, p. 193.
18. Proust, letter of mid-August 1909 to Alfred Vallette, in *Selected Letters*, vol. II, p. 442.
19. See Proust, letter to Paul Souday, 17 December 1919, in *Correspondence de Marcel Proust*, vol. XVIII, p. 536.
20. Proust, *Le Temps retrouvé*, in *A la recherche*, vol. IV; the three expressions are on pp. 475–6.
21. Ibid., pp. 474–5.
22. Ibid., p. 478. The subsequent quotations in this paragraph are on p. 474.
23. Ibid., p. 476.
24. Ibid., p. 486.
25. Ibid., vol. I, p. 179.
26. Proust, 'Journées de lecture', in *Pastiches et mélanges*, p. 250.
27. Proust, *A la recherche*, vol. II, pp. 76–7.
28. See Proust, letter from the first fortnight in July 1908 to Francois de Pâris, in *Correspondance de Marcel Proust*, vol. VIII, pp. 172–3.
29. Proust, letter of 12 June 1908 to Francois Vicomte de Pâris, in *Selected Letters*, vol. II, p. 376.
30. Letter of 23 May 1909 to Georges de Lauris, in ibid., p. 435.
31. Proust, *A la recherche*, vol. I, p. 133.
32. Ibid., vol. IV, p. 267. The next two quotations are on p. 268.
33. Proust, *Du côté de chez Swann*, in ibid., vol. I, p. 133.
34. Painter, *Marcel Proust*, p. 23.
35. As cited by Coulon, *Promenades en Normandie*, p. 91.
36. Proust, *A la recherche*, vol. II, p. 19.
37. Proust, letter of mid-August 1907 to Emile Mâle, in *Selected Letters*, vol. II, p. 322.

38. Proust, *A l'ombre des jeunes filles en fleurs*, in *A la recherche*, vol. II, p. 6.
39. Proust, letter to Jacques de Lacretelle, 14 December 1917, in *Correspondance de Marcel Proust*, vol. XVI, p. 358.
40. Barthes, 'The Death of the Author', p. 144.
41. Ellison, 'Who is Marcel?', p. 85.
42. Proust, *A la recherche*, vol. IV, p. 494.
43. Proust, letter to Mme Straus, 3 June 1914, in *Correspondance de Marcel Proust*, vol. XIII, p. 231.
44. Maurois, *Proust*, p. 152.
45. Proust, letter to Emile Straus, 3 June 1914, in *Correspondance de Marcel Proust*, vol. XIII, p. 228.
46. Gide, *Journal: 1889–1939*, p. 692.
47. Proust, *Le Temps retrouvé*, in *A la recherche*, vol. IV, p. 487.
48. Proust, letter to Alfred Vallette, about mid-August 1909, in *Correspondance de Marcel Proust*, vol. IX, p. 155.
49. Proust, *Esquisse, I* to *Sodom et Gomorrhe, I*, in *A la recherche*, vol. III, pp. 930–1.
50. Pierre-Quint, *Marcel Proust*, p. 172.
51. *A l'ombre des jeunes filles en fleurs, II*, in *A la recherche*, vol. II, Pléiade, pp. 190–1.

5: The Stylised Quotidian in James Joyce

1. Gillet, *Claybook for James Joyce*, p. 133.
2. S. Joyce, *My Brother's Keeper*, p. 32.
3. Joyce, 'Drama and Life', in *The Critical Writings of James Joyce*, p. 45.
4. Diary entry of 2 Feb. 1904, in S. Joyce, *The Complete Dublin Diary of Stanislaus Joyce*, p. 12. The next quotation (entry of 29 March 1904) is on p. 20.
5. S. Joyce, *My Brother's Keeper*, p. 17.
6. Joyce, *Stephen Hero*, p. 211. The quotations in the next paragraph are from the same page.
7. Joyce *Ulysses*, vol. I, ch. 9, ll. 184–6. As in this instance, subsequent quotations from *Ulysses* are cited by chapter and line number from the Gabler text. The traditional chapter designations are used in the discussion although there are no chapter titles in the Gabler edition.
8. Letter of March 1901 to Henrik Ibsen in *Letters of James Joyce*, ed. Gilbert, p. 52.
9. Mayoux, *Joyce*, p. 44.
10. Joyce, *Dubliners*, p. 32.
11. Letter of 15 October 1905 to Grant Richards, in *Letters of James Joyce*, ed. Ellmann, vol. II, p. 122.
12. Letter of c. 24 September 1905 to S. Joyce, in ibid., p. 109.
13. See S. Joyce's letter of 10 October 1905 to J. Joyce, in ibid., pp. 114–15.
14. Letter of 13 November 1906 to S. Joyce, in ibid., p. 192.
15. Letter of 5 May 1906 to Grant Richards, in ibid., p. 134.

16. S. Joyce, *My Brother's Keeper*, p. 62. The next quotation in this paragraph is from p. 226. The quotation in the following paragraph is reported by Stanislaus in the same volume, pp. 103–4.
17. Joyce, *Dubliners*, ed. Scholes, p. 38. The subsequent quotations in this paragraph are from pp. 61, 97, 150.
18. Ibid., p. 40.
19. Letter of 3 Dec. 1904 to S. Joyce, in *Letters of James Joyce*, ed. Ellmann, vol. II, p. 72.
20. Letter of 6 August 1909 to Nora Barnacle Joyce, in ibid., p. 232. The next quotation, from the letter of 22 August 1909, is on p. 239.
21. Letter of 26 August 1909 to Nora Barnacle Joyce, in ibid., p. 240. The next quotation is from a letter of 31 August 1909 to Nora on p. 242.
22. Joyce, *Dubliners*, p. 219. The subsequent quotations in this paragraph and the next are on p. 223.
23. Letter of 7 August 1912 to S. Joyce, in *Letters of James Joyce*, ed. Ellmann, vol. II, p. 300.
24. Joyce, *Stephen Hero*, p. 78.
25. S. Joyce, *My Brother's Keeper*, p. 134. The next quotation is on pp. 134–5.
26. Joyce, *Stephen Hero*, p. 163.
27. Joyce, *A Portrait of the Artist as a Young Man*, p. 224. The quotation in the next paragraph is on p. 169.
28. Ibid., p. 169. The next quotations in this paragraph are on pp. 172, 174, 215.
29. Ibid., p. 66. The subsequent quotations in this paragraph are on pp. 96, 99.
30. Ibid., p. 252.
31. As quoted in Gorman, *James Joyce*, p. 108.
32. Ellmann, *James Joyce*, p. 129.
33. Joyce, *Ulysses*, vol. I, ch. 1, 101–10.
34. Ibid., l. 278. The next quotation is in vol. II, Ch. 15, ll. 4191–2.
35. Ibid., vol. II, ch. 15, ll. 4191–2.
36. Entry of 14 September 1904, in S. Joyce, *The Complete Dublin Diary of Stanislaus Joyce*, pp. 85–6.
37. Letter of 29 August 1904 to Nora Barnacle Joyce, in *Letters*, ed. Ellmann, vol. II, p. 48.
38. Maddox, *Nora*, p. 92.
39. Borach, 'Conversations with James Joyce', pp. 325–6.
40. Hassan, *The Postmodern Turn*, p. 102.
41. Joyce, *Ulysses*, vol. I, ch. 8, ll. 108–10.

6: Distancing and Displacement in Virginia Woolf

1. Introduction to Woolf, *Mrs. Dalloway*, First Modern Library edition, p. vi.
2. Q. Bell, 'Introduction' to *Virginia Woolf*, p. viii.
3. Diary entry of 8 Feb. 1926, *The Diary of Virginia Woolf*, vol. III, p. 58.

4. 'Autobiography', reprinted in Leslie Stephen, *Hours in a Library*, vol. III, p. 237.

5. L. Woolf, *Downhill All the Way*, p. 13.

6. Woolf, 'The New Biography', in *Collected Essays*, vol. IV, p. 229.

7. Woolf, 'A Sketch of the Past', in *Moments of Being*, p. 81.

8. Woolf, 'Mr Bennett and Mrs Brown', in *Collected Essays*, vol. I, p. 320. The next quotation is on the same page.

9. Fry, *Vision and Design*, p. 239.

10. Woolf, 'Mr Bennett and Mrs Brown', in *Collected Essays*, vol. I, pp. 336–7.

11. Woolf, 'Modern Fiction', in *The Common Reader* (First Series), p. 150. The next quotation is on p. 149.

12. C. Bell, *Proust*, p. 62.

13. Woolf, 'Phases of Fiction', in *Collected Essays*, vol. II, p. 83. The quotation in the next paragraph is on p. 100.

14. See Q. Bell, *Virginia Woolf*, vol. II, p. 209.

15. L. Woolf, *Downhill All the Way*, p. 169.

16. Woolf, 'A Sketch of the Past', in *Moments of Being*, p. 81.

17. Entry of 26 Jan. 1920, in *The Diary of Virginia Woolf*, vol. II, p. 14.

18. Entry of 18 November 1924, in ibid., p. 321. The next quotation is on the same page.

19. See letter of 13 May 1927 to Vita Sackville-West, in *The Letters of Virginia Woolf*, vol. III, p. 374.

20. Woolf, 'A Sketch of the Past', in *Moments of Being*, p. 72. The subsequent quotations in this paragraph and the next are on pp. 122, 73.

21. Ibid., p. 84. The quotations in the next paragraph are on pp. 64–67.

22. Ibid., p. 112. The next quotations are on pp. 81–3.

23. Ibid., pp. 80–1.

24. Entry of 14 May 1925, in *The Diary of Virginia Woolf*, vol. III, pp. 18–19.

25. Letter of 13 May 1927 to Vita Sackville-West, in ibid., p. 374.

26. Letter of 11 May 1927 from Vanessa Bell to Virginia Woolf, in ibid., Appendix, p. 572.

27. Letter of 25 May 1927 to Vanessa Bell, in ibid., p. 383.

28. Woolf, *To the Lighthouse*, p. 132. The next quotation is on p. 133.

29. Woolf, 'A Sketch of the Past', in *Moments of Being*, p. 117.

30. *The Hyde Park Gate News*, 12 September 1892, as quoted in Q. Bell, *Virginia Woolf*, vol. I, p. 32.

31. Woolf, 'A Sketch of the Past', in *Moments of Being*, p. 83.

32. Ibid., p. 117.

33. Woolf, *To the Lighthouse*, pp. 125–6.

34. Letter of 25 June 1938 to Vanessa Bell, in *The Letters of Virginia Woolf*, vol. VI, pp. 243–4.

35. Letter of May 3, 1938 to Vita Sackville-West, in ibid., p. 225.

36. Letter of 22 May 1927 to Vanessa Bell, in ibid., vol. III, p. 379.

37. Letter of 5 June 1927 to Violet Dickinson, in ibid., p. 389.

38. Woolf, *To the Lighthouse*, pp. 12–13.

39. Letter of 27 May 1927 to Roger Fry, in *The Letters of Virginia Woolf*, vol. III, p. 385.

40. Letter of 17 May 1927 from Roger Fry to *Virginia Woolf*, as quoted in Q. Bell, Virginia Woolf, vol. II, p. 129.
41. Woolf, 'A Sketch of the Past', in *Moments of Being*, p. 121. The quotations in the next paragraph are on p. 122.
42. Woolf, *To the Lighthouse*, p. 63.
43. Ibid., p. 53. The quotations in this paragraph and the next are on pp. 150, 53, 52.
44. Fry, *Vision and Design*, p. 175. Fry had made these observations in a 1901 essay on the Florentine painter Giotto, who, interestingly, had painted scenes of Christ and the Virgin. Such subject matter is one of the many allusions in Lily Briscoe's painting.
45. Fry, *Transformations*, p. 8.
46. Woolf, *To the Lighthouse*, p. 128. The next quotation is on pp. 128–9.
47. Ferrer, *Virginia Woolf and the Madness of Language*, p. 10.
48. Entry of 14 October 1922, in *The Diary of Virginia Woolf*, vol. II, pp. 207–8.
49. Diary entry of 17 Feb. 1922, in ibid., p. 167.
50. Trombley, *All that Summer She was Mad*, p. 225. The next quotation is on p. 228.
51. T. B. Hyslop, 'Post-Illusionism and Art in the Insane', as cited in ibid., p. 229.
52. Ibid., p. 95.
53. Letter of 26 November 1904 to Violet Dickinson, in *The Letters of Virginia Woolf*, vol. I, p. 159.
54. Woolf, *Mrs Dalloway*, p. 99.
55. Ibid., p. 84.
56. Ibid., p. 31. The next quotations in this paragraph are on the same page. The quotation in the next paragraph is on p. 184.
57. Ibid., p. 184. The next quotation is on p. 127.
58. Letter of 9 October 1927, in *The Letters of Virginia Woolf*, vol. III, pp. 428–9. Vita's response of 11 October 1927 is in the footnote on p. 429.
59. Entry of 21 December 1925, in *The Diary of Virginia Woolf*, vol. III, p. 52.
60. Entry of 5 October 1927, in ibid., p. 161.
61. Woolf, *Orlando*, p. 309.
62. Entry of 21 December 1925, in *The Diary of Virginia Woolf*, vol. III, p. 52.

7: The Mythification of Selfhood in Anaïs Nin

1. Nin, *Collages*, pp. 65–6.
2. Entry of Fall 1937, in *The Diary of Anaïs Nin*, vol. II, p. 252.
3. Nin, *A Woman Speaks*, p. 162.
4. Entry of Winter 1947–8, in *The Diary of Anaïs Nin*, vol. V, p. 10.
5. Entry of April 1936, in ibid., vol. II, p. 76.

6. Nin, *The Novel of the Future*, pp. 145–6. The quotation in the next paragraph is on p. 133.

7. Entry of April 1946 in *The Diary of Anaïs Nin*, vol. IV, p. 142.

8. Entry of August 1937, in ibid., vol. II, p. 232.

9. Nin, *The Novel of the Future*, p. 164. The quotation in the next paragraph is on p. 158.

10. Spencer, *Collage of Dreams*, p. 187.

11. Entry of August 1936, in *The Diary of Anaïs Nin*, vol. II, p. 106.

12. Nin, 'Ragtime', in *Under a Glass Bell*, p. 61.

13. Nin, *House of Incest*, p. 52. The quotations in the next paragraph are on pp. 70, 56.

14. Ibid., p. 62. The next quotation is from the Prologue to *House of Incest*.

15. Entry of August 1936, in *The Diary of Anaïs Nin*, vol. II, p. 113.

16. Nin, *House of Incest*, p. 17.

17. Nin, *Henry and June*, p. 116.

18. Entry of March 1933, in *The Diary of Anaïs Nin*, vol. I, p. 202. The next quotation is on the same page.

19. Nin, *Linotte*, p. 365.

20. Entry of March 1933, in *The Diary of Anaïs Nin*, vol. I, p. 202. The next two quotations are on pp. 202, 203.

21. Entry of May 1933, in ibid., p. 206. The next quotations are on pp. 207, 209.

22. Entry of August 1936, in ibid., vol. II, p. 110. The next quotation is on p. 112.

23. Entry of Feb. 1939, in ibid., pp. 328–9.

24. The 1992 unexpurgated version (entitled *Incest*) of volume I of *The Diary of Anaïs Nin* does add virtual incest to this relationship. Regardless of such sensational material, however, the fundamental fact is that Nin falls 'out of love' – whatever kind it may have been – and that it is this disillusionment that is transferred to the icy, fictional atmosphere of the *Winter of Artifice*.

25. Nin, *Winter of Artifice*, pp. 94–5. The next quotations are on p. 119.

26. There has been controversy over the nature of this birth since the 1992 publication of *Incest*, the unexpurgated version of volume I of *The Diary of Anaïs Nin*.

27. Nin, *Winter of Artifice*, p. 119.

28. Entry of August 1934, in *The Diary of Anaïs Nin*, vol. I, p. 342.

29. Nin, *Henry and June*, p. 116.

30. Nin, *Winter of Artifice*, p. 173.

31. Nin, *Ladders to Fire*, in *Cities of the Interior*, p. 64. The quotations in the next paragraph are on pp. 90, 103, 90, 104.

32. Nin, *The Novel of the Future*, p. 134. The next quotation is on p. 157.

33. Entry of September 1939, in *The Diary of Anaïs Nin*, vol. II, p. 347.

34. Entry of Winter 1947–8, in ibid., vol. V, p. 10. The next quotation is on p. 7.

35. Nin, *Seduction of the Minotaur*, in *Cities of the Interior*, p. 468. The subsequent quotations in this paragraph and the next are on pp. 465–6, 478, 531.

36. Ibid., p. 565.

37. Nin, *Children of the Albatross*, in ibid., p. 142. The subsequent quotations in this paragraph and the next are on pp. 143, 145, 196, 148, 196, 170.
38. Nin *The Novel of the Future*, p. 125.
39. Nin, *The Four-Chambered Heart*, in *Cities of the Interior*, p. 273. The quotation in the next paragraph is on the same page.
40. Entry of September 1948, in *The Diary of Anaïs Nin*, vol. V, p. 33. The subsequent quotations in this paragraph and the next are on the same page.
41. Nin, *The Four-Chambered Heart*, in *Cities of the Interior*, p. 343. The next quotation is on the same page.
42. Nin, *A Spy in the House of Love*, in ibid., p. 410. The next quotations are on pp. 411, 439, 452.
43. Entry of June 1932 in *The Diary of Anaïs Nin*, vol. I, p. 118. The next quotations are on pp. 272, 284.
44. Nin, *Linotte*, p. 263.

References

Editions of the Works of Joyce, Nin, Proust, and Woolf:

Joyce, James, *The Critical Writings of James Joyce*, ed. Ellsworth Mason and Richard Ellmann (New York; Viking, 1964).

——, *Dubliners*, ed. Robert Scholes and A. Walton Litz (New York: Viking Critical Library Edition, 1969; rpt. Penguin, 1976).

——, *Letters of James Joyce*, ed. Stuart Gilbert (New York: Viking, 1957).

——, *Letters of James Joyce*, ed. Richard Ellmann, 2 vols (New York: Viking, 1966).

——, *A Portrait of the Artist as a Young Man*, ed. Chester G. Anderson (New York: Viking Critical Library Edition, 1964; rpt. Penguin, 1982).

——, *Stephen Hero*, ed. Theodore Spencer (New York: New Directions, 1944; rpt. 1963).

——, *Ulysses: A Critical and Synoptic Edition*, ed. Hans Walter Gabler *et al.*, 3 vols (New York: Garland, 1984).

——, *The Workshop of Daedalus: James Joyce and the Raw Materials for 'A Portrait'*, ed. Robert Scholes and Richard M. Kain (Evanston, Ill.: Northwestern University Press, 1965).

Nin, Anaïs, *Cities of the Interior* (1959; Chicago, Ill.: Swallow Press, 1974).

——, *Collages* (Chicago, Ill.: Swallow Press, 1964).

——, *The Diary of Anaïs Nin*, ed. Gunther Stuhlmann, 7 vols (New York: Harcourt Brace, 1966–80').

——, *Henry and June: From the Unexpurgated Diary of Anaïs Nin* (New York: Harcourt Brace, 1986).

——, *House of Incest* (New York: Swallow Press, 1958).

——, *Incest: The Unexpurgated Diary of Anaïs Nin, 1932–34* (New York: Harcourt Brace, 1992).

——, *Linotte: The Early Diary of Anaïs Nin, 1914–1920*, trans. from the French by Jean L. Sherman (New York: Harcourt Brace, 1978).

——, *The Novel of the Future* (New York: Macmillan, 1968).

——, *Under a Glass Bell* (New York: Gemor Press, 1944).

——, *Winter of Artifice* (Chicago, Ill.: Swallow Press, 1948).

——, *A Woman Speaks: The Lectures, Seminars, and Interviews of Anaïs Nin*, ed. Evelyn J. Hinz (Chicago, Ill.: Swallow Press, 1975).

Proust, Marcel, *A la recherche du temps perdu*, vols 1–4, ed. Jean-Yves Tadié (Paris: Gallimard, Pléiade, 1987–9).

——, *Contre Sainte-Beuve, Pastiches et mélanges; Essais et articles*, ed. Pierre Clarac (Paris: Gallimard, Pléiade, 1971).

——, *Matinée chez la princesse de Guermantes: Cahiers du temps retrouvé*, ed. Henri Bonnet and Bernard Brun (Paris: Gallimard, 1982).

——, *Pastiches et mélanges* (Paris: Gallimard, 1919).

——, *Correspondance de Marcel Proust*, ed. Philip Kolb, 10 vols (Paris: Librairie Plon, 1970–92).

——, *Selected Letters*, vol. 2: *1904–1909*, ed. Philip Kolb, trans. Terence Kilmartin (New York: Oxford University Press, 1989).

Woolf, Virginia, *Collected Essays*, 4 vols (London: Hogarth Press, 1966–7).

——, *The Common Reader*, ed. Andrew McNeillie, first series (New York: Harcourt Brace, 1925; rpt. 1984).

——, *The Complete Shorter Fiction of Virginia Woolf*, ed. Susan Dick (New York: Harcourt Brace, 1985).

——, *The Diary of Virginia Woolf*, ed. Anne Oliver Bell, 5 vols (New York: Harcourt Brace, 1977–84).

——, *The Letters of Virginia Woolf*, ed. Nigel Nicolson and Joanne Trautman, 6 vols (New York: Harcourt Brace, 1975–80).

——, *Mrs. Dalloway* (New York: Harcourt Brace, 1925; rpt. 1981).

——, *Mrs. Dalloway* (New York: First Modern Library Edition, 1928).

——, *Moments of Being: Unpublished Autobiographical Writings*, ed. Jeanne Schulkind (New York: Harcourt Brace, 1976).

——, *Orlando: A Biography* (New York: Harcourt Brace, 1928; rpt. 1956).

——, *Roger Fry: A Biography* (New York: Harcourt Brace, 1940).

——, *A Room of One's Own* (New York: Harcourt Brace, 1929; rpt. 1981).

——, *To the Lighthouse* (New York: Harcourt Brace, 1927; rpt. 1981).

Other References

Augustine, Saint, *Confessions*, trans. R. S. Pine-Coffin (Harmondsworth, Middx: Penguin, 1961; rpt. 1987).

Barthes, Roland, 'The Death of the Author' [original French version, 1968], trans. Stephen Heath, in *Image – Music – Text* (New York: Hill & Wang, 1977) pp. 142–8.

Beaujour, Michel, *Miroirs d'encre: rhétorique de l'autoportrait* (Paris: Seuil, 1980).

Bell, Clive, *Proust* (London: Hogarth Press, 1928).

Bell, Quentin, *Virginia Woolf: A Biography*, 2 vols (New York: Harcourt Brace, 1972).

Bonnet, Henri, *Proust de 1907 à 1914* (2nd edn [1959]; Paris: Nizet, 1971; 1st edn, 1959).

Borach, Georges, 'Conversations with James Joyce', trans. Joseph Prescott, *College English*, vol. XV (March 1954) pp. 325–27.

Brée, Germaine, 'Michel Leiris: Mazemaker' in James Olney (ed.), *Autobiography: Essays Theoretical and Critical* (Princeton, N.J.: Princeton University Press, 1980.) pp. 194–206.

Brewer, William F., 'What is Autobiographical Memory?', in David C. Rubin (ed.), *Autobiographical Memory* (Cambridge: Cambridge University Press, 1986) pp. 25–49.

Brown, Roger and Kulik, James, 'Flashbulb Memories', *Cognition*, vol. 5 (March 1977) pp. 73–99.

Bruss, Elizabeth W., *Autobiographical Acts: The Changing Situation of a Literary Genre* (Baltimore, Md: Johns Hopkins University Press, 1976).

Buckley, Jerome Hamilton, *The Turning Key: Autobiography and the Subjective Impulse since 1800* (Cambridge, Mass.: Harvard University Press, 1984).

Cellini, Benvenuto, *The Life of Benvenuto Cellini Written By Himself*, ed. and trans. John Addington Symonds, 2 vols (New York: Tudor Publishing Co., 1934).

Cockshut, A. O. J., *The Art of Autobiography in Nineteenth and Twentieth Century England* (New Haven, Conn. : Yale University Press, 1984).

Coe, Richard N., *When the Grass Was Taller: Autobiography and the Experience of Early Childhood* (New Haven, Conn.: Yale University Press, 1984).

Coulon, Bernard, *Promenades en Normandie avec un guide nommé Marcel Proust* (Condé-sur-Noireau: Editions Charles Corlet, 1986).

Deleuze, Gilles, *Proust et les signes* (Paris: Presses Universitaires de France, 1964).

De Man, Paul, *Allegories of Reading: Figural Language in Rousseau, Nietzsche, Rilke, and Proust* (New Haven, Conn.: Yale University Press, 1979).

——, 'Autobiography as De-facement', *Modern Language Notes*, vol. 94 (1979) pp. 919–30.

Eakin, Paul John, *Fictions in Autobiography: Studies in the Art of Self-Invention* (Princeton, N. J.: Princeton University Press, 1985).

——, 'Narrative and Chronology as Structures of Reference and the New Model Autobiographer' in James Olney (ed.), *Studies in Autobiography* (New York: Oxford University Press, 1988) pp. 32–41.

——, *Touching the World: Reference in Autobiography* (Princeton, N.J.: Princeton University Press, 1992).

Egan, Susanna, *Patterns of Experience in Autobiography* (Chapel Hill, N.C.: University of North Carolina Press, 1984).

Eliot, T. S., *Selected Prose*, ed. Frank Kermode (New York: Harcourt Brace, 1975).

Ellison, David R., 'Who is "Marcel"? Proust and the Question of Autobiographical Identity', *L'Esprit créateur*, vol. 20 (Fall 1980) pp. 78–85.

Ellmann, Richard, *James Joyce* (Oxford: Oxford University Press, 1959; rev. 1982).

Ferré, Andre, *La Géographie de Marcel Proust* (Paris: Le Sagittaire, 1933).

Ferrer, Daniel, *Virginia Woolf and the Madness of Language*, trans. Geoffrey Bennington and Rachel Bowlby (London: Routledge, 1990).

Fleishman, Avrom, *Figures of Autobiography: The Language of Self-writing in Victorian and Modern England* (Berkeley, Cal.: University of California Press, 1983).

——, *Virginia Woolf: A Critical Reading* (Baltimore, Md: Johns Hopkins University Press, 1975).

Foucault, Michel, 'What is an Author?', trans. Josué Harari (original French version, 1969), in David Richter (ed.), *The Critical Tradition: Classical Texts and Contemporary Trends* (New York: St Martin's Press, 1989) pp. 978–88.

Franklin, Benjamin, *The Autobiography of Benjamin Franklin*, ed. Leonard W. Labaree *et al.* (New Haven, Conn.: Yale University Press, 1964).

Freud, Sigmund, *The Standard Edition of the Complete Psychological Works of Sigmund Freud*, trans. and ed. James Strachey, vol. XIII (London: Hogarth Press and the Institute of Psycho-analysis, 1953; rpt. 1978).

Fry, Roger, *Transformations: Critical and Speculative Essays on Art* (New York: Brentano's, 1926).

——, *Vision and Design* (1920; New York: Brentano's, 1924).

Frye, Northrop, *Anatomy of Criticism* (Princeton, N.J.: Princeton University Press, 1957).

Genette, Gerard, *Figures III* (Paris: Seuil, 1972).

Gide, André, *Journal: 1889–1939* (Paris: Gallimard, Pléiade, 1951).

——, *Si le grain ne meurt* (Paris: Gallimard, 1955).

Gillet, Louis, *Claybook for James Joyce* (London: Abelard-Schuman, 1958).

Gorman, Herbert, *James Joyce* (1940; New York: Octagon Books, 1974).

Gosse, Edmund, *Father and Son* (1907; Harmondsworth, Middx: Penguin, 1949; rpt. 1982).

Gusdorf, Georges, 'Conditions and Limits of Autobiography' (original French version 1956), trans. James Olney, in James Olney (ed.), *Autobiography: Essays Theoretical and Critical* (Princeton, N.J.: Princeton University Press, 1980) pp. 28–48.

Hassan, Ihab, *The Postmodern Turn: Essays in Postmodern Theory and Culture* (Columbus, Ohio: Ohio State University Press, 1987).

Hayman, Ronald, *Proust: A Biography* (New York: Harper Collins, 1990).

Henke, Suzette A., *James Joyce and the Politics of Desire* (New York and London: Routledge, 1990).

Joyce, Stanislaus, *My Brother's Keeper: James Joyce's Early Years* (New York: Viking Press, 1958).

——, *The Complete Dublin Diary of Stanislaus Joyce*, ed. George H. Healey (Ithaca, N.Y.: Cornell University Press, 1971).

Jung, Carl, *Collected Works of C. G. Jung*, trans. R. F. C. Hull, vol. XV (New York: Bollingen Foundation, 1953).

Kershner, R. B., *Joyce, Bakhtin, and Popular Literature* (Chapel Hill, N.C.: University of North Carolina Press, 1989).

Leiris, Michel, *Manhood: A Journey from Childhood into the Fierce Order of Virility*, trans. Richard Howard (1946; San Francisco: North Point Press, 1984).

——, *Scratches*, trans. Lydia Davis (1948; New York: Paragon House, 1991).

Lejeune, Philippe, *Le Pacte autobiographique* (Paris: Seuil, 1975).

Leonard, Diane R, 'Proust and Virginia Woolf, Ruskin and Roger Fry: Modernist Visual Dynamics', *Comparative Literature Studies*, vol. 18 (Sept. 1981) pp. 333–43.

Maddox, Brenda, *Nora: The Real Life of Molly Bloom* (Boston, Mass.: Houghton Mifflin, 1988).

Mallarmé, Stéphane, *Oeuvres complètes* (Paris: Gallimard, Pléiade, 1945).

Maurois, André, *Proust: Portrait of a Genius*, trans. Gerard Hopkins (1950; New York: Carroll & Graf, 1984).

Mayoux, Jean-Jacques, *Joyce* (Paris: Gallimard, 1965).

Mehlman, Jeffrey, *A Structural Study of Autobiography: Proust, Leiris, Sartre, Lévi-Strauss* (Ithaca, N.Y.: Cornell University Press, 1974).

Neuman, S. C., *Gertrude Stein: Autobiography and the Problem of Narration*, ELS Monograph Series (Victoria, B.C.: University of Victoria, 1979).

Olney, James, 'Autobiography and the Cultural Moment: a Thematic, Historical, and Biographical Introduction' in *Autobiography*, ed. James Olney, pp. 3–27.

——, *Metaphors of Self: The Meaning of Autobiography* (Princeton, N.J.: Princeton University Press, 1972).

——, 'Some Versions of Memory/Some Versions of Bios: The Ontology of Autobiography', in *Autobiography*, ed. James Olney, pp. 237–67.

—— (ed.), *Autobiography: Essays Theoretical and Critical* (Princeton, N.J.: Princeton University Press, 1980).

——, *Studies in Autobiography* (New York: Oxford University Press, 1988).

Painter, George D., *Marcel Proust* (1959, 1965); rev. and updated ed. in 1 vol. (New York: Random House, 1989).

Pascal, Roy, *Design and Truth in Autobiography* (Cambridge, Mass.: Harvard University Press, 1960).

Peterson, Linda H., *Victorian Autobiography: The Tradition of Self-Interpretation* (New Haven, Conn. : Yale University Press, 1986).

Pierre-Quint, Léon, *Marcel Proust: sa vie, son oeuvre* (1925; Paris: Le Sagittaire, 1946).

Poulet, Georges, *L'Espace proustien* (Paris: Gallimard, 1963).

Rank, Otto, *Art and Artist: Creative Urge in Personality Development* (New York: Alfred A. Knopf, 1932).

Renza, Louis A., 'The Veto of the Imagination: a Theory of Autobiography' in James Olney (ed.), *Autobiography: Essays Theoretical and Critical* (Princeton, N.J.: Princeton University Press, 1980) pp. 268–95.

Ricouer, Paul, *A Ricoeur Reader: Reflection and Imagination*, ed. Mario J. Valdés (Toronto: University of Toronto Press, 1991).

——, *The Rule of Metaphor*, trans. Robert Czerny (original French version, 1975; Toronto: University of Toronto Press, 1977).

——, *Time and Narrative*, trans. Kathleen McLaughlin and David Pellauer, 3 vols (original French version, 1983–5; Chicago: University of Chicago Press, 1984–8).

Rimbaud, Arthur, *Oeuvres complètes* (Paris: Gallimard, Pléiade, 1972).

Rousseau, Jean-Jacques, *The Confessions*, trans. J. M. Cohen (1781; Harmondsworth, Middx: Penguin, 1953; rpt. 1982).

Rubin, David C. (ed.), *Autobiographical Memory* (Cambridge: Cambridge University Press, 1986).

Sainte-Beuve, Charles-Augustin, *Oeuvres choisies de Sainte-Beuve*, ed. Marcel Hervier (Paris: Librairie Delagrave, 1926).

Sartre, Jean-Paul, *The Words*, trans. Bernard Frechtman (1964; New York: Vintage Books, 1981).

Sekora, John, 'Is the Slave Narrative a Species of Autobiography?', in James Olney (ed.), *Studies in Autobiography* (New York: Oxford University Press, 1988) pp. 99–111.

Soyinka, Wole, *Aké: The Years of Childhood* (New York: Random House, 1981).

Spencer, Sharon, *Collage of Dreams: The Writings of Anaïs Nin*, expanded edn (New York: Harcourt Brace, 1981).

Spengemann, William C., *The Forms of Autobiography: Episodes in the History of a Literary Genre* (New Haven, Conn.: Yale University Press, 1980).

Sprinker, Michael, 'Fictions of the Self: the End of Autobiography', in James Olney (ed.), *Autobiography: Essays Theoretical and Critical* (Princeton, N.J.: Princeton University Press, 1980) pp. 321–42.

Stephen, Leslie, *Hours in a Library*, vol. III (New York: G. P. Putnam's Sons; London: Smith, Elder, 1899).

Szegedy-Maszák, Mihály, 'The Life and Times of the Autobiographical Novel', Budapest: *Neohelicon*, vol. XIII (1985) pp. 83–104.

Taine, Hippolyte, *Histoire de la litterature anglaise*, vol. I (Paris: Librairie Hachette, 1877).

Théorie d'ensemble, Collection *Tel Quel* (Paris: Seuil, 1968).

Thibaudeau, Jean, 'Le Roman comme autobiographie' in *Théorie d'ensemble* (Paris: Seuil, 1968).

Trombley, Stephen, *All that Summer She was Mad; Virginia Woolf: Female Victim of Male Medicine* (New York: Continuum, 1982).

Watson, Julia, 'Shadowed Presence: Modern Women Writers' Autobiographies and the Other', in James Olney (ed.), *Studies in Autobiography* (New York: Oxford University Press, 1988).

Weintraub, Karl Joachim, *The Value of the Individual: Self and Circumstance in Autobiography* (Chicago, Ill.: University of Chicago Press, 1978).

Woolf, Leonard, *Downhill All the Way: An Autobiography of the Years 1919 to 1939* (New York: Harcourt Brace, 1967).

Index

This index lists the names of people, characters and places real and fictional that are mentioned in the text.

Woolf, Virginia, viii, x, 3, 21, 25, 40, 43, 46–8, 50–60, 67, 80, 82–4, 101, 105, 115, 123, 124, 130, 131, 132, 134–69, 177–8, 181, 187
    novels: *Jacob's Room*, 135, 146, 149, 159; *Mrs Dalloway*, 54, 55, 58, 59, 60, 134, 138, 158–65, 168; *Orlando*, 57, 135, 136, 165–8; *To the Lighthouse*, 46, 47, 48, 51, 53, 55, 56, 59, 60, 124, 135, 136, 140–58, 161, 162, 165, 168
    essays: 'Mr Bennett and Mrs Brown', 137, 138; 'Modern Fiction', 55, 138; 'The New Biography', 136; 'Phases of Fiction', 139; *A Room of One's Own*, 134, 165, 168, 184; 'A Sketch of the Past', 52, 135, 136, 141, 147, 153
Woolman, John, 6
Wordsworth, William, 1, 3, 30, 31, 33, 149
Wright, Richard, 37

Yeats, W. B., 17

Zora (Nin character), 192
Zurich, 100, 129